Airlife's Commuter Aircraft and Airliners

A Boeing 737-341, PP-VOO, of VARIG taxies out at Rio's Galeao international airport.

Airlife's Commercial Aircraft and Airliners

Rod Simpson

Airlife
England

Copyright © 1999 Rod Simpson

First published in the UK in 1999
by Airlife Publishing Ltd

British Library Cataloguing-in-Publication Data
A catalogue record for this book
is available from the British Library

ISBN 1 84037 073 4

Typeset by Phoenix Typesetting, Ilkley, West Yorkshire.
Printed in Hong Kong

Airlife Publishing Ltd
101 Longden Road, Shrewsbury, SY3 9EB, England
E-mail: airlife@airlifebooks.com

CONTENTS

INTRODUCTION

Airlife's Commercial Aircraft and Airliners joins *Airlife's General Aviation* and *Airlife's Helicopters and Rotorcraft* to form a quick and comprehensive source of key information to the manufacturers of post-war civil aircraft and the aircraft they have designed and built. This volume covers the principal transport aircraft built in production quantities together with details of many prototypes which did not manage to reach commercial service. While primarily concerned with civil aircraft, the book refers to military transports manufactured by the various companies and, in many cases, such types have gone into civil operation after release from military service.

It is not the task of *Airlife's Commercial Aircraft and Airliners* to provide detailed specifications of the aircraft described which are well documented in other publications. Its purpose is to explain the progression of the manufacturing companies, to detail the individual models of each aircraft so as to identify the differences between each model and to provide information on the production quantities and the serial number systems used by each manufacturer. The data is, so far as possible, correct to mid-1998.

Today's passenger on a Boeing 747, high above the Indian Ocean, will give little thought to the journey he or she might have made to Sydney in 1946. Today, there are more than thirty direct flights and connections between London and Sydney with over 12,000 seats available every day. The flight time is twenty-two hours – which may be tedious for the passenger but compares favourably with the four days of the 1946 Qantas journey in a Lockheed Constellation. One refuelling stop at Singapore is all that is necessary for the '747 but the 1946 airliner called at up to eight points, including Cairo, Karachi, Colombo, and Singapore on its trans-global journey.

The aircraft today are, also, more reliable. Expansion of air transport in the immediate postwar years resulted in piston engines for the long-range airliners being stretched to ever higher power output – and it was a common occurrence for Stratocruisers and Constellations to arrive at their destinations on three rather than four engines. By contrast, modern turbofan engines have a negligible in-flight shutdown record and have now grown to such a size and power output that aircraft such as the Boeing 777 can carry six times the 1946 passenger load on half the number of engines at twice the speed.

In 1946, the backbone of many short-haul airline routes was the extraordinary Douglas DC-3 (C-47) Dakota. Manufactured in large numbers during the war, the DC-3 was tough, reliable and affordable for the fledgling postwar operators. The following fifty years have seen a continual stream of 'DC-3 replacements' but many of the Douglas transports still soldier on. Turbine engines brought the first major advance in the twenty to thirty seat airliner category and reliable turboprops such as the Rolls-Royce Dart, Allison 501, Pratt & Whitney PT6 and Garrett AiResearch TPE331 provided the improved economy and higher speeds required by local and regional airlines. The advent of the Fokker F.27 and Vickers Viscount brought about a major expansion in medium-haul routes in the United States and the arrival of many new carriers. These operators progressively grew out of the turboprops into short-haul jet and turbofan airliners such as the Boeing 727 and 737 and the Douglas DC-9. This growth opened up a market for further new companies to serve local communities with new turboprops such as the Embraer Bandeirante, Shorts 330 and British Aerospace Jetstream. The major carriers in the United States saw this as an opportunity to give passengers integrated connections from their trunk services by forming commuter affiliates operated by independent companies within a larger reservations and codesharing system. Many networks were created including American Eagle, Northwest Airlink, United Express and Delta Connection which allowed the major airlines to exploit 'hub and spoke' route structures. For the passenger, this was generally advantageous although it often meant that any journey on American Airlines involved flying through Dallas and any Delta journey involved a plane change in Atlanta.

As the airlines became increasingly successful, the aircraft manufacturers offered new products and became more concentrated. With the enormous cost of developing new airliners it was inevitable that some manufacturers would succumb. In the United States, Lockheed disappeared, Convair abandoned airliner manufacture and McDonnell Douglas was acquired by the giant of the industry, Boeing. Remarkably, the European decision to start a new company from scratch has proved to be successful, despite the market power of Boeing. Airbus Industrie has pressed forward with a full model range and, while its output is still much smaller than that of the American market leader, it has acquired a good reputation and sales to many major customers.

Such concentration into the hands of a few manufacturers is not without its challenges. In 1999, both Boeing and Airbus are faced with large order books and pressure on production capacity and manpower. Possibly, this gives an opening for the producers from the former Soviet Union to gain ground with the demanding airlines. In the past, Tupolev, Antonov and Ilyushin have built aircraft to very different specifications and economic criteria from those of the west. Strenuous efforts are now being made to achieve recognition of factories in the CIS under western certification criteria and to equip airliners such as the Tu-204 with western engines so as to make them more marketable in competition with Airbus and Boeing products. What is certain is that customer demand for air transportation will continue unabated and the manufacturers will continue to build ever larger and more efficient airliners to provide this service in airspace which will become increasingly crowded and difficult to control.

Airlife's Commercial Aircraft and Airliners has had the advantage of expert assistance from a number of friends and expert aviation historians. I am particularly grateful to Tony Eastwood for his advice on the content of the book, for a number of the illustrations and for the information I have accessed in his excellent series of *Airliner Production List* volumes published by The Aviation Hobby Shop. I also much appreciate the help of John Zimmerman and Dave Richardson of Aviation Data Service who have made considerable information sources available to me. The photographs in *Airlife's Commercial Aircraft and Airliners* come from the aircraft manufacturers, The Aviation Hobby Shop (AHS), Aviation Photo News (APN), Mike Hooks (MJH) and from my own collection. Finally, I have to thank my patient and understanding wife, Valerie, who has, again, been deserted on countless occasions under pressure from the word processor!

R. W. Simpson

ABBREVIATIONS

A number of abbreviations are used in the book. Definitions or explanations of these are shown below. For convenience, the title 'Soviet Union' has been used as a general term in the sections on manufacturers who now operate in the Commonwealth of Independent States. To maintain historical consistency and to keep the data tables as simple as possible, metric measures have not been included. This is in line with current standards used by the main world manufacturers and the procedures used in air transport. For the assistance of readers, rates of conversion to metric equivalents are shown at the end of the list of abbreviations.

a/c	=	Aircraft
ACARS	=	Airline Communications & Reporting System
ALOTS	=	Airborne Lightweight Optical Tracking System
ANG	=	Air National Guard
APU	=	Auxiliary Power Unit
ATR	=	Avions de Transport Regional
AWACS	=	Airborne Warning & Control System
A&AEE	=	Aircraft & Armament Experimental Establishment
AI(R)	=	Aero International (Regional)
BAC	=	British Aircraft Corporation
BBJ	=	Boeing Business Jet
BEA	=	British European Airways Corp.
BOAC	=	British Overseas Airways Corp.
CAA	=	Civil Aviation Authority
c/n	=	Construction Number
DDR	=	Deutsche Democratische Republik

DHC	=	de Havilland Aircraft of Canada
ECM	=	Electronic Countermeasures
EFIS	=	Electronic Flight Information System
ELINT	=	Electronic Intelligence
ETOPS	=	Extended-range Twin Operations
FAA	=	Federal Aviation Administration
FDCDS	=	Flight Direction & Control System
FF	=	First Flight
FLA	=	Future Large Aircraft
FLIR	=	Forward-Looking Infra-Red
GE	=	General Electric
GPS	=	Global Positioning System
HAL	=	Hindustan Aircraft Ltd.
h.p.	=	Horsepower
IAE	=	International Aero Engines
JASDF	=	Japanese Air Self Defence Force
lb	=	pounds
lb.s.t.	=	pounds static thrust
LNG	=	Liquid Natural Gas

MAD	=	Magnetic Anomaly Detector	RAF	=	Royal Air Force
MBB	=	Messerschmitt-Bölkow-Blohm	RCAF	=	Royal Canadian Air Force
MLW	=	Maximum Loaded Weight	RR	=	Rolls-Royce
mod	=	modified	shp	=	shaft horsepower
MTOW	=	Maximum Takeoff Weight	SIGINT	=	Signals Intelligence
MZFW	=	Maximum Zero-Fuel Weight	SLAR	=	Sideways-Looking Airborne Radar
NATO	=	North Atlantic Treaty Organisation	s/n	=	Serial Number
NEACP	=	National Emergency Air Command Post	STOL	=	Short Takeoff and Landing
NVS	=	Noise & Vibration Suppression System	TACAMO	=	Take Command and Move Out
pax	=	passengers	TCA	=	Trans Canada Airlines
Prot	=	Prototype	TCAS	=	Traffic Alert & Collision Avoidance System
P&W	=	Pratt & Whitney	TOGW	=	Takeoff Gross Weight
QC	=	Quick Change	u/c	=	Undercarriage
			USAF	=	United States Air Force
			USG	=	U.S. Gallons

Metric Conversions

1 foot	=	0.3048 metres
1 nautical mile	=	1.8532 kilometres
1 square foot	=	929.03 square centimetres
1 knot	=	1.85 km/h or 1.15 m.p.h.
1 pound	=	0.453 kilograms
1 imperial gallon	=	4.546 litres
1 U.S. Gallon	=	3.785 litres
1kN	=	225 lb.s.t.
1kW	=	1.34 h.p.

PRODUCTION OF AIR CARRIER AIRCRAFT
BY WESTERN MANUFACTURERS 1980 TO 1996

Aircraft Type	1996	1995	1994	1993	1992	1991	1990
Airbus A300	8	14	23	23	24	23	21
Airbus A310	2	2	3	13	20	27	17
Airbus A319/320/321	103	88	55	62	107	133	59
Airbus A330	12	14	17	3	2		
Airbus A340	30	22	25	23	6		
ATR42/72	40	38	52	47	62	64	49
BAC 111							
BAe. ATP				6	12	12	13
BAe. HS.748							
BAe. Jetstream 31			1	7	18	38	46
BAe. Jetstream 41	19	22	16	19	6	1	
BAe.146	22	19	18	19	12	19	36
Beech Be.1900	69	65	50	45	29	39	48
Beech Be.99							
Boeing 727							
Boeing 737	138	140	119	149	219	218	174
Boeing 747	38	40	39	57	59	64	68
Boeing 757	70	67	62	78	95	80	80
Boeing 767	42	35	36	56	61	63	61
Boeing 777	30	15	6				
Bombardier CRJ	44	35	27	22	9		
Bombardier DHC-6							
Bombardier DHC-7							
Bombardier DHC-8	24	25	29	22	37	61	64
CASA C-212	15	22	26	22	18	20	12
CASA CN.235	10	10	8	10	15	13	15
Dornier Do.228	6					21	24
Dornier Do.328	22		18				
Embraer EMB.110					2	10	4
Embraer EMB.120	17	10	7	15	21	24	54
Embraer EMB-145	4						
Fairchild Metro	7	7	16	20	14	10	14
Fokker F-28/F-100			27	46	59	61	32
Lockheed 1011							
McDD MD-80/DC-9			28	27	87	147	150
MDD MD-11/DC-10		6	17	35	38	27	14
Shorts 330/360					6	5	7
Total	**772**	**696**	**725**	**826**	**1038**	**1180**	**1062**

1989	1988	1987	1986	1985	1984	1983	1982	1981	1980
20	20	9	6	6	17	30	48	40	39
23	26	20	21	23	27	24	5		
67	21	8							
45	46	40	31	3	2				
1	2		2	1	3	1	2	1	4
10	7	2	1						
	2			4	6	3	4	8	8
36	48	55	47	38	24	19	7		
31	26	28	22	19	12	8	5	1	
42	41	15	17	21	30				
			10	5	5	20	19	16	
*					7	10	25	87	137
144	166	164	145	110	73	70	104	105	96
42	28	26	37	24	14	18	21	50	83
49	48	39	36	34	20	20	9		
37	53	40	28	24	28	48	26	4	
	9		5	13	13	3	21	47	73
	4	1	6	7	4		19	36	18
61	37	27	39	17	4	3			
8	19	10	23	26	16	37	51	33	25
16	10	7	4			2			
15	20	37	33	26	22	17	6	2	
8	7	4	5	7	26	31	43	63	65
61	41	38	20	6	1	2			
12	29	38	36	30	23	33	30	47	50
26	9	4	9	12	14	14	14	15	10
					1	9	15	25	26
102	119	112	80	70	53	33	45	71	39
	7	5	4	1			8	12	37
13	17	22	28	42	36	31	14	23	21
869	**862**	**751**	**689**	**568**	**484**	**490**	**541**	**686**	**731**

PRODUCTION OF AIR CARRIER AIRCRAFT
BY WESTERN MANUFACTURERS 1963 TO 1979

Aircraft Type	1979	1978	1977	1976	1975	1974	1973
Airbus A300	27	12	13	18	12	5	3
AW.650 Argosy							
BAC 111		3	5	1	1	4	2
BAC/Sud Concorde	1	3	2	4	4	1	2
BAe. HS.748	10	7	9	9	12	3	6
Beech 99					3	8	1
Boeing 707/720	2	1	4	9	6	22	11
Boeing 727	137	120	68	60	90	88	87
Boeing 737	80	39	25	38	53	54	22
Boeing 747	68	36	16	24	24	23	26
Bombardier DHC-6	55	39	46	42	34	46	46
Bombardier DHC-7	10	4	2		2		
Canadair CL.44							
CASA C.212	12	28	24	29	29	11	7
Convair 990							
Dassault Mercure					3	6	1
DH.106 Comet							
DH.114 Heron							
Douglas DC-8							
Embraer EMB.110	43	36	27	53	40	29	12
Fairchild Metro	42	32	22	12	7	8	6
Fokker F.28/F-100	14	11	14	13	14	10	15
HS.121 Trident		3	7	9	6	4	7
Lockheed 1011	15	9	8	14	28	42	35
McDD DC-9	43	28	20	46	39	50	30
McDD DC-10	42	21	14	15	30	51	59
SAL Twin Pioneer							
Sud Caravelle							3
Shorts 330/360	15	11	6	5	2	1	
VFW-614		2	6	5	3		
Vickers VC-10							
Total	**616**	**445**	**338**	**406**	**442**	**466**	**381**

1972	1971	1970	1969	1968	1967	1966	1965	1964	1963
1									
						1	4	2	
5	7	25	39	30	22	44	27	10	2
	1		2						
8	18	19	19	27	19	15	15	9	11
3	2	11	71	65	1				
5	10	19	54	112	119	80	63	39	33
40	30	62	112	162	159	136	112	82	22
24	18	45	114	108	6				
28	72	90	12						
11	44	22	83	98	69	21	1		
							1	3	1
1	2								
									6
1	1								
								1	2
								3	2
4	9	29	81	98	37	30	21	19	20
3									
18	17	14	11	1	3				
11	10	5	7	11	3	9	10	9	3
19	3	1							
36	33	46	127	207	148	69	19		
58	19	3							
									2
5	3	8	21	14	21	15	17	25	23
2	1								
		1	2	7	10	7	9	9	6
283	**300**	**400**	**755**	**940**	**617**	**427**	**299**	**211**	**133**

PRODUCTION OF AIR CARRIER AIRCRAFT
BY WESTERN MANUFACTURERS 1946 TO 1962

Aircraft Type	1962	1961	1960	1959	1958	1957	1956
Airspeed Ambassador							
Avro Tudor							
AW.650 Argosy		2	2	6			
BAe. HS.748	11	3	1				
Boeing 377							
Boeing 707/720	66	82	87	80	11	1	
Breguet Deux Ponts				3	1		
Bristol 170						4	6
Bristol Britannia			10	19	26	15	9
Canadair CL.44	8	20	5	1			
Canadair C.54M							
Convair 240/340/440					41	98	72
Convair 880/990	44	29	19	4			
DH.106 Comet	11	16	17	20	7	4	6
DH.114 Heron	1	2	1	4	10	14	17
Douglas DC-4							
Douglas DC-6					64	44	36
Douglas DC-7					43	132	73
Douglas DC-8	30	82		43	3		
H Page Hermes							
H Page Marathon							
HS.121 Trident	3						
Lockheed L049/749							
Lockheed L1049/1649					48	119	46
Martin 202/404							
Saab Scandia							
SAL Twin Pioneer	5	7	2	17	37	13	3
Sud Est Languedoc							
Sud Est Armagnac							
Sud Caravelle	33	43	39	18	1		1
Vickers VC-10	3						
Vickers Viking							
Total	**215**	**286**	**183**	**215**	**292**	**444**	**269**

1955	1954	1953	1952	1951	1950	1949	1948	1947	1946
			13	7	1		1	1	
						1	6	13	10
					3	49	3	1	
	4	6	2	1	2	1			
9	38	22	26	10	8	4	28	30	27
3	1	1	1						
					1	25	8	35	2
188	207	182	97	33	29	37	117	8	
1	2	10	9	4	1	1			
34	20	31	7		1				
								12	63
81	57	116	90	44	16	5	52	91	7
31	38	21							
				1	18	7	1	1	
			12	28				1	1
				16	39	11	14	59	36
57	35	34	10	14					
			87	16	13		13	21	1
	6			4	6	1			
1									
			3	6	12	9	18	15	17
		2	5		1				
1									
						7	23	94	46
406	**408**	**425**	**362**	**184**	**151**	**158**	**284**	**382**	**210**

One of the Airbus lines at Toulouse is seen here with a group of Airbus A320s in final assembly. In the foreground is an A320-321 ordered by International Lease Finance Corporation and delivered to Mexicana in 1993.

AÉROSPATIALE

FRANCE

Aérospatiale was formed on 1 January 1970 through amalgamation of Sud-Aviation, Nord Aviation and the guided missile and space products manufacturer, SEREB. Each of these companies had a long pedigree and Sud Aviation (originally a combination of SNCASE or Sud-Est and SNCASO or Sud-Ouest) and Nord (originally SNCAN) both developed air transports during the post-war period. At the time of the Aérospatiale amalgamation, Sud Aviation was building the SE-210 Caravelle and Nord was in production with the Nord 262. Once production of these two types came to an end, Aérospatiale continued with the development of the Concorde in conjunction with British Aircraft Corporation and then moved into position as a major part of the Airbus consortium, turning over the former Caravelle production facility at Toulouse to Airbus production.

The Société Nationale de Constructions Aéronautique Sud Est (SNCASE)

In 1941 the nationalised Sud Est company was given a French Government order to construct a batch of SE-161 airliners, derived from the Marcel Bloch MB-160. The SE-161 Languedoc was a low-wing four-engined aircraft capable of transporting thirty-three passengers. As it turned out, the course of the war meant that production of the Languedoc was delayed until 1945 at which time the first aircraft flew and was quickly followed by deliveries to Air France for European services. Four Languedocs were also sold to the Polish airline, LOT. In service, the Languedoc was troubled by the problems of its Gnôme Rhône engines and the fleet was soon re-engined with Pratt & Whitney R-1830s. In practice, the Languedoc was very much an interim aircraft for Air France and was soon replaced by the DC-4 with the SE-161s passing on to Aviaco, Air Liban and to the Armée de l'Air and Aéronavale who also received some new production aircraft.

With the success of the Constellation and the DC-4 in mind, Sud-Est embarked on the design of a four-engined, 100-seat airliner which was designated SE-2010. It had the general appearance of a DC-4 with a tricycle undercarriage and mid-set wing – but was somewhat larger. Taking a highly nationalistic approach, the French Government ordered fifty Armagnacs to be built for use by Air France. Teething problems resulted in the national airline becoming unenthusiastic about the Armagnac and gradually the planned production total slipped back until only eight machines (including the prototype) were actually completed. These served with SAGETA, an airline created purely to operate the aircraft and, not surprisingly, the whole project was a financial disaster which absorbed large amounts of state funding. The Armagnac was an adequate rather than brilliant design and by 1968 the last machine, used for experimental engine testing, was withdrawn and scrapped.

COMMERCIAL AIRCRAFT AND AIRLINERS

The true success story for SNCASE resulted from a 1951 specification issued by the French Government (SGACC) for a medium range jet airliner. Among submissions from the whole French aircraft industry, the Sud-Est X-210 project, powered initially by three of the new Atar engines which had been launched by SNECMA, was accepted for development. The final design, which was to become the Caravelle, was modified to use two Rolls-Royce Avon engines mounted on the sides of the rear fuselage. The elegant SE-210 had a highly streamlined fuselage with a nose section taken directly from the de Havilland Comet. The Caravelle prototype made its first flight in the spring of 1955 and greater enthusiasm was expressed by Air France than had been evident with the Armagnac with the result that a launch order was placed for twelve aircraft with twelve options. On 2 April 1958, the Caravelle was awarded its French type certificate but the definitive production Series I aircraft emerged with a slightly longer fuselage and a higher gross weight as a result of which the first delivery was not made until March 1959.

The Caravelle final assembly line was established at the Toulouse factory at St Martin du Touch and the company, which had become Sud Aviation on 1 March 1957 with the merger of SNCASE and SNCASO, pressed forward with a sales drive which yielded early orders from SAS and VARIG. Interest in the Caravelle came from many world airlines with, inevitably, different requirements and Sud Aviation was quick to seek further developments of the aircraft, primarily with more powerful variants of the Avon engine. In particular the needs of airlines operating in hot and high environments had to be addressed and, with increased thrust engines, Sud was also able to increase the range and gross weight of successive Caravelle variants. Further customers included Aerolineas Argentinas, Finnair, Swissair, Alitalia and Sabena.

An order from United Airlines for twenty Caravelle 6Rs was placed in 1960 and this seemed to position the aircraft for its breakthrough into the North American market. In order to offer an American engine on the Caravelle, Sud and General Electric converted an aircraft with CJ.805 engines but this failed to attract an expected order from TWA and a follow-on batch for United. Strong competition from the DC-9 and Boeing 727 had appeared and orders for the Caravelle were coming in twos and threes from European airlines. This prompted Sud Aviation to launch the Super Caravelle 10B with a modified wing profile, double slotted flaps, cabin windows positioned at a higher level and a modified tailplane junction with a shock fairing. The 'Super B', which was fitted with Pratt & Whitney JT8D-1 turbofans, gained orders from Finnair, and the Danish operator, Sterling Airways.

By 1972, orders for the Caravelle had largely dried up and the production line was closed with delivery of the 280th aircraft to Air Inter. Caravelles continued to give excellent service into the 1990s and passed to the charter market but by 1997 fewer than fifteen aircraft remained in operation.

Details of the transport aircraft produced by the Sud Est company are as follows.

Sud Est SE-2010 Armagnac, F-BAVE

Type No.	Name	No. Built	Notes
SE-161/1	Languedoc	101	Pre-war Bloch-designed low-wing 44-pax airliner with twin fin tail unit, tailwheel u/c and four 900 h.p. Gnôme Rhône 14N radial piston engines. Prot. F-ARTV FF. Sep. 1939.
SE-161R	Languedoc		SE-161 with 1220 h.p. Gnôme Rhône engines.
SE-161/P7	Languedoc		SE-161 for Air France with 1220 h.p. Pratt & Whitney R-1830 SIC-3G engines.
SE-200		2	Large long range transport flying boat powered by six Wright Cyclone 2600 radial engines. Prot. F-BAHE (c/n 1) FF 1942/43. Abandoned post-war after testing.
SE-2010	Armagnac	8	104-pax airliner with mid-wing and tricycle u/c powered by four 2687 h.p. Pratt & Whitney R4360-B13 radial piston engines. Prot. F-WAVB (c/n 1) FF. 30 Dec. 1950. F-WAVB later mod. to SE-2060 as SNECMA Atar testbed F-ZWSQ.
SE-210	Caravelle	2	52-pax pressurised airliner with low wing, cruciform tail, tricycle u/c, teardrop-shaped cabin windows and two 10,000 lb.s.t. Rolls-Royce Avon RA.26 Mk.521 turbojets in rear fuselage mounted pods. 90,400 lb. TOGW. Prot. F-WHHH (c/n 01) FF. 27 May 1955.
SE-210	Caravelle I	20	SE-210 with 4ft 6in fuselage stretch giving max 99-pax seating, 95,920 lb. TOGW and two Avon RA./291 Mk.522 turbojets. All later upgraded to Caravelle III.
SE-210	Caravelle IA	12	Caravelle I with Avon RA.29/1 Mk.526 engines.
SE-210	Caravelle III	78	Caravelle I with 11,400 lb.s.t. Avon RA.29/3 Mk.527 engines incorporating noise suppressors in lengthened nacelles. 101,000 lb. TOGW.
SE-210	Caravelle VI-N	53	Caravelle III with 12,200 lb.s.t. Avon RA.29/6 Mk.531 engines. 105,840 lb. TOGW.
SE-210	Caravelle VI-R	56	Caravelle III with 12,600 lb.s.t. Avon RA.29/6 Mk.533R engines with thrust reversers, modified cockpit with enlarged windows, no dorsal fin fairing, additional wing spoilers, 110,250 lb. TOGW.
SE-210	Caravelle VII		Caravelle III (N420GE c/n 42) re-fitted with two 16,100 lb.s.t. General Electric CJ805-23C engines, 114,660 lb. TOGW.
SE-210	Caravelle 10A	1	'Caravelle Horizon' based on Caravelle VII with modified wing root profile, higher cabin window line, shock bullet behind tailplane junction and double slotted flaps.
SE-210	Caravelle 10B1.R	20	Caravelle VI-R with 14,000 lb.s.t. JT8D-1 turbofans, strengthened u/c, modified underfloor cargo area and 119,000 lb. TOGW. Also known as Caravelle 10R.

COMMERCIAL AIRCRAFT AND AIRLINERS

Type No.	Name	No. Built	Notes
SE-210	Caravelle 10B.3	22	Caravelle Super B with strengthened u/c, 123,480 lb. TOGW and 14,500 lb.s.t. JT8D-9 turbofans.
SE-210	Caravelle 11R	6	Caravelle 10R with 2ft 9in forward fuselage stretch, port-side cargo door and strengthened floor for pax/cargo operations.
SE-210	Caravelle 12	12	Caravelle 10R with fuselage stretch of 6ft 7in for ward and 4ft aft of wing, strengthened structure 140-pax seating and 127,900 lb. TOGW. Powered by two 14,500 lb.s.t. JT8D-9R turbofans.

Serial numbers for the Languedoc were c/n 01 (prototype) and c/n 1 to 100 and for the Armagnac, c/n 01 (prototype) and c/n 1 to 8. The Caravelle had two prototypes (c/n 01 and 02) and production aircraft from c/n 1 to 280. The Caravelles were also allocated line numbers from 1 to 280 which may sometimes be quoted – and were not in exactly the same sequence as the serial numbers.

In April 1960, Sud Aviation and Dassault formed a consortium to develop a Mach 2.2 supersonic airliner which was named the Sud-Dassault Super Caravelle. This was to be a seventy-six-passenger airliner with transatlantic range and preliminary designs showed it to have a curved delta wing with four high performance turbojet engines in double under-wing pods. Maximum take-off weight would be 170,000 lb. During design development the Super Caravelle grew to 198,400 lb. gross weight and 100-passenger capacity and by 1962 discussions between the British and French governments had reached the point of a cooperation agreement being signed for its joint development. Under the agreement, Aérospatiale and British Aircraft Corporation, together with the engine manufacturers, SNECMA and Rolls-Royce/Bristol Siddeley would jointly produce a new supersonic transport which would incorporate the design work carried out on the Super Caravelle and the very similar Bristol 223 project.

The Concorde which finally emerged was, again, larger than either of the original projects with a maximum take-off gross weight of 408,000 lb. and seating capacity for up to 144 passengers. The engines selected were the Rolls-Royce/SNECMA Olympus 593 rated at an enormous 32,825 lb.s.t. and the Concorde incorporated many innovative technical features such as the drooping nose to improve visibility on take-off and landing. The problems associated with high speed flight, including airframe expansion from surface friction heating, had to be solved by the design teams but the programme moved remarkably quickly for such a complex undertaking and the first prototype (the French-built F-WTSS, c/n 001) flew on 2 March 1969 followed on 9 April by the first British-built aircraft (G-BSST c/n 002/13520). These were followed by two pre-production Concordes (G-AXDN, c/n 01/13522 and F-WTSA, c/n 02) which had a fuselage stretch of 19ft 6 in, higher powered engines (the 38,050 lb.s.t. Olympus 593 Mk. 610), changes to the ogival wing leading edge design, increased fuel capacity, a longer rear fuselage overhang and an improved nose visor. Two further production test examples were also built as Concorde 100s (F-WTSB c/n 201 and G-BBDG c/n 202/13523).

Following type certification on 13 October 1975 the first Concordes for Air France and British Airways commenced revenue services on 21 January 1976. Seven production aircraft were delivered to each of the national airlines from the Toulouse and Bristol production lines, designated Concorde 101 (Air France) and Concorde 102 (British Airways). A single serial number sequence was used covering both production lines (c/n 201 to 216). Despite efforts by the manufacturers and the British and French governments, no orders were forthcoming for Concordes for other airlines – largely because of the enormous cost of acquiring a fleet of the aircraft and the uncertainty of the commercial viability of the supersonic concept. However, several airlines did set up joint services with the Concorde operators. An arrangement with Braniff resulted in both French and British Concordes changing their registered identity at Washington on each occasion for the onward stage to Dallas. For this purpose, hybrid registrations (e.g. G-N94AF) were used

Sud Est SE-161 Languedoc, F-BATQ

and adjusted each time. Singapore Airlines operated a joint service with British Airways between London and Singapore via Bahrein, using G-BOAB with Singapore Airlines livery on one side and British Airways colours on the other. In 1999, the active fleet of six Air France and seven British Airways aircraft are engaged on a mixture of scheduled transatlantic services (Paris–New York and London–Washington respectively) and charter operations.

The Société Nationale de Constructions Aéronautique Sud Ouest (SNCASO)

SNCASO was formed in the nationalisation reorganisation of 1936 and despite its activities being strictly controlled during the war the small design team based in Cannes designed and constructed the prototype of a small transport aircraft – the SO-90. The SO-90 was flown in August 1943 and taken to Algeria from where it eventually returned to France to become the basis for the production SO-90. A series of conflicting government decisions resulted in a stop-start progression for the aircraft and it was only the SO-94 and SO-95 Corse which were produced in any numbers. Intended as a civil feeder liner and postal transport, the Corse failed to gain any commercial orders although examples were evaluated by some operators including Air Maroc. The completed Corses were eventually delivered to the French Navy as crew trainers.

Also emanating from the wartime design team in Cannes was a larger thirty-passenger transport, the SO-30N Bellatrix. In this case, the prototype was constructed during the mid-war years but hidden from German occupying forces and not flown until February 1945 after hostilities had ceased. The all-metal SO.30N was a streamlined aircraft with a circular section fuselage, twin tail fins and a retractable tailwheel undercarriage and was very modern in its design with a top speed of 300 m.p.h. The second Bellatrix which flew in the following autumn was equipped with a tricycle undercarriage with a large single nosewheel – and this was the standard used on the production SO.30P Bretagne. A batch of Bretagnes was laid down in contemplation of deliveries to Air France, but, as with the SO.95 Corse, it seems that the national airline saw little use for the Bretagne. A number of SO.30Ps did go into commercial operation with nine being delivered to Air Algerie and twelve to Air Maroc. Others flew with Aigle Azur in French Indo-China and with Air Laos, Iranian Airways, Aero Cargo – and Air France who used one Bretagne for cargo operations. However, the majority of the forty-five aircraft (c/n 1 to 45) were passed over to the French Air Force and Aéronavale for use as general transports and for various experimental testbed applications at Bretigny and Istres. The Bretagnes were finally withdrawn in the late 1970s.

Type No.	Name	No. Built	Notes
SO-90		3	Low-wing 8-pax all-metal transport with retractable tailwheel u/c and two 325 h.p. Béarn 6D-07 piston engines. Prot. FF 16 Aug. 1943.
SO-93		1	SO-90 with tricycle u/c and Renault 12S engines.
SO-94		15	10-pax version of SO-93. Radar trainer SO-94R with lengthened nose.
SO-95	Corse	45	SO-94 with tailwheel u/c and two SNECMA 12S-02 engines. Max 13-pax capacity. All delivered as military SO-95M.
SO-30N	Bellatrix	1	All-metal low-wing 22-pax airliner with retractable tailwheel u/c, twin fin tail unit and powered by two wing-mounted 1020 h.p. Gnôme Rhône 14N radial engines. Prot. F-WALY (c/n 01) FF. 26 Feb. 1945.
SO-30R	Bellatrix	2	Developed 30-pax SO-30R with single fin tail unit, tricycle u/c and two 1600 h.p. SNECMA 14R engines. Prot F-WAYA (c/n 01) FF. 6 Nov. 1945. Second a/c, F-WAYB with twin fins and later fitted with two Rolls-Royce Nene turbojets.
SO-30P	Bretagne	45	SO-30R with twin fin tail unit, max 43-pax capacity and fitted with two 2400 h.p. Pratt & Whitney R2800–CA18 engines. Prot. F-WAYC (c/n 1) FF. 11 Dec. 1947.
SO-30C		1	SO-30R built as military freighter with belly cargo hatches and 1850 h.p. SNECMA 14R-206 engines. Prot. F-WAYN (c/n 01) FF. 6 Jan. 1950.

The Société Nationale de Constructions Aéronautique du Nord (SNCAN)

SNCAN (Nord Aviation) was merged into Aérospatiale on 1 January 1970. As with the other constituent companies of Aérospatiale, Nord had been formed through government nationalisation of the aviation industry in 1937 and it produced a variety of German designed aircraft (Me.108 derivatives etc.) during and after the war. The first original post-war design was the abortive Nord N.2100 Norazur ten-passenger light transport but Nord was also working on a larger aircraft aimed at a French Air Force requirement for a mid-sized freighter and SNCAN came up with a solution which was remarkably similar to the contemporary Fairchild Packet.

Sud Ouest SO.30P, No 20

Nord 262, F-GBEJ

The Nord 2500 had a high wing, twin booms and a main fuselage pod with rear loading doors. It was an attractive and practical design which had the flexibility to carry passengers or paratroops and could also be sold to civil operators. Following the initial test period of the five prototype/pre-production aircraft, Nord put considerable effort into achieving overseas sales, particularly in South America, but the French Air Force order became the main outlet for the N-2501 Noratlas and 208 were produced with the final delivery being made in late-1961. A few examples of the Noratlas reached commercial service – particularly with UAT-Aeromaritime who took delivery of seven Nord 2502s and Air Algerie which took over an N-2502B in 1958 and used it for four years before selling it on to the Portuguese Air Force.

The Noratlas was also built in Germany by Flugzeugbau Nord for the West German Air Force. One hundred and eighty-seven examples were delivered between 1956 and 1964 with the first twenty-five coming from the SNCAN factory and the balance being locally constructed at Hamburg-Finkenwerder. A number of German aircraft were sold to civil operators, particularly German cargo companies and Ecuador, when the Noratlas was retired from Luftwaffe service in the early 1970s.

In 1961, Nord absorbed part of Avions Max Holste under an arrangement which left Reims Aviation as an independent company devoted to Cessna licence production and passed the heavy aircraft programmes of Holste to Nord. Holste had developed a twin piston-engined light transport, the MH-250 Super Broussard, which eventually went into production as the turboprop MH-260. Only a handful of MH-260s were produced and at the time Nord took over the programme commercial prospects were poor and Holste was in financial difficulty over the aircraft. Under Nord, the MH-260 was redesigned with a new pressurised fuselage, increased passenger capacity and more powerful Turboméca Bastan engines.

Sales of the new Nord 262 started with an order for four aircraft from Air Inter and Nord also achieved a significant breakthrough with the sale of twelve aircraft to Lake Central Airlines in the USA which were put into service with the Allegheny Commuter network in 1966. Further orders came in ones and twos from various carriers including Air Ceylon, Linjeflyg, Alisarda, Cimber Air and Air Comores. The Nord production line at Bourges started to be filled out with French military aircraft in order to attempt to make the programme financially viable. In the end a total of 110 Nord 262s was completed with fifty-three going to commercial customers and the balance to the French Government, Armée de l'Air and Aéronavale.

The Nord 262 was always a victim of its Turboméca Bastan engines which, in the initial stages, had a very poor reliability record. In 1975 Frakes Aviation announced a programme to re-engine the aircraft as the Mohawk 298. This involved fitting the Nord 262 with a pair of Pratt & Whitney PT6A-45 engines and at least nine aircraft were converted for use by Allegheny. Production of the Nord 262 ended in 1976 but a number remain in service with the French military forces. Detailed information on the Noratlas and Nord 262 series is as follows.

Type No.	Name	No. Built	Notes
N-2500	Noratlas	1	Cargo aircraft of all metal construction with high wing, twin booms, tricycle u/c and fuselage pod incorporating hinged rear loading door. Powered by two 1600 h.p. SNECMA 14R piston engines. Prot. F-WFKL (c/n 01) FF. 10 Sep. 1949.
N-2501	Noratlas	213	N-2500 with 2040 h.p. Bristol Hercules 739 engines. Two a/c converted to N-2502B.
N-2501A	Noratlas	2	Civil version of N-2501 for UAT (c/n 1 and 2). Converted to N-2502.
N-2501D	Noratlas	187	N-2501 for German Air Force.
N-2501E	Noratlas		Initial designation for N-2506. Prot. No.40. FF after conversion 9 Aug. 1956.
N-2502	Noratlas	5	N-2501 with supplementary wingtip-mounted Turboméca Marboré turbojets. (c/n 3 to 7).
N-2502B	Noratlas	3	Civil N.2502 for Air Algerie. F-OBDZ (c/n 3) plus N-2501 conversions c/n 148/1 and 149/2.
N-2502C	Noratlas	1	Civil N.2502. F-BGKG (c/n 2).
N-2502F	Noratlas	1	N-2501 for French Navy.
N-2503	Noratlas	1	N-2501 fitted with two 2500 h.p. Pratt & Whitney R2800-CB17 engines. F-WFRG (c/n 01). FF 31 Jan. 1956.
N-2504	Noratlas	1	French Navy variant of N-2501. One prot. only (c/n 01).
N-2506	Noratlas	1	N-2502 with Hercules 759 engines, improved flaps, height-adjustable u/c and rear fuselage airbrakes. Initially designated N-2501E. Prot. F-WIEX (c/n 01) FF. 22 Aug. 1957.
N-2508	Noratlas	2	N-2503 with supplementary wingtip-mounted Turboméca Marboré II turbojets. (c/n 01 & 02).

Noed N.2501 Noratlas, No.9, Armée de l'Air

Type No.	Name	No. Built	Notes
MH-250	Super Broussard	1	High-wing all-metal 26-pax light transport with retractable tricycle u/c and powered by two 600 h.p. Pratt & Whitney R-1340 radial piston engines. 14,600 lb. TOGW. Prot. F-WJDA (c/n 001) FF. 20 May, 1959.
MH-260	Nord 260	10	MH-250 with two 986 shp Turboméca Bastan III turboprop engines. 20,723 lb. TOGW. Prot. F-WJDV (c/n 01) FF. 27 Jul. 1960. Production version fitted with Bastan IV engines.
N-262	Nord 262	1	Pressurised version of MH-260 with redesigned fuselage, taller tail unit, 29-pax interior and 1065 shp Bastan VIB.2 turboprops. 21,715 lb. TOGW. Prot. F-WKVR (c/n 01) FF. 24 Dec. 1962.
N-262A	Nord 262	75	Production N-262 with fin leading edge fairing and 1065 shp Bastan VIC engines. 23,370 lb. TOGW. (except N-262A-12 at 22,930 lb.)
N-262B	Nord 262	4	N-262A with detail modifications for Air Inter.
N-262C	Frégate	8	N-262A with 1145 shp Bastan VII turboprops, modified wingtips. 23,810 lb. TOGW.
N-262D	Nord 262	21	N-262C for Armée de l'Air with military interior and equipment.
N-262E	Nord 262	1	N-262 upgraded with Bastan VII engines
N-262	Mohawk 298		N-262C converted by Frakes Aviation with two Pratt & Whitney PT6A-45 turboprops. Nine conversions.

Every Nord 262 carried a specific designation which identified the original delivery customer. A number of aircraft sold second-hand received new customer numbers if they were modified to a new internal or equipment specification. These specific designations and their customers are shown below.

Model	Customer	Model	Customer
N-262A12	Lake Central	N-262A36	Air Comores
N-262A14	Japan Domestic	N-262A38	Tunis Air
N-262A15	Europe Aero Svce.	N-262A40	ENSA
N-262A20	SNIAS	N-262A41	CEV
N-262A21	Alisarda	N-262A42	Danish CAA
N-262A22	Air Ceylon	N-262AG43	Dan Air
N-262A24	Rousseau Aviation	N-262A45	Air Alsace
N-262A26	Linjeflyg	N-262C50P	U.Volta AF
N-262A27	Cimber Air	N-262C61	SFA
N-262A28	French Navy	N-262C62	Gabon AF
N-262A29	French Navy	N-262C63	E.African DCA
N-262A30	IFG	N-262C64	Gabon AF
N-262A32	SFA	N-262C65	U.Volta AF
N-262A33	Air Madagascar	N-262C66	Congo AF
N-262A34	French Air Force	N-262C67	Bouraq Indonesia
N-262A35	SFA	N-262D51	French Air Force

COMMERCIAL AIRCRAFT AND AIRLINERS

Each model of the Nord Noratlas had its own serial number sequence. Those built in small numbers are detailed in the Model Table, but the main production model, the N-2501, had c/n 02 to 05 for the prototype and pre-production aircraft followed by c/n 1 to 208 for the main production batch. The German production aircraft were c/n 001 to 187. Production Holste/Nord MH-260s were c/n 1 to 9 and the Nord 262 batch ran from c/n 1 to 110 (plus prototypes referred to in the Model Table).

SE-210 Caravelle 11R, 9Q-CLD

Concorde G-N94AD

SE-210 Caravelle VIR, N1004U

AIRBUS INDUSTRIE INTERNATIONAL

Airbus Industrie must be counted as a success story – and yet its success is the result of its people building a business and a product line despite the organisation being a pawn in an international political game. Airbus has often been accused of being highly subsidised by France and the other governments of the constituent partners. It will probably never be known if Airbus (both as an organisation and through the manufacturing activities of its partner companies) has ever made a profit – but it can also be said that its major competitor, Boeing, might never have built such a successful line of airliners without the massive initial orders for military '707s from the United States government.

Whatever the truth, Airbus Industrie has become the clear challenger to Boeing in the international air transport market place and it has won orders from Boeing based on the excellence of its products and by filling market niches which have been left open by its American competitor. Few would have believed this possible when the first Airbus A300 was rolled out in 1972. The Airbus project had been launched in 1965 when an Anglo-French working party produced the specification of a 225-seat medium range wide-body airliner to meet the needs of European airlines. Over a period of eighteen months project definition work was done by a number of European manufacturers which culminated on 26 September 1967 in a Memorandum of Understanding being agreed between the British, French and German governments.

A300-600, B-2315

COMMERCIAL AIRCRAFT AND AIRLINERS

This Memorandum established government-sponsored participation in the development of the new project by Hawker Siddeley (37.5%), Sud-Aviation (37.5%) and the German organisation Arge-Airbus (25%). This structure was soon disrupted by the withdrawal of British Government support for the project in 1969 but Hawker Siddeley decided to continue as a manufacturing participant in the programme, undertaking the design and manufacture of the wings on a private venture basis. The formal Airbus programme was established on 18 December 1970 as a French GIE ('Groupement d'Interet Economique') and at this time Fokker-VFW was brought into the partnership with a 7% share of manufacturing activity. The two major partners each retained 37.5% of the Airbus work. The partnership was further adjusted in October 1971 by the inclusion of CASA. Hawker Siddeley's wing contract constituted 20% of the production work and eventually British Aerospace was able to convert this into a full membership share of the GIE. As a result, the final constitution of Airbus in 1979 was Aérospatiale 37.9%, Deutsche Airbus 37.9%, British Aerospace 20% and CASA 4.2%.

The Airbus A300 as originally conceived was a 300-seater to be powered by a pair of Rolls-Royce RB.207 engines which were then under development but the insolvency of Rolls-Royce in 1971 meant that the aircraft would, instead, have to be powered by General Electric CF6 or Pratt & Whitney JT9D turbofans. This resulted in Airbus redefining the A300 as a smaller aircraft with 250 seats in which form it was designated A300B (although it probably should have been called the A250). The first Airbus, which flew on 28 October 1972 was the A300B1 variant and only one further example was completed since Airbus decided that the initial production model should be the larger A300B2 with an additional thirty-passenger capacity. This was necessary to meet the needs of the lead customer, Air France. The majority of A300s were powered by General Electric CF6 turbofans, but later aircraft were sold with the JT9D engines. The A300 received French and German certification on 15 March 1974 by which time the first delivery had already been made to Air France. However, it was not until 1977 that a strong flow of orders started to be achieved and allowed Airbus to move up to respectable production rates.

An important breakthrough came with an order from Eastern Airlines which gave Airbus a much needed stepping stone into the North American market. Further A300 orders were received from key European airlines including SAS, Iberia and Alitalia and far eastern

A310-325, F-WWCF (S2-ADE)

A320-233, F-WWBX (VP-BVA)

operators such as Pakistan International, Indian Airlines and Singapore Airlines. Laker Airways, which had pioneered the low-cost Skytrain services with DC-10s also ordered the A300 but went out of business before the aircraft could be delivered. In 1980, Airbus launched the A300-600 which provided a lengthened rear fuselage and redesigned EFIS cockpit. The first of this version was delivered to Saudia in 1984 and all subsequent A300s were built to this standard or as the A300-600R with additional fuel capacity in tailplane tanks. American Airlines became the first customer for the A300-600R, receiving the first of an order for twenty-five in December 1987.

One of the most remarkable developments of the A300 came in 1991 with the announcement of the A300-600ST Beluga. Throughout the history of the Airbus project, the problem of manufacture of large components in different factories had been resolved by the use of the turboprop Super Guppy outsized transporters which were based on Boeing Stratocruiser airframes. With these nearing the end of their useful lives, Airbus formed a separate subsidiary, SATIC (Super Airbus Transport International) to develop the A300 airframe as the basis for replacement. The lower half of the fuselage and the wings were retained but the cockpit section was lowered and a completely new bulbous cargo compartment built in place of the upper fuselage, incorporating forward clamshell doors for loading. The tail was enlarged with a leading edge fin fillet and with endplate fins on the tailplane. Initially, SATIC built four Belugas for Airbus operations and it is not marketing the aircraft to third-party customers – but, doubtless this may change if there is sufficient demand. SATIC is currently studying the use of the A340 airframe for a larger Beluga variant.

While the A300 had been coming off the Toulouse final assembly line, Airbus had developed a smaller capacity version with a shortened fuselage and seating for 210 passengers together with a redesigned wing and the upgraded EFIS cockpit which was installed in the A300-600R. The first A310 flew in April, 1982 and was certificated on 11 March 1983 with deliveries to the lead customers, Lufthansa, KLM and Swissair commencing in the following August. At about the same time, Airbus announced the alternative long-range A310-300 and the first example of this version was handed over to Swissair at the end of 1985. The A310 series has been delivered to a wide range of users including Kuwait Airways, Cyprus Airways, Singapore Airlines, Wardair Canada and Pan American. A specialised freight model, the A310-200F is in service with Federal

Express, the aircraft having been converted from former Lufthansa, KLM and PanAm passenger aircraft.

The spring of 1984 saw Airbus launching the third model in an expanding product line. The 150-seat A320 was a completely new design which owed little to the A300/310. Airbus saw that it needed to compete with the Boeing 737 and McDonnell Douglas DC-9 so the A320 was the first of a new family which could meet a range of capacity needs in the smaller short/medium haul market. The A320 was technologically advanced with an EFIS cockpit with a fly-by-wire control system and side sticks in place of the conventional control yokes. In general layout, the design was conventional with a low wing and a pair of CFM56 turbofans mounted on short underwing pylons.

With many existing satisfied A300/310 operators Airbus soon accumulated orders for the A320 with Air France, once again, being the launch operator. When the A320 prototype was flown in February 1987 Airbus could claim 439 orders and the first two deliveries were made to Air France and British Caledonian in March 1988. Some questions were raised over the sophisticated computer-controlled systems when the ninth A320 crashed while demonstrating at an air show at Habsheim in June of that year but Airbus deliveries built up rapidly with Air Inter, Cyprus Airways, and Ansett all taking their initial aircraft in the first year. Airbus had gained a major North American order for the A320 from Northwest Airlines and this was followed by sales to America West, Air Canada and United. By the end of 1997, over 100 A320s were flying in the United States. Airbus has progressively upgraded the A320 and offers the aircraft with a choice of CFM56 engines or the V.2500 series turbofans from International Aero Engines.

The A320 was the central model in what is now a three-aircraft family. The first A320 development was the A321 which was announced in November 1989 and raised passenger capacity to 180 seats by stretching the A320 fuselage by 22ft 9in. Deliveries to the first customer, Lufthansa, followed on from JAA certification which took place on 17 December 1993. Alitalia has also taken the first of an order for forty aircraft and other substantial operators will be CAAC, Asiana, Aero Lloyd and Iberia (who have ordered a mixed fleet of A319s, A320s and A321s totalling fifty aircraft with twenty-six options). Over 200 A321s had been sold by the spring of 1998. Airbus followed the stretched A321 with a reduced capacity A320, the A319, which is a 124-seat version with the fuselage shortened by 12ft 3in. The A319 was certificated in April 1996 and, again, there was high customer demand with 500 aircraft on order or delivered to fifteen airlines by September, 1998. Northwest Airlines has been a major customer with fifty due to be received to add to the fleet of seventy A320s. Airbus has also offered the A319 as the A319CJ 'Corporate Jetliner' for executive use with an interior layout of separate cabins and a port-side corridor to give access to the individual areas.

In 1986, the Airbus product line was comprehensive but, essentially composed of

A319-112, D-AKNF

A321-131, TC-ONH

short/medium haul aircraft. To compete effectively with Boeing, Airbus needed a long haul widebody aircraft with the range to fly London to Singapore or Los Angeles or Sydney to Los Angeles. While the A320 was a completely new model, the new long range A340 design started from an existing Airbus design base with the A300B11 which was an outgrowth of the standard Airbus 300. Otherwise known as the TA11 the four-engined A340 was developed in parallel with a twin-engined model designated TA9 (or Airbus A.330) which was a slightly shorter version with reduced range. New engines or uprated derivatives of existing powerplants were offered by CFM, Rolls-Royce (Trent), General Electric and Pratt & Whitney (PW4000) to power the new models. International Aero Engines proposed an ultra-high bypass version of their V2500 which would have been highly suitable for the A340 but this development was abandoned and Airbus had to revert to existing engines.

Airbus flew the first A340 in October 1991 and the A330 followed a year later. The JAA type certificates were awarded in December 1992 and October 1993. They followed these basic models with the long range A330-200 and the A340-200 and intend to build further payload and range offerings with the A340-500 and A340-600. The A340-500, which will be slightly longer than the standard A340 will have a range of 9800 miles – or 35% more than the similar capacity Boeing 767-300ER. Around 230 each of the A330 and A340 had been ordered by the summer of 1998 with major operators of the A340 including Lufthansa, Singapore Airlines and Virgin Atlantic and the A330 being requested by Malaysia Airlines, Northwest, Cathay Pacific and Emirates Airlines.

Production details

Airbus have allocated separate serial number batches to each of the main production models. These batches are as follows:

Models	Batch	Notes
A300 and A310 Series	c/n 001 to 796 (current)	Some c/ns not used due to order cancellations
A320, 321 and 319	c/n 001 to 0918 (current)	Some c/ns not used due to order cancellations
A330 and A340	c/n 001 to 250 (current)	

Model Information

From May 1978 Airbus introduced a new system of designations. A typical designation would be A300B4-203-06. The separate parts of the designation were made up as follows:

COMMERCIAL AIRCRAFT AND AIRLINERS

Example: A300B4-203-06

A300	Basic Aircraft designation	A300, A310, A320, A330, A340 etc.
B	Aircraft Function	B=Passenger, C=Convertible, F=Freighter
4	Model category	1=Low weight prototype, 2= 302,033 lb. TOGW, 4= 330,687 lb. TOGW and centre section fuel tank
2	Primary series depending on major weight or design changes	100 series with basic airframe. 200 series with leading edge slats etc.
03	Engine type	e.g. 01= GE CF6-50C, 02=CF6-50C1, 03= CF6-50C2, 20= P&W JT9D-59A, 21= P&W JT9D-59B
06	Design weight category	For example, categories for the A300B2-100 included:

Category		MTOW (tonnes)	MLW (t)	MZFW (t)
00	=	137	127.5	116.5
01	=	137	130	120.5
02	=	142	130	120.5
03	=	142	134	124

In practice, the last code section for weight categories has not been used. The number of aircraft using the 'C' and 'F' designation has been quite small.

Details of the individual designations allocated are as follows.

Type No.	No. Built	Notes
A300		Original 1969 wide body medium haul airliner design with low wing and twin turbofans in pylon-mounted underwing pods.
A300B		Definitive production Airbus A300 design with reduced capacity.
A300B1	2	Initial production A300B powered by two 49,000 lb.s.t. General Electric CF6-50A turbofans. 291,000 lb. TOGW. Prot. F-WUAB (c/n 001) FF. 28 Oct. 1972.
A300B2-100		B2 Basic short-haul version based on A300B1 with fuselage lengthened by 8ft 7in to give max 269-pax. capacity. 302,033 lb. TOGW.
A300B2-101	24	A300B2 production aircraft with two 50,400 lb.s.t. GE CF6-50C turbofans. Also known as A300B2-1C and A300B2-1C/101. 302,033 lb. TOGW. Max. 345-pax. capacity.
A300B2-103	1	A300B2-101 with two 50,400 lb.s.t. GE CF6-50C2 turbofans.
A300B2-1A	5	A300B2-101 with two 48,400 lb.s.t. GE CF6-50C2A turbofans.
A300B2-200		Special hot and high performance version with leading edge Kruger slats at wing root for higher gross weight operations. Max. 330,687 lb. TOGW. Also known as A300B2K.
A300B2-201		A300B2-200 with 50,400 lb.s.t. GE CF6-50C turbofans. 313,056 lb. TOGW.
A300B2-202	2	A300B2-200 with GE CF6-50C1 turbofans.
A300B2-203	9	A300B2-200 with 51,800 lb.s.t. CF6-50C2 turbofans. 315,040 lb. TOGW. Also known as A300B2K-3C.
A300B2-320	4	A300B2-200 with two Pratt & Whitney JT9D-59A turbofans and modified A300B4 wing. Later redesignated A300B4-220.
A300-B2K-3C	13	Initial designation for A300B2-203.

Type No.	No. Built	Notes
A300B4-100		B4 Basic medium haul version with additional centre-section fuel tank and 330,687 lb. TOGW.
A300B4-102	6	A300B4-100 with two 51,800 lb.s.t. GE CF6-50C1 turbofans.
A300B4-103	51	A300B4-100 with two 51,800 lb.s.t. GE CF6-50C2 turbofans. Also known as A300B4-2C and A300B4-2C/103.
A300B4-120	8	A300B4–100 with two 51,800 lb.s.t. Pratt & Whitney JT9D-59A turbofans.
A300B4-200		Transcontinental long-range variant with strengthened airframe. 315,040 lb. TOGW.
A300B4-203	108	A300B4-200 with two 51,800 lb.s.t. GE CF6-50C2 turbofans. 363,760 lb. TOGW.
A300B4-220	13	A300B4-200 with two 51,800 lb.s.t. Pratt & Whitney JT9D-59A turbofans.
A300C4		A300B4 Combi passenger/freight derivative with main deck forward port side cargo door and 41 tonne payload.
A300C4-203	4	A300B4-203 Combi passenger/freight aircraft with strengthened floor and forward port cargo door.
A300B4-600		600 series with modified rear fuselage, 21in fuselage stretch and EFIS cockpit as used on A310. 363,760 lb. TOGW.
A300B4-601	6	A300B4-600 with 57,860 lb.s.t. CF6-80C2A1 turbofans.
A300B4-603	11	A300B4-600 with 58,950 lb.s.t. CF6-80C2A3 turbofans.
A300B4-605R	77	Long-range A300B-600 with additional tailplane fuel tanks, computerised fuel trimming system and 60,100 lb.s.t. CF6-80C2A5 engines. 378,530 lb. TOGW.
A300F4-605R	21	A300-605R all-freight aircraft with no cabin windows, single forward entry door, cargo door in forward port side, strengthened floor and cargo handling system.
A300C4-605R	2	A300B4-605R Combi passenger/freight aircraft with strengthened floor and forward port cargo door.
A300B4-608ST	4	A300B4 converted to Super Transport with bulbous upper fuselage, low level cockpit, enlarged fin, tailplane end plates and two 59,000 lb.s.t General Electric CF6-80C2AB turbofans. Prot. F-WAST (c/n 655) FF. 13 Sep. 1994.

A330-322, 9M-MKY

Type No.	No. Built	Notes
A300B4-620	68	A300B4-600 with 56,000 lb.s.t. Pratt & Whitney JT9D-7R4H1 turbofans.
A300C4-620	4	A300B4-620 Combi passenger/freight aircraft with strengthened floor and forward port cargo door.
A300B4-621	1	A300B4-600 with Pratt & Whitney JT9D-7R4D1 turbofans.
A300B4-622	2	A300B4-600 with 58,950 lb.s.t. Pratt & Whitney PW4158 turbofans.
A300B4-622R	25	A300B4-600R with 58,950 lb.s.t. Pratt & Whitney PW4158 turbofans.
A300B10		Initial designation for A310.
A310-200		A300 with redesigned wing of smaller area and fuselage shortened by 22ft 8in fore and aft of wing, redesigned rear fuselage. Max. 280-pax. capacity. 305,560 lb. TOGW. Powered by various GE, P&W engines. Prot. F-WZLH (c/n 162) FF. 3 Apl. 1982. Some converted as A310-200F all-freight aircraft.
A310-203	44	A310 with two GE CF6-80A3 turbofans.
A310-203C	1	A310-203 Combi passenger/freight aircraft with forward port cargo door and strengthened floor.
A310-204	7	A310 with two GE CF6-80C2A2 turbofans.
A310-221	10	A310 with two Pratt & Whitney JT9D-7R4D1 turbofans.
A310-222	23	A310 with two Pratt & Whitney JT9D-7R4E1 turbofans.
A310-240		A310 with two Rolls-Royce RB211-525B4 turbofans. Not built.
A310-300		Long-range A310 with additional tailplane fuel tanks, computerised fuel trimming system and max. 361,600 lb. TOGW.
A310-304	76	A310-300 with two GE CF6-80C2A2 turbofans.
A310-307	1	A310-300 with two GE CF6-80C2A7 turbofans.
A310-308	26	A310-300 with two GE CF6-80C2A8 turbofans.
A310-322	6	A310-300 with two Pratt & Whitney JT9D-7R4E1 turbofans.
A310-324	49	A310-300 with two Pratt & Whitney PW4152 turbofans.
A310-324ET	1	A310-324 with ETOPS mods inc. hold fire suppression system and additional generator.

A340-211, F-WWJM (VR-HMR)

Type No.	No. Built	Notes
A310-325	7	A310-300 with two Pratt & Whitney PW4156A turbofans.
A310-325ET	1	A310-325 with ETOPS mods.
A320-100		New short-haul 150-passenger narrow body airliner with low wing and two CFM engines on underwing pylons, modernised CRT-based flight deck with side sticks. 149,915 lb. TOGW. Prot. F-WWAI (c/n 0001) FF. 22 Feb. 1987.
A320-111	21	A320-100 production model with two CFM56-5A1 turbofans.
A320-200		Longer range A320 with wing centre section fuel tank, wingtip winglets and 162,040 lb. TOGW.
A320-211	276	A320-200 with two CFM56-5A1 turbofans.
A320-212	32	A320-200 with two CFM56-5A3 turbofans.
A320-214	13	A320-200 with two CFM56-5B4 turbofans.
A320-231	146	A320-200 with two IAE V2500-A1 turbofans.
A320-232	50	A320-200 with two IAE V2527-A5 turbofans.
A320-233	2	A320-200 with two IAE V2500-A5 turbofans.
A319-100		A320 with fuselage shortened by 63in forward and 84in aft of wing and 124-passenger capacity. Wing modified with removal of inboard spoilers. Max. 154,323 lb. TOGW. Prot. F-WWDB (c/n 0546) FF. 28 Aug. 1995.
A319-112	3	A319 with two CFM56-5B6/2P turbofans.
A319-113		A319 with two CFM56-5A4 turbofans.
A319-114	3	A319 with two CFM56-5A5 turbofans.
A319-131		A319 with two IAE V2522-A5 turbofans.
A319CJ		Corporate jet version of A319 with executive interior and engine choice.
A319-M5		Proposed 100-seat A319 with shorter fuselage.
A321-100		A320 with fuselage stretched by 14ft forward and 8ft 9in. aft of wing, repositioned emergency exits, modified fuel system, double-slotted flaps and strengthened u/c. 200-passenger capacity. 183,000 lb. TOGW. Prot. F-WWIA (c/n 0364) FF. 11 Mar. 1993.
A321-111	20	A321 with two CFM56-5B1 turbofans.
A321-112	13	A321 with two CFM56-5B turbofans.
A321-131	21	A321 with two IAE V2530-A5 turbofans.
A321-200		Longer range A321 with up to two additional fuel tanks in rear cargo hold and 205,000 lb. TOGW. Prot. F-WWJA (c/n 0633).
A321-231		A321 with two IAE V2533-A5 turbofans.
A330-300		Long-range development of A300 with fly-by-wire systems, enlarged wing with increased sweep and wingtip winglets, fuselage lengthened by 32ft 10in. for 433-pax capacity, two-crew six-screen EFIS cockpit and powered by two underwing pylon-mounted Rolls-Royce Trent 700 (or Pratt & Whitney PW4000 or General Electric CF6-80E1) turbofans. 491,630 lb. TOGW. Prot. F-WWKA (c/n 0012) FF. 2 Nov. 1992.
A330-200		A330-300 with 3ft 7in. reduction in fuselage length, increased fuel and max 381-pax capacity. Max. 507,150 lb. TOGW. Prot. F-WWKA (c/n 181) FF. 13 Aug. 1997.
A330-301	10	A330 with two G.E. CF6.80E1A2 turbofans.

Type No.	No. Built	Notes
A330-321	9	A330 with two Pratt & Whitney PW.4168 turbofans.
A330-322	16	A330 with two Pratt & Whitney PW.4168 turbofans.
A330-341	1	A330 with two Rolls-Royce Trent 772-60 turbofans.
A330-342	10	A330 with two Rolls-Royce Trent 772 turbofans.
A340-200		Extended range A330 with four engines and related modified systems, 14ft shorter fuselage. 566,575 lb. TOGW. and Max. 253-pax capacity. Prot. F-WWAI (c/n 0001) FF. 25 Oct. 1996.
A340-211	17	A340-200 with four CFM56-5C2 turbofans.
A340-212	3	A340-200 with four CFM56-5C4 turbofans.
A340-300	1	A340-200 with lengthened (A330) fuselage and associated systems changes. 295-pax capacity.
A340-311	31	A340-300 with four CFM56-5C2 turbofans.
A340-312	14	A340-300 with four CFM56-5C3 turbofans.
A340-313	27	A340-300 with four CFM56-5C4 turbofans.
A340-341	3	A340-300 with four Rolls-Royce Trent 77s-60 turbofans.
A340-342	2	A340-300 with four Rolls-Royce Trent 772 turbofans.
A340-500		A340 with enlarged wing and increased 313-pax. capacity.
A340-600		A340-500 with increased fuel load and 380-pax capacity. To be powered by four Rolls-Royce Trent 500 and FF. Jan. 2001.
A340-8000		Very long-range version of A340-200 with additional rear cargo hold fuel tanks and increased gross weight to 606,375 lb.
A3XX		Projected double-deck airliner with four RR Trent 900 or GE-PW GP7000 turbofans. A3XX-100 standard version with 555-pax. seating, A3XX-100R long range version, A3XX-50 with 16ft 8in shorter fuselage for 480-pax. and A3XX-200 stretched version with 656-pax seating. Also cargo (A3XX-100F) and combi (A3XX-100C) variants with forward and aft freight doors. Prototype to fly in 2002.
AE31X		Projected 95/115 regional jet under development by Airbus, AVIC and Singapore Technologies.

A300-608ST, Beluga F-WSTC

ANTONOV

UKRAINE

While the Ilyushin and Tupolev bureaux have dominated Soviet passenger transport since the war, the field of utility and cargo aircraft has largely been served by the Antonov Design Bureau. Named after Oleg K. Antonov, the OKB was formed in 1945 following Antonov's career with the Yakovlev bureau. The first design of Antonov's new group was, perhaps, its most famous and certainly the longest-lived. The An-2 utility biplane was urgently required to provide support to the remote parts of the Soviet Union and to replace the smaller and less capable Polikarpov Po-2 biplanes.

The An-2 could have been considered old fashioned when it was introduced in 1947 but it had thoroughly modern construction with a tubular forward fuselage frame and stressed aluminium structure from the cockpit to the tail, and fulfilled the prime requirements of being extremely tough and capable of operation from the roughest of fields and having good short field performance and abundant power from a mighty ASh-621R radial engine. Following its first flight in August 1947, the An-2 went into production at Kiev–Svyetoshino. Numerous variants were produced but, while there were a few highly specialised applications for atmospheric sampling and similar roles, most versions differed from the basic An-2 only in terms of equipment. Large numbers went to the Soviet military forces and Aeroflot based the An-2 widely across the Soviet Union as a 12/14 passenger transport. They were used as ambulance aircraft, for fire fighting, parachute

An-2, D-FBAW

dropping, powerline patrol, fishery spotting, mapping and agricultural spraying and dusting.

An-2s were delivered to all the other Warsaw Pact countries and, in 1960, production of the aircraft was passed to PZL at Mielec in Poland where production continued until the mid-1990s. Total production is believed to be just under 16,000 of which Antonov's plant completed nearly 4000 An-2s and nearly 12,000 have come from Mielec. Indeed, Mielec still maintains a large stock of components to enable it to deliver An-2s on an 'as required' basis. The An-2 was also built in China but, contrary to some reports, none were constructed in East Germany. The An-3 was a new version of the aircraft developed by the parent factory at Kiev in 1959 and fitted with a Glushenkov TVD-10B turboprop engine. It was intended that this engine could be retrospectively fitted to existing An-2s but it appears that few if any aircraft have been so modified. The An-3 is still being promoted by the Antonov factory although no production appears to be in hand.

In the early 1950s Antonov was awarded the task of designing a new utility transport for the Soviet forces and the An-8 which emerged was to set the pattern for a range of highly capable cargo and passenger aircraft which became standard equipment for the Soviet Union and its satellites. The An-8 was a high wing aircraft with the (then) unique feature of an upswept rear fuselage incorporating a ventral rear loading ramp. The tricycle under-carriage utilised retractable four-wheel bogies enclosed in lower fuselage fairings and the military role of the aircraft was supported by a tail-mounted gun turret containing an NR-23 cannon. Antonov fitted the An-8 with two AI-20D turboprops and outside its cargo role the aircraft could carry up to forty-eight troops on folding seats. Approximately 200 An-8s were delivered and a number still operate with civil users – primarily in Africa.

The success of the An-8 led to Antonov devising an eighty-five-seat passenger version which had a redesigned circular-section pressurised fuselage and four engines. This An-10 Ukraina was first flown in March 1957 and went into service with Aeroflot in July 1959 between Moscow and Simferopol. They brought much increased capacity to Aeroflot's routes and were responsible for a substantial increase in passenger traffic throughout the Soviet network. With the introduction of the stretched An-10A up to 110 passengers could be carried and An-10 operations continued until 1972 when the type was withdrawn and replaced by the Il-18 and Tu-134 as a result of a poor accident record culminating in a major crash at Kharkov in May of that year.

In 1962, the first An-12 entered service with Aeroflot. Based on the An-10, the An-12 was a pure cargo aircraft and it featured a ventral rear loading ramp similar to that used on the An-8. As with the An-10 it had a glazed nose section incorporating a navigator's position and it also had a tail turret similar to that of the An-8 although this was faired

An-12, CU-T-827

An-22, CCCP-67691

over in the civil versions of the aircraft. An-12s entered service on Siberian routes in February 1963 and large numbers were subsequently delivered to the Soviet forces from the factories at Tashkent and Voronezh. The An-12 was also built in China as the Y-8. An-12s became standard equipment throughout the Warsaw Pact and civil air cargo users included LOT in Poland, TABSO in Bulgaria, CAAC, Iraqi Airways and Cubana. Batches were also delivered to the Indian, Egyptian, Algerian, Polish and Iraqi air forces.

In the late 1960s, the introduction of jet regional airliners such as the Tu-124 highlighted the increasing age of the short haul Aeroflot fleet of Il-12s and Il-14s. This resulted in Antonov being assigned the task of designing a new turboprop local service airliner. As with the An-2 and An-10, part of the specification was for an aircraft capable of operating from the worst of unprepared airfields in the most remote parts of the Soviet Union. The An-24 followed a similar layout to that of the Fokker F.27 and Handley Page Herald with a high wing, conventional tail unit and retractable tricycle undercarriage although its more rugged design was aimed at different operating criteria and its commercial economics did not match those of its western counterparts. Powered by a pair of Ivchenko AI-24A turboprops, the An-24 was intended as a thirty-two-passenger aircraft but it was finally configured to carry up to fifty-two passengers in four-abreast seating. With the emphasis on reliability and low maintenance the An-24 had straightforward systems and this allowed it to move fairly rapidly from its first flight in December 1959 to entering passenger service in the summer of 1962.

Production of the passenger versions of the An-24 took place at Kiev-Svyetoshino and later at Ulan Ude and dedicated freight variants (An-24T, An-24TV and An-24RT) were built from 1968 onwards at Irkutsk. The An-24TV incorporated a ventral rear loading ramp and this was to become a feature on later models based on the An-24 design. Large numbers were delivered to Aeroflot and a number of improvements in power and performance were incorporated as the production line matured. The An-24 was a standard transport for the Soviet Air Force together with other Warsaw Pact air arms including those of Poland, Hungary and Czechoslovakia. It became a popular and reliable choice for foreign airlines such at MIAT Mongolian, Lebanese Air Transport, United Arab Airlines, LOT, Cubana, TABSO and Air Mali. Antonov built special variants to meet the need for executive transports, casualty evacuation, parachuting, geophysical survey, cloud seeding and firefighting. It is believed that over 1300 examples of the different models were finally completed by the time production ceased in 1978.

The An-24 provided a basis for a range of further twin-engined models of which the An-26 cargo aircraft was the first development. This featured a pressurised cargo hold and a

An-24B, EW-46404

modified rear access ramp and cut-back rear fuselage. The majority of An-26s were delivered as military transports to the Soviet forces and other users but a substantial number have reached commercial customers including LOT, Tarom, MIAT-Mongolian and CAAC. Antonov also devised a specialised aerial survey and mapping variant, the An-30, with an extensively glazed nose and raised flight deck, and the stretched An-32 utility/freighter aircraft with much improved hot and high performance and revised engine nacelles with a higher thrust line. First deliveries of the An-32 were made from Kiev in 1984 and it has also been marketed as the An-32P Firekiller firefighting model with large tanks mounted externally on the lower fuselage. Many of the 370-odd An-32s delivered to date have been acquired by military customers including the Indian, Peruvian, Angolan, Afghan and Sri Lankan air forces but the aircraft has been widely exported to civil users in the CIS and Latin America.

With the An-24 fleet becoming increasingly geriatric, the Antonov Bureau commenced the design of a replacement during the early 1990s. The An-140 followed a similar high wing layout with a pressurised fuselage containing up to fifty-two passenger seats but the engine-mounted undercarriage layout of the An-24 is replaced by a main undercarriage housed in fuselage pods. The elegant unswept wing mounts a pair of 2470 shp TV-117VMA turboprops but the An-140 may be offered to Western customers with Pratt & Whitney PW127As. A cargo version is under development with a forward freight door. The An-140 prototype entered its flight test programme at Kiev-Svyetoshino in September 1997 and production aircraft will be built at Kharkov and at the Samara plant in Russia, initially to meet an order for forty aircraft placed by Ukrainian Airlines and a possible requirement by Diamond Sakha. A licence agreement has also been entered into for production of the aircraft by the Iranian company, HESA.

Antonov's innovative approach to aircraft design was well illustrated in the An-72 twin-engined STOL jet transport. As with other Antonov designs, the An-72 is a high-wing aircraft and has a pressurised fuselage with a high-set T-tail. A rear cargo ramp is incorporated and the An-72 is mainly used in the cargo role although high density seating for fifty-two passengers can be provided. The two Progress D-36 turbofans are mounted above and ahead of the wing centre section, close to the fuselage, and provide a high lift coefficient due to their jet exhaust discharging over the centre wing surface. Primarily a military model, the An-72 has been used by a number of commercial operators including Aviaenergo, Aviacor and Helitaxi Colombia. A higher powered version is designated An-74 and Antonov has also built an airborne early warning variant, the An-71 with a large radar rotodome mounted on an enlarged forward-swept fin. It is believed that nearly 300 examples of the An-72 and An-74 have been completed at the Kharkov factory.

Perhaps the best known of Antonov's designs have been the oversize transports which were first initiated in the 1960s. The Soviet Air Force and Aeroflot had a requirement for a very large aircraft which could carry loads such as a mobile missile unit or the principal Soviet battle tank. The Antonov Bureau designed the An-22 Antei with a high wing, twin tail fins, rear fuselage ventral ramp loading and a carrying capacity of up to 300,000 lb. The An-22 was powered by four 15,000 shp Kuznetsov NK-12MA turboprops driving contra-rotating propellers. It had an unpressurised main hold but the cockpit and forward fuselage was pressurised and could be fitted with up to twenty-nine passenger seats. The prototype Antei was first flown in early 1965 and a total of sixty-eight were built (mostly at Tashkent) between 1971 and 1974. Some were fitted with a cradle above the centre fuselage to allow carriage of oversize loads including wings for the An-124. No An-22s were exported and it is believed that around forty are still in service.

The An-22 was followed by the An-124 which was intended as its turbofan-powered successor and closely mirrored the specification of Lockheed's C-5 Galaxy military freighter. Again, the high wing layout was adopted and the An-124 (initially known as the An-400) had a conventional fin and tail-plane and both a rear ventral ramp and an upward-opening nose door to allow through-loading of freight. The whole fuselage was pressurised and an upper deck situated above the cargo compartment could accommodate up to eighty-eight passengers. Antonov designed a very clean wing which was heavily anhedralled and carried the four D-18T turbofans on underwing pylons. The main undercarriage was housed in lower fuselage fairings and consisted of five double wheel units on each side with twin two-wheel nose units incorporating kneeling mechanisms. The An-124, which became the largest production aircraft in the world, was built, initially at Kiev and later at Ulyanovsk with first deliveries to Aeroflot taking place in 1985. Approximately sixty have been completed and up to half of these are employed on commercial heavylift charter work with Heavylift/Volga Dnepr, Air Foyle and other independent Russian cargo operators. Antonov also built one example of the even larger An-225 Mriya which combines a stretched An-124 fuselage with longer span wings, two additional engines and a twin-fin tail unit. The An-225 was specially designed as a carrier for the Buran space shuttle which is mounted on a cradle above the wing centre section. This unique aircraft is no longer in service and construction of a second aircraft has been abandoned.

Showing the versatility of the Bureau's designers, Antonov has also designed successful small aircraft. In the mid-1950s they responded to an Aeroflot request for a small local service aircraft capable of carrying up to eight passengers and equipped to transport stretcher cases and light freight. The An-14 Pchelka was a strut-braced high wing machine with a fixed tricycle undercarriage, twin AI-14M radial engines and an upswept rear fuselage with a twin-fin tail unit and rear loading doors giving access to the main cabin. The

An-32, UR-48086

An-14 underwent a fairly extended development period and eventually reached Aeroflot users in 1965. A production total of 339 has been quoted by official sources, all of which were built at Arsenyev. Most of the production An-14s served in the Soviet Union but a handful made their way to Bulgaria, Yugoslavia and Mongolia.

The An-14 provided the basis for Antonov to develop further light transport designs. The first of these was the An-28 (originally An-14M) which featured a modified fuselage in which the original pod and boom layout of the An-14 gave way to a deeper and longer shape which expanded passenger capacity to seventeen seats. The An-28 gained a pair of TVD-10B turboprops which markedly improved performance. The first An-28 flew in 1969 but it was not until 1984 that the first production aircraft flew and, as with the An-2, this was produced by PZL-Mielec in Poland under the devolved production plan which transferred responsibility for many secondary aircraft to other Warsaw Pact countries. The principal customer was Aeroflot and around 200 An-28s had been built by 1996. The An-28 was followed by the An-38 which retained the basic wing and tail structure of the An-28 but had a stretched fuselage which added three additional seat rows, raising passenger capacity to twenty-six. This aircraft was entirely developed in the Ukraine and the prototype first flew in June 1994 from the Novosibirsk factory where the production line was subsequently established.

The greatest investment by Antonov in its new financially independent situation is the An-70 heavy military freighter which has been developed as an enlarged replacement for the An-12. This four-turboprop tactical transport is larger than the equivalent western C-130 Hercules and there was discussion as to whether it could fulfil the FLA military freighter requirement under consideration for NATO forces. The first An-70 was flown in December 1994 but was destroyed in a mid-air collision shortly after. The flight test programme was resumed in 1997 using the second aircraft (intended for static tests) and the Russian and Ukrainian air forces are said to require approximately 500 examples.

Production Details

Serial numbers for Antonov aircraft are issued by the factory assigned to produce the individual model. The system used in the PZL factory at Mielec is distinctive and consists of a number/letter prefix followed by a batch number and individual aircraft in the batch. For the factories in the Ukraine (and in Russia), the principal system (referred to in the table as the Standard system) is to have a four-part serial consisting of the Year Built (one digit indicating the last number of the year), Factory Number (two digits, e.g. 99 for factory GAZ-99 at Ulan Ude), Batch number (two digits) and the Individual Aircraft in the batch (two digits). A typical example would be an An-24B manufactured in 1977 at Ulan Ude with the construction number 7 99 013 06. There are, however, many variations with parts of the serial structure frequently being omitted. In recent times, the factories

An-28, YL-KAD

have issued individual numbers which appear to be computer-generated and which have no clear sequential relationship. The systems used for each of the Antonov types are as follows.

Model	C/n example	Serial – Part 1	Serial – Part 2	Notes
An-2	10847303	Prefix 1, Batch number (up to 3 digits, factory number 473)	Individual a/c in batch (2 digits)	Kiev-Svyetoshino built. No factory code on export aircraft.
An-2M	701519	Year built (one digit), Batch number (3 digits)	Individual a/c in batch (2 digits)	Built a Kiev-Svyetoshino
An-2	1G27-21	Prefix 1G, Batch number (up to 3 digits)	Individual a/c in batch (2 digits)	Polish production at PZL Mielec
An-8	9340308	Standard system	Standard system	Built at Tashkent (34)
An-8	0G3410	Batch number (0 plus Cyrillic letter), Factory number (34)	Individual a/c in batch (2 digits)	Built at Tashkent (34)
An-10	9401602	Standard system	Standard system	Built at Voronezh (40)
An-12	2340407	Standard system	Standard system	Built at Irkutsk (90), Tashkent (34), Voronezh (40)
An-14	601609	Year built (two digits), Batch number (2 digits)	Individual a/c in batch (2 digits)	Built at Arsenyev
An-22	8340110	Standard system	Standard system	Built at Tashkent (34). Prots. c/n 0101 to 0103 built at Kiev-Svyetoshino
An-22A	43482282	Year built (one digit), Factory number (34)	5-digit random number	Built at Tashkent
An-24	69900404	Standard system	Standard system	Built at Svyetoshino (73) and Ulan Ude (99)
An-24T	8910607	Standard system	Standard system	Built at Irkutsk (91)
An-24T	1022806	Type code (102), unident code (one digit), Year built (one digit)	Individual a/c serial (2 digits)	Built at Irkutsk
An-26	47302105	Standard system	Standard system	Built at Svyetoshino (73)
An-28	1AJ 002-04	Type prefix (1AJ), batch (3 digits)	Individual a/c serial (2 digits)	Built at PZL, Mielec
An-30	0604	Batch number (2 digits)	Individual a/c serial (2 digits)	Built at Svyetoshino (73)
An-32	1407	Batch number (2 digits)	Individual a/c serial (2 digits)	Built at Svyetoshino (73)
An-38	380100	Type number (38), Batch (2 digits)	Individual a/c serial (2 digits)	Built at Novosibirsk-Chkalowa
An-72	36572096914	Project number (365), Type number (720)	5-digit random number	Built at Kharkov (GAZ-135)

COMMERCIAL AIRCRAFT AND AIRLINERS

Model	C/n example	Serial – Part 1	Serial – Part 2	Notes
An-74	36547096919	Project number (365), Type number (470)	5-digit random number	Built at Kharkov (GAZ-135)
An-76	36576096915	Project number (365), Type number (760)	5-digit random number	Built at Arsenyev (GAZ-116)
An-124	9773054516003	Factory project number (977305), quarter and year (2 digits)	5-digit random number	Built at Ulyanovsk
An-124	19530502012	Factory project number (195305), batch number (2 digits)	3-digit random number	Built at Kiev
An-140				Built at Kharkov (GAZ-135) and Samara

Model Information

Details of all Antonov designs are as follows.

Type No.	Name	No. Built	Notes
An-2		3986	Large all-metal biplane with fixed tailwheel u/c, fully enclosed cabin with porthole windows and powered by one ASh-621R radial piston engine. Prot. FF. 31 Aug. 1947. NATO name 'Colt'.
PZL An-2		11900	An-2 built under licence in Poland by PZL at Mielec.
An-2T			Utility version for 12-pax or 1500kg cargo load. Also PZL-built.
An-2TD			Parachute training variant. Also PZL-built.
Yunshuji Y-5			An-2T built in China.
An-2TP			10-pax local service passenger version of An-2T with improved trim, soundproofing and toilet. Some with rectangular windows.

An-38, 3810001

Type No.	Name	No. Built	Notes
An-2P			High density transport version for 14-pax. Also PZL-built.
An-2R			Agricultural model with lengthened u/c, cabin hopper and underwing spraybars or belly mounted duster. PZL-built. Also known as An-2Skh.
An-2S			Ambulance version of An-2TP with provision for six stretchers and attendants. Also PZL-built.
An-2Geo			Geophysical survey version of An-2T with the TS-1230 infrared survey system.
An-2L			Firefighting version of An-2T with cabin-mounted water tank.
An-2M			Improved agricultural model with air conditioned cockpit and larger squared-off tail surfaces. Prot. FF. 20 May 1964.
An-2PK			VIP version of An-2P with 6-pax seats. PZL-built.
An-2PF			Aerial photography version of An-2P. PZL-built.
An-2PR			An-2T fitted with TV-relay equipment. PZL-built.
An-2F	Fedya		An-2 for night reconnaissance with dorsal gun turret and new tapered boom rear fuselage and twin fin tail. Also known as An-2NRK or An-2K.
An-2PP			An-2V seaplane version fitted with water scoops in the floats to carry water for forest fire suppression.
An-2V			Revised designation for An-4.
An-2W			Improved utility model based on An-2TP with alternative wheel, float or ski u/c. PZL-built.
An-3			Upgraded An-2 for agricultural work with 940 shp Glushenkov TVD-10B turboprop engine, repositioned air-conditioned cockpit, longer rear fuselage and modified tail unit. Prot. CCCP-30576, FF. 1982.
An-4			Twin float seaplane version of An-2T. Became An-2V.

An-70

Type No.	Name	No. Built	Notes
An-6			High altitude version of An-2 with turbocharged ASh-621R engine. Later designated An-2ZA Meteo and fitted with observer cabin on fin leading edge.
An-8		200	Military freighter with high wing, upswept rear fuselage with ventral loading ramp, retractable tricycle u/c, tail gun turret and powered by two AI-20D turboprop engines. Prot. FF. 1955. Some used by Aeroflot. NATO name 'Camp'.
An-10	Ukraina	100	Developed An-8 for Aeroflot with 75-pax capacity, circular section fuselage, fully pressurized cabin, modified main u/c housings, tailplane-mounted fins and powered by four Ivchenko AI-20 turboprops. 119,050 lb. TOGW. Prot. CCCP-U1957 FF. 7 Mar. 1957. NATO name 'Cat'.
An-10A	Ukraina		An-10 with fuselage stretched by 6ft 7in, 100-pax seating, reversing propellers and increased fuel. 121,473 lb. TOGW.
An-10V			See An-16.
An-12		1243	Military freighter version of An-10 with ventral rear fuselage loading doors, increased fuel capacity and 134,480 lb. TOGW. Four 4000 shp Kuznetsov NK-4 turboprops. 119,050 lb. TOGW. Prot. FF. 12 Dec. 1957. NATO name 'Cub'.
An-12A			Improved An-12 with four 4000 shp Ivchenko AI-20A and increased fuel capacity. 123,460 lb. TOGW.
An-12B			Civilian version of An-12 without tail gun turret and fitted with improved soundproofing. Powered by Ivchenko AI-20A engines with APU in port nacelle. Also referred to as An-12V.
An-12BP			Military An-12 parachute transport with unpressurised cabin and no ventral rear loading doors. An-12BPL has fixed ski u/c for Arctic operations.
An-12BK			An-12B with increased fuel capacity, redesigned cargo compartment with larger loading doors.
An-12PS			An-12B for air-sea rescue with droppable motor-boat.
An-12PP			Military electronic warfare variant. Also An-12PPS.
An-12BSh			Navigation trainer equipped for 10 trainees.
Yunshuji Y-8			An-12 built in China.
An-14	Pchelka	339	Light all-metal military utility aircraft with high strut-braced wing, fixed tricycle u/c, upswept rear fuselage with ventral freight doors and twin-fin tail. Powered by two 260 h.p. AI-14R radial piston engines. Prot. CCCP-L1958, FF. 15 Mar. 1958. NATO name 'Clod'.
An-14M			Development of An-14 with deeper fuselage with stretched rear section, modified wing shape, larger tailfins and powered by two TVD-850 turboprop engines. Redesignated An-28.

Type No.	Name	No. Built	Notes
An-16		1	An-10 with 9ft 10in fuselage stretch and high density interior. FF. 1963.
An-22	Antei	68	Very large high wing freighter with pressurised forward section for 29-pax and unpressurised rear load compartment with internal crane system and ventral doors, twin fin tail unit, tricycle u/c with twin six-wheel main bogies, nose radome with glazed navigator station. Powered by four NK-12MA turboprops. 496,000 lb. TOGW. Prot. CCCP-46191. FF. 27 Feb. 1965. Also referred to as An-22M. NATO name 'Cock'.
An-22A	Antei		An-22 with altered electrical system, on-board engine starting and modified avionics.
An-24		1360	44-seat pressurised local service airliner with high wing, retractable tricycle u/c and powered by two Ivchenko AI-24VT turboprops. Prot. CCCP-L1959 FF. 20 Dec. 1959. NATO name 'Coke'.
An-24B			Export version of An-24 with improved soundproofing and minor systems modifications.
An-24P			An-24 for aeromedical evacuation with internal stretcher provision etc. or firefighting version with internal and external water tanks.
An-24V			An-24 with extended cabin and 50-pax capacity. Ivchenko AI-24BV or AI-24T engines with water injection.
An-24RV			An-24V with RU-19-300 auxiliary jet engine in starboard nacelle to provide improved takeoff power.

An-74

Type No.	Name	No. Built	Notes
An-24T			An-24 freighter without rear pax entry door, four porthole cabin windows each side, and fitted with inward-retracting ventral rear cargo hatch, dual rear ventral fins and reinforced cargo floor. Originally designated An-24TV.
Yunshuji Y-7			An-24 built in China.
An-26		1440	Pressurized cargo version of An-24 without cabin windows, fitted with new scissor-lift rear loading ramp and bulged observer window in forward fuselage side. NATO name 'Curl'.
An-26B			An-26 modified with rollamat loading system to handle standard cargo pallets. Some AN-26B used as military intelligence gathering platforms (An-26ST and An-26T).
An-26M			Military medical evacuation version.
An-26PS			Military staff transport with upgraded communications.
An-26P			An-26 fitted for firefighting.
An-26RT			Military An-26 airborne communications relay aircraft.
An-26Sh			Military navigation trainer.
An-26Z			Electronic listening aircraft with external belly-mounted radomes and associated aerials.
Yunshuji Y-7H			An-26 built in China.
An-28		200	An-14M with further stretched fuselage for 17-pax. and powered by two PZL TWD-10B turboprops. Prot. CCCP-1968. FF. Sep. 1969. Built by PZL – Mielec. NATO name 'Cash'.
An-28PT			An-28 fitted with Pratt & Whitney PT6A turboprops. Prot. SP-DDF. FF. 22 Jul. 1993.
An-28RM			Military An-28 for coastal patrol with radome under forward fuselage.
An-28TD			Military cargo and paratroop transport variant.
M-28	Skytruck		An-28 with higher powered PT6A-65A engines, improved avionics, new air conditioning, additional wing fuel tanks, enlarged fins, belly-mounted cargo pod and increased gross weight.
An-30		123	An-24T for photographic survey with glazed framed nose, domed cockpit enclosure, two cabin portholes each side and belly-mounted doors for vertical cameras. NATO name 'Clank'.
An-30M			An-30 with equipment for dry ice cloud seeding. Named 'Sky Cleaner'.
An-32		350	An-24T for operation from unprepared hot and high airfields with two 5042 shp AI-20D-5 turboprops in new nacelles with higher thrust line, enlarged ventral fins, leading edge slats and enlarged flaps. Prot. FF. 9 Jul. 1976. NATO name 'Cline'.
An-32B			An-32 with upgraded 5250 shp engines and higher gross weight.

Type No.	Name	No. Built	Notes
An-32P	Firekiller		An-32 equipped for firefighting with two external belly tanks for fire retardant. Prot. UR-48004.
An-38-100		1	Development of An-28 with 8ft 1in fuselage stretch forward and aft of wing giving 24-pax capacity, 19,400 lb. TOGW. Powered by two 1500 shp Allied Signal TPE331-14GR-801E turboprops. Prot. 381001 FF. 23 Jun. 1994.
An-38-200			An-38 powered by two Omsk Mars TVD-20 turboprops.
An-38K			An-38 with rear port cargo door and strengthened freight floor.
An-40			Very large four-turbofan freighter. Redesignated An-124.
An-70		2	Medium-capacity military freighter with high wing, ventral rear loading ramp and 12-wheel main bogie u/c. Powered by four Ivchenko D-27 propfan engines with counter-rotating 6/8 blade props. 271,190 lb. TOGW. Prot. FF. 16 Dec. 1994.
An-70T			Civil version of An-70. An-70TK will be convertible pax/freighter.
An-71		3	An-72 carrier-borne AEW aircraft with much enlarged forward-swept vertical tail mounting large rotating radar. NATO name 'Madcap'.
An-72		100	Medium-capacity STOL utility transport with circular section fuselage with two small porthole windows each side, T-tail, fuselage mounted 4-wheel main u/c and high wing with two closely mounted Lotarev D-36-1A turbofans positioned above and forward of wing leading edge. Prot. CCCP-19774. FF. 31 Aug. 1977. NATO name 'Coaler'.
An-72A			Production An-72 with increased wingspan, lengthened fuselage and increased gross weight.
An-72AT			Cargo version of An-72A with provision for pallet handling etc.

An-124, CCCP-82042

Type No.	Name	No. Built	Notes
An-72P			Military armed maritime patrol version, with underwing rocket pods and u/c fairing-mounted 23mm cannon. Also known as An-76.
An-72S			VIP version of An-72 with extra cabin windows, improved sound-proofing, three-cabin executive interior and galley.
An-74A		160	An-72 with increased fuel capacity, cabin windows, enlarged nose radome, ski/wheel u/c and new avionics for polar operations. NATO name 'Coaler A'. An-74T freighter and An-74TK convertible pax/freighter variants.
An-74P-100			VIP version of An-74.
An-74-200			An-74 with improved D-36 engines.
An-76			Alternative designation for An-72P.
An-77			Proposed westernised version of An-70 to compete with FLA.
An-124-100	Ruslan	58	Very large military/civil freighter with high-set supercritical wing, upward-opening nose loading door and ventral tail ramp, 20-wheel dual bogie main u/c, FBW control system, upper passenger deck for 88-pax and powered by four 51,590 lb.s.t. Lotarev D-18T turbofans in underwing pylon-mounted pods. 892,860 lb. TOGW. Prot. CCCP-680125 FF. 26 Dec. 1982.
An-124-100M			An-124-100 with upgraded avionics including TCAS-2, ACARS, Litton GPS/IRS etc.
An-124-102			An-124 with upgraded glass cockpit for 3-crew operation.
An-124FFR			Proposed firebombing version of An-124.
An-140		2	High-wing pressurised 81-pax local service airliner powered by two 1800 shp Klimov TV3-117VMA turboprops. Prot. UN-NTD FF. 17 Sep. 1997.
An-180			Proposed 150-seat airliner with two propfan engines mounted on tailplane.

An-225, CCCP-82060 with Buran space shuttle

Type No.	Name	No. Built	Notes
An-225	Mriya	1	An-124 with 47ft 10in fuselage stretch, new wing centre section with two additional pylon-mounted Lotarev D-18T turbofans, mounting points on fuselage roof for carrying Buran space shuttle, enlarged 28-wheel twin-bogie main u/c, twin-fin tail unit and 1,322,750 lb. TOGW. Prot. CCCP-480182 FF. 21 Dec. 1988.

PZL M-26 Skytruck, N5091L

Antonov An-30, 1107, Czech AF

ATR   INTERNATIONAL

During the 1970s, many manufacturers embarked upon design of mid-range commuter aircraft to bridge the gap between the established light twenty-seaters such as the Twin Otter and Embraer Bandeirante and the larger turboprop class dominated by the F.27 Friendship. Aérospatiale was one of the companies to address this market with an aircraft designated AS.35 – a high wing twin turboprop with forty seats and capable of future growth into larger passenger-carrying variants. At the same time, Aeritalia was also actively pursuing the same goal with its AIT230 project.

Discussions between the two companies led to an agreement being signed in July 1980 for them to pool their efforts and form a new company, ATR (Avion de Transport Regional). The new aircraft was titled the ATR 42 (signifying forty-two-passenger seating) and it was launched at the 1981 Paris Show with the Boards of Aérospatiale and Aeritalia authorising construction of two prototypes in the following October, safe in the knowledge that over fifty aircraft had been ordered by fourteen airlines.

ATR's first prototype was flown in August 1984 and its design closely followed the Aérospatiale AS.35 concept with the tailplane lowered and with rectangular rather than round windows. After flight testing at Toulouse it received French and Italian certification on 24 September 1985. Component production is carried out in Italy and France with the fuselage and tail coming from Pomigliamo d'Arco near Naples and the landing gear being added at Aeritalia's Capodichino plant. Centre wing boxes are built at St Nazaire and

ATR 72, B-22707

outer wings at Nantes with final assembly of the aircraft taking place at Aérospatiale's factory in Toulouse.

December 1985 saw the first customer aircraft being accepted by Air Littoral with further early deliveries to Cimber Air, Brit Air, Finnair, Holland Aero Lines, Air Queensland and Air Calédonie. ATR soon achieved a breakthrough into the American commuter market with sales to Simmons Airlines which put a substantial fleet to work on the American Eagle network and Continental Express which uses a fleet of over thirty ATR 42s. More than 300 of the standard ATR 42 were in service at the end of 1997.

With the ATR 42 in production, the company moved on to an enlarged variant – the ATR 72 which was announced in 1985 and differed from the basic aircraft in having longer wings and a stretched fuselage to accommodate up to seventy-four passengers. This received French certification on 25 September 1989 with the FAA certificate following shortly after. The first deliveries were made in Europe to Finnair, Binter Canarias and the German operator, NFD with initial American aircraft reaching Trans States Airlines in March 1991. Over 180 examples of the ATR 72 were in service in early-1998 with Simmons Airlines, again, having the largest fleet. ATR has also had various plans over the years for a military freighter variant of the ATR 42. The ATM 42L was a rear-loading utility version of the ATR 42 proposed to the French Air Force in 1986 and current plans include the ATR 52C with an upswept tail and rear cargo ramp but ATR will have to find sufficient customer interest in an already crowded market before this receives approval.

In early 1995, the ATR partners, Aérospatiale and Alenia together with British Aerospace decided to form Aero International (Regional) – AI(R) – as a marketing vehicle for their range of regional and commuter aircraft. These included the British Aerospace BAe.146 series and the BAe. Jetstream 41 together with the ATR 42 and ATR 72. The formation of AI(R) was achieved by merging the support services and sales and marketing divisions of Avro International, Jetstream and ATR with each of the partners holding equal shares in the new enterprise. Production responsibility remains with the original organisations.

While the original products formed the backbone of the new organisation the AI(R) partners had a clear wish jointly to develop new aircraft models to expand the range offered by the consortium. This resulted in the start of design studies on a new seventy-seat regional jet titled AI(R)JET 70 which was a low-wing, T-tailed design with new technology turbofans to be selected from the General Electric CF34-8, Allison AE.3012, BMW/Rolls-Royce BR700 or Pratt & Whitney/SNECMA SPW14. By the middle of 1997 many elements of the programme were becoming questionable, particularly the development of the SPW14 engine which was the preferred powerplant. AI(R)'s risk-sharing partners started to have second thoughts and the AI(R)JET 70 was eventually abandoned

ATR 42, F-WWEM

in December 1997. This action threw into question the whole logic of AI(R) and prompted the individual partners to consider whether they would be better off in some other trading grouping. As a consequence, early in 1998 it was decided that the consortium should be wound up with marketing responsibility passing back to ATR and British Aerospace.

Production Details

All ATR 42s and ATR 72s receive simple serial numbers in a common series which started at c/n 001 and had reached approximately c/n 550 by the end of 1997. The only exception was c/n 13 which was allocated as c/n 12A. The first production ATR 72 was c/n 108.

Model Information

Details of the ATR 42 and ATR 72 variants are as follows.

Type No.	No. Built	Notes
ATR42-200	2	High-wing pressurised 50-pax commuter airliner with retractable tricycle u/c, T-tail and powered by two 1800 shp Pratt & Whitney PW120 turboprops. 34,725 lb. TOGW. Prot. F-WEGA (c/n 001) FF. 16 Aug. 1984.
ATR42-300	177	ATR42-200 with strengthened structure and 35,605 lb. (later 36,815 lb.) TOGW.
ATR42F-300	1	Convertible pax/cargo version with port rear cargo door and hardened interior and freight floor. One a/c F-WWEB (c/n 131).
ATR42-310	32	Production designation for ATR42-300.
ATR42-320	76	ATR42-300 with 1900 shp PW121 engines and 4-blade props.
ATR42-400	1	ATR42 with 1900 shp PW121A engines and 6-blade Ratier props.
ATR42-420	3	Production designation for ATR42-400
ATR42-500	1	ATR42 with 2400 shp PW127E engines and 6-blade Ratier props ATR72 tail, upgraded cockpit, improved soundproofing, redesigned cabin fit and 41,005 lb. TOGW. Prot. F-WWEZ (c/n 443) FF. 16 Sep. 1994.
ATR42-510	36	Production designation for ATR42-500
ATR72-200	108	ATR with 14ft 9in fuselage stretch for 74-pax capacity, longer outer wing panels to give 8ft 1in wingspan increase, optional port forward cargo door, enlarged tail, increased fuel, two 2160 shp Pratt & Whitney PW124B turboprops and 47,400 lb. TOGW. Prot. F-WWEY (c/n 098) FF. 27 Oct. 1988.
ATR72-210	83	ATR72-200 with 2480 shp PW127 engines and new 4-blade props.
ATR72-210A		ATR72-200 with 2480 shp PW127F engines and 6-blade HS568F props.
ATR72-510	4	ATR72 with 6-blade Ratier props and improved cruise performance.
ATR82TF		Proposed ATR72 with stretched fuselage, 78-seat capacity and two General Electric CF34 turbofans in underwing nacelles. Not built.

BOEING   UNITED STATES

There can be no argument that the Boeing Company is the world's largest and most successful postwar producer of transport aircraft. With a range covering multiple variants of the Boeing 737, 747, 757, 767 and 777 and the new Douglas-derived Boeing 717 and with a large order backlog for both civil and military users the company has the most diversified range and the greatest user penetration of any manufacturer. Boeing has become skilled in stretching and improving all of its base models so that as each model becomes obsolete there is a replacement available to customers which will provide improved technical and economic advantages. In 1946, however, nobody would have predicted that Boeing was to become so powerful in the commercial aviation market even though they had a prewar record of production of the Stratoliner, the Model 247 and the Model 314 passenger-carrying flying boat. Douglas with its DC-4 and Lockheed with the Constellation had a head start and the virtual concession by British and other allied manufacturers that transport aircraft would be the prerogative of American industry gave Boeing's rivals a clear way ahead with commercial passenger carriers.

The arrival of peacetime, however, meant that there was already the realisation that a huge transportation market existed, particularly in the United States and that there was room for several manufacturers of modern airliners. The technology leap achieved during the war moved the air transport industry from reliance on twenty-five-seat short-haul aircraft in the DC-3 category to being able to achieve transcontinental operations with four-engined airliners. Boeing had spent the war in large-scale production of large aircraft such as the B-17 and later the B-29 and was well positioned in terms of engineering ability and manufacturing facilities to move across into transport aircraft. With the sudden conclusion of war with Japan, orders for the B-29 were immediately under threat but Boeing had already established a project for a military transport based on the Superfortress and orders for three prototypes of this XC-97 (Boeing Model 367) had been placed as early as 1942. The Model 367 used the wings, undercarriage, tail and Wright R-3350 radial piston engines of the B-29 married to a completely new pressurised fuselage which was unusual in having lower and upper half-shells providing a lower freight section and an upper deck for passengers and heavy military cargo. In this respect it laid the ground for all the later modern jet transports which incorporate large underfloor baggage and freight holds.

The XC-97 prototype was flown in November 1944 and it yielded excellent performance being able to operate at 25,000 feet flying at 350 m.p.h. over a range in excess of 3000 miles – which meant that it could fly coast-to-coast in the United States with a 20,000 lb. payload. Built at Boeing's Renton plant, the C-97, now powered by Pratt & Whitney R-4360 engines, entered full service in 1949 and was produced in several configurations including the KC-97 which soldiered on with Air National Guard units on aerial refuelling missions until the late 1970s. The Model 367 was soon developed by Boeing into the Model

377 Stratocruiser for commercial use. It differed from the military model in having a full set of passenger cabin windows (initially round portholes but later available as square windows) and an additional passenger area in the lower rear hold which was accessed by a circular staircase and used as a bar and lounge for first class passengers. The Stratocruiser entered service on the North Atlantic with Pan American in 1949. They eventually operated twenty-nine Stratocruisers and the other twenty-six aircraft built by Boeing were delivered to Northwest Airlines, BOAC and United Air Lines. When they were finally sold in the mid-1950s to be replaced by jet transports the Stratocruisers went to a variety of other carriers including Transocean Airlines and the Venezuelan operator, RANSA. A number of Stratocruiser and C-97 airframes were used to manufacture the Guppy series of outsize cargo transports which were designed by Aero Spacelines of Van Nuys, California and seven of the nine Guppies were fitted with Allison 501 turboprop engines. More details of these conversions are given in the data tables.

With the advent of the jet engine Boeing was in no doubt that the piston-engined transports had had their day and work was put in hand to develop a jet airliner which would replace the DC-7s, Super Constellations and Stratocruisers. The B-47 jet bomber and the C-97 were both used as a development basis and the eightieth major study based on the Stratocruiser, the 367-80, emerged as the preferred configuration for the new model. Subsequently, this was redesignated with the model number 707 but the prototype flew in July 1954 as the Model 367-80 and has always been referred to as the 'Dash-80'. It was a pressurised all-metal aircraft with a swept low-mounted wing and a conventional tail and it introduced the highly unusual feature of having four Pratt & Whitney JT3 turbojet engines mounted in pods on underwing pylons. This solution to mounting four jet engines was followed by Douglas with the DC-8 and it avoided the complex alternative solution of burying the engines in the wing roots and allowed Boeing to design a much more elegant wing which could be modified to meet many subsequent requirements for high lift performance. It was noticeable that as a result of Boeing's complex engineering solutions the wing of the '707 appeared to disassemble into many separate sections of flaps, slats, ailerons and spoilers during the landing process with, apparently, little remaining in place other than the main spar.

There is no doubt that the success of the '707 set Boeing on the track to its future dominant position. Whether or not it was a brilliant design, the '707 put Boeing in this position through its success in being selected as a military programme by the United States Air Force to meet their requirement for an aerial tanker/transport and evaluation of the 367-80 resulted in an order being placed for the Model 717 which was designated KC-135 in military service. Eventually, the United States forces received 776 examples of the various military Boeing 707s and, while the accounting for military and civil programmes was maintained separately this undoubtedly assisted Boeing financially in the overall Boeing 707 programme. The last '707s which were completed were the final examples of

Boeing 707-312, G-AYVE

sixty-six E-3 AWACS surveillance aircraft which were developed as a result of the remarkable reliability and aerodynamic stability of the '707 airframe for use with the U.S. Air Force and with NATO, France, the RAF and the Royal Saudi Air Force. The U.S. Air Force has also modified many C-135 airframes as airborne command posts and for electronic surveillance and countermeasures with external SLAR pods and other special antennae. From the outset, however, Boeing marketed the civil '707 aggressively to the airlines although they were forced to modify the Dash-80 by designing a wider and longer fuselage which could accommodate a maximum of 180 economy passengers in six-abreast seating with a centre aisle. Airlines also started to require mixed first and economy interior layouts to give optimum revenue yield and airliners such as the '707 were configured with two or more interior cabins. They were also fitted with substantial underfloor holds as pioneered in the Stratocruiser so that third party freight could be carried in addition to passenger baggage.

Pan American, a loyal user of the Stratocruiser, was the first commercial customer for the '707 and it received its first aircraft on 15 August 1958 putting it into service immediately. The major international carriers queued up to buy the aircraft with early deliveries of the Boeing 707-100 going to Continental Air Lines, American Air Lines, Qantas and TWA. Every customer was able to determine its own internal layout of seating, galleys and flight deck equipment and this could differ substantially from one aircraft to another depending on whether it was to be used on American domestic service or long-haul international routes. Inevitably, the design became refined and changed over time with changes in engine power and a progressive increase in passenger capacity resulting from the stretching of the '707 fuselage.

Boeing also built the Model 720 which had a shortened fuselage and a much modified wing with increased sweep on the leading edges. The Boeing 720 was designed to operate on short/medium range routes and from secondary airfields and was eventually replaced by Boeing's next design – the Model 727. The '707 and '720 became early victims of the ICAO Annex 16 and FAR.36 noise regulations which decreed the phasing out of heavy airliners which were not capable of meeting 'Stage 2' noise limits. These regulations started to come into force in 1990 and were designed to reach an effective total ban by 1999 in the United States and 2002 in Europe. This meant that affected aircraft either had to be sold outside the regulated territories and progressively face a worldwide embargo or be scrapped. The other alternatives were the fitting of hushkits such as those offered by Comtran or quiet Nacelle Corp or the more costly solution of re-equipping with modern turbofans. Most of the United States military C-135s and KC-135s were refitted with TF33-PW102 and, later, CFM56 turbofans and a number of commercial Boeing 707s received similar treatment but the availability of the more modern long range Boeing 767 which offered lower twin-engine operating costs meant that this was generally not an attractive option for the airlines.

The appetite of the world's airlines was sufficiently excited by the '707 and other first generation long-haul jet airliners for them to demand solutions for their medium and short range requirements. The Boeing 727 was a completely new 130-passenger model although it followed the same family design and engineering style established by the '707 and had a forward fuselage which was substantially the same. It was evident at an early stage that the most economical power specification was for use of three of the new Pratt & Whitney JT8D turbofans and Boeing fitted these, equipped with thrust reversers, neatly into a tail cluster with two engines in external pods and one buried in the rear fuselage with an air intake within the fin leading edge. As a consequence, the '727 had a T-tail and it was also provided with a passenger entry staircase which retracted beneath the rear fuselage.

The Boeing 727 achieved immediate acceptance from customers who included most of the world's leading airlines. Large fleets were built up by United, Braniff, American, Northwest, Continental and TWA. Foreign airlines which bought the '727 included Lufthansa, Air France, Aerolineas Argentinas, TAA, Alitalia and Iberia. British Airways, despite its successful operation of the '707 was obliged to use the DH.121 Trident but was to return to Boeing to acquire the '737 and '757 when the Tridents came up for replacement. The '727 was used by some military customers including the RNZAF and the

Boeing 377 Stratocruiser (C-97), YV-C-ERH

Belgian Air Force but the USAF only acquired a small number of used aircraft for Air National Guard transportation tasks. In total 1832 examples of the Boeing 727 were completed between 1964 and 1984 and over 1300 are still in revenue operation in 1998. The '727 was delivered initially as the Series 100 and this was supplemented in 1967 by the Series 200 with a stretched fuselage which increased maximum passenger seating to 189. Variants offered by Boeing included a convertible passenger/cargo model with a port-side forward freight door and the '727 became a popular all-cargo aircraft with the small package carriers such as Federal Express and UPS. A number of passenger '727s have been converted as freighters by companies such as Pemco. Boeing 727s which started to reach the end of their useful lives were mostly replaced in service by the stretched 737-400 which provided equivalent passenger capacity with more modern systems and lower operating costs. Some Boeing 727s have been re-engined with Rolls-Royce Tay turbofans and several have been fitted by Valsan with wingtip winglets which provides improved fuel consumption.

For some airlines, the '727-100 was still too large for short-haul low-density routes and the next move by Boeing was to develop a small twin-engined aircraft to challenge the successful Douglas DC-9. The Boeing 737, unflatteringly nicknamed 'Fat Albert', was designed for six-abreast seating with a centre aisle for up to 107 passengers. It had a high level of commonality with the '727 in its nose and upper fuselage structure but had a conventional tail unit with a fuselage-mounted tailplane and two Pratt & Whitney JT8D turbofans which were fitted immediately under the wings without pylons. Later variants of the aircraft which used the larger-diameter CFM56 engine introduced a small support pylon which moved the engine forward of the wing and gave a slightly higher thrust line and maintained clearance between the engines and the ground without involving a major undercarriage redesign.

The first delivery to launch customer Lufthansa was made in April 1968 and other major users of the original Series 100 and 200 variants included United, Piedmont, Sabena, South African Airways, Aer Lingus, Pacific Western and All Nippon. The low-cost carrier Southwest acquired 42 examples for its no-frills services and charter operators such as Britannia Airways built up large fleets to handle European inclusive tour business. Again, Boeing offered a convertible passenger/cargo version with a forward freight door and operators of this variant included Wien Alaska, Nordair, Iraqi Airlines and Air Zaire.

In 1981, Boeing introduced its 'second generation' '737-300 which featured an 8ft 8in fuselage stretch, CFM56 engines in oval-section nacelles and a modified vertical tail. The Series 300 could carry an additional forty-two passengers and the capacity of the aircraft was further enhanced with the announcement of the further stretched Series 400 which had two fuselage plugs totalling 9ft 6in so as to increase maximum seating capacity to 170. This made the aircraft an ideal replacement for older Boeing 727-200s although the new aircraft were technologically much improved with the EFIS cockpit systems which Boeing had pioneered in the development of the larger '757 and '767 and it did require flight deck crews to learn new systems. The first 737-300 was delivered in November 1984 and, again the major users were Southwest, United, Lufthansa and Continental. Large orders were placed for the new 737s by the leasing companies such as GPA, Ansett Worldwide and ILFC as a result of which these aircraft became available to smaller carriers such as Air Berlin, Hispania and Istanbul Airlines. Boeing also replaced the original short fuselage 737-100 and -200 with the 737-500 which introduced the CFM56 engines and improved systems of the -300 and -400.

The third generation of 737s was announced in November 1993. These aircraft, with varying fuselage lengths, designated 737-600, 737-700 and 737-800 replace the existing -300, -400 and -500 although fuselage stretch and therefore passenger capacity is not exactly the same as in the earlier models. Changes from the second generation 737s include a larger wing, increased range, higher cruise speed and new CFM56-7 engines giving improved thrust, fuel burn and noise levels. Boeing has also introduced the Boeing Business Jet ('BBJ') for corporate users which combines the fuselage of the medium-capacity 737-700 with the strengthened wings and undercarriage of the 737-800 and this results in a business aircraft with a large cabin area and a range of over 7000 miles which allows it to fly from New York to Tokyo or London to Johannesburg. The BBJ was certificated in November 1997.

For many people the name 'Boeing' is synonymous with the Boeing 747 – popularly entitled the Jumbo Jet. When the company initiated the '747 programme in 1964 they were responding to the rapidly expanding demand for long-range air travel and planned a leap in passenger capacity from the 180 seats of the '707 to the extraordinary total of 550 seats which can be accommodated in a Boeing 747-100. In technical terms, the 747 was based on a scaled up Boeing 707 but with a wide body fuselage with main cabin tourist seating in a two-aisle ten-abreast layout. One of Boeing's motives for establishing the 747 project was to respond to the C-5 super large military freighter tender which was eventually won by Lockheed with its Galaxy and the '747 was designed from the outset with a flight deck set above the forward fuselage so as to allow for an upward-opening nose to provide cargo loading. This separate flight deck module incorporated a rear cabin which could accommodate twenty business class passengers or a crew rest area and it was accessed by a circular staircase positioned to the rear of the forward first class cabin. In the later 747-300 and -400 series the upper deck has been extended to give a capacity of up to ninety-nine tourist passengers although most airlines use the space for premium class seating. The original cargo nose concept was used as planned on the all-cargo versions of the '747.

Boeing 727-223, N6827

COMMERCIAL AIRCRAFT AND AIRLINERS

The prototype '747 was flown in February 1969 and despite its revolutionary size it moved rapidly through the test programme and was certificated on 30 December 1969. At the time of its introduction to service in 1970 the '747 was the largest passenger aircraft ever built and its arrival required enormous changes to ground handling equipment and to airport design. Boeing had carefully engineered the wings of the '747 so as to keep the span as short as possible to accommodate the aircraft within existing airport docks but many taxiways had to be strengthened to take the 735,000 lb. gross weight of the '747 which was double that of its '707 predecessor. As it turned out, Boeing's competitors – Douglas and Lockheed decided to take a more conservative approach to the demand for widebody jets and the DC-10 and Lockheed 1011 were smaller aircraft with up to 340 seats. The result was that Boeing found itself without any true competition for the '747 and until the Airbus A3XX reaches the market the '747 will continue to be the only option for airlines needing 500-plus seat capacity for high demand routes.

Initial predictions were that, at a unit price of $21 million demand for the '747 would be limited to a handful for each of the major air carriers. The reality was a rapidly accelerating order book. Pan Am started with an order for twenty-five aircraft and this was followed quickly with fourteen for United, ten for American, nineteen for TWA, sixteen for British Airways and other orders from Air Canada, Northwest, Iberia, Braniff, Eastern and Japan Air Lines. The 'Jumbo Era' had truly arrived and the '747 probably ranks near the top of any list of technological innovations which have brought major world change. It suddenly brought the dream of mass international transport into reality. The '747 also brought with it the concept of separate powerplant choice. Initial 747-100s were equipped with the Pratt & Whitney JT9D very large turbofan but with the introduction of the improved 747-100B in 1977 customers could choose between the JT9D, the General Electric CF6 or the Rolls-Royce RB.211. The '747 was also available in mixed passenger/freight 747C 'Combi' configuration with a rear fuselage cargo door or as a 747F pure freighter with an upward-opening nose loading door to take straight-through loading of up to six standard 40ft. containers. A number of standard '747s have been converted by third party modifiers for freight or small package operation.

Perhaps the most radical version of the Boeing 747 came early in the development cycle with the introduction of the 747SP ('Special Performance'). This long-range variant was shortened by virtually the whole length of the rear fuselage in order to reduce the structural gross weight and increase range by 1700 miles. The passenger load was, surprisingly, reduced by only fifty at high density and Boeing sold fifty-two 'SPs to carriers such as Saudia, Pan American, Iran Air and South African Airways. They also built a specialised short-range high density version of the '747B, designated 747SR for use by Japan Airlines and All-Nippon on domestic very high density operations where up to 550 passengers could be carried. Only twenty-nine were built.

The next major external change to the '747 was enlargement of the cockpit bubble with a rear extension providing space for up to ninety economy passengers. In practice, many carriers decided to use this area for business or first class accommodation and some users of earlier Series 100 and 200 aircraft had them modified to 747-300 standard. The new upper deck has its own galley and lavatories and emergency doors with escape slides and the change of layout also involved removal of the spiral stairway which gives access to the upper deck on the '100 and '200 models and fitting a straight staircase near to the forward main passenger entry door.

In August 1988, Boeing flew the first of the extensively redesigned Model 747-400. Externally, this was similar to the '300 but identifiable by the addition of wingtip winglets. The structure was lightened by the use of new materials, the cockpit incorporated the five-screen EFIS system developed on the Boeing 757 and 767 allowing two-crew operation and new tailplane tanks assisted the aerodynamic alterations in extending range to 8400 nautical miles. This long-range capability was enhanced by enlarged crew rest areas and the passenger cabin was redesigned. One of the first Qantas 747-400s demonstrated the new capabilities of the aircraft in August 1989 by setting the world distance record for commercial airliners, flying the 11,185 miles from London to Sydney in twenty hours nine minutes although this was with minimum payload and maximum fuel and is not practical for normal operations. The 747-400 remains the high capacity large aircraft standard and Boeing had delivered approximately 400 examples by the end of 1997.

The advent of more fuel-efficient engines in the mid-1970s and a search for a successor to the '727 resulted in Boeing initiating two projects which ran in parallel and sometimes seemed to be competing for a similar market. Both the '757 and the '767 were twin turbofan aircraft with the '757 being a single aisle short/medium range aircraft with maximum accommodation for 230 passengers and the '767 as a larger twin-aisle wide body aircraft for medium/long ranges with up to 289 passengers seats in a 2-4-2 layout or the lower density 2-3-2 layout for 221 passengers. Because of their parallel development, the '757 and '767 shared many parts and systems including the modernised two-crew flight deck which was also adopted for the 747-400.

The '767 actually preceded the '757 in development and it offered a fuel burn of 110 lb. per passenger seat compared with 165 lb. for the Boeing 727-100 which was a major advance in the operating cost base. The capacious underfloor hold became highly productive by being able to accommodate the large LD8 containers or palletised cargo. The first '767 order was placed by United Airlines in July 1978 and the prototype '767 made its first flight at Everett on 26 September 1981. Boeing gained the type certificate for the Model 767 on 30 July 1982 with United starting revenue services in the following month and further handovers taking place thereafter to China Airlines, American, Delta, Air Canada Ansett and TWA. The '767 was subsequently offered in stretched 767-300 form which was announced in 1983 and the -300ER extended range model with a 6600 mile range which appeared in 1987. Early in its career the '767 was approved for ETOPS extended range Atlantic and Pacific operations and airlines such as TWA, United and British Airways routinely operate the '757, '767 and '777 on Transatlantic routes. Boeing also used the '767 airframe as the platform for a specialised military AWACS version. First flown in August 1996 following modification at the Boeing plant at Wichita, Kansas, this has a rear fuselage mounted rotodome and deliveries to the first customer, the Japanese Air Self Defence Force who have ordered four E-767s, were made from Seattle in early-1998. Some '767s have also been delivered as dedicated freighters with a forward port-side upper deck cargo door. The 500th '767 was delivered to American Airlines in June 1993 and a further 150 had been delivered by the beginning of 1998.

Over 800 examples of the Boeing 757 have also been handed over to airline customers. Again, the operating economics of the '757, using high bypass ratio CF6 or RB.211 engines were substantially better than those of the earlier '727 with a fuel burn of up to 35% less than that of the first generation turbofans. Again, the 757 could be ETOPS approved and was designed from the outset for two-crew operation. The launch customer

Boeing 737-2H4, N82SW

was Eastern Airlines which put the aircraft into service on 1 January 1983 and other users include British Airways who use many of their forty-eight-strong fleet on shuttle operations, American, Delta and United who all have fleets of around ninety aircraft and United Parcel Service which is taking delivery of seventy-five of the Model 575-200PF package freighter variant.

With the enlargement of capacity offered by the Boeing 747-400, Boeing was faced with a gap in capacity between the 767-300ER with just under 300 seats and the '747 with over 500 seats. Market studies for the resultant Model 777 started in 1986 with the aircraft being launched as an official project in October 1990. Externally, the '777 is similar to an enlarged '767 with two engines in the 71,000 to 74,000 lb.s.t. class. Passenger capacity is up to a maximum of 440 in all-economy ten-abreast two-aisle seating, although most long-range carriers opt for a three-class layout for up to 328 passengers. As with other Boeing models, a fair amount of the '777 is built by subcontractors with final assembly taking place at Everett. Japan Aircraft Industry (a consortium of Mitsubishi, Kawasaki and Fuji) has designed and builds the majority of the fuselage and the wing centre section.

The first Boeing 777 was flown on 28 October 1994 and the first delivery was made to United Airlines, who had placed an order for thirty-four aircraft with thirty-four options, in May 1995. Boeing had delivered ninety aircraft, including a number of IGW (increased gross weight) variants by the beginning of 1998 to seventeen airlines including British Airways, All Nippon, Malaysian, Thai International and United. Boeing is also accumulating a large order book for the stretched '777-300 which increases the economy class seating to 550 and fits the '777 even more closely in below the '747-400 and offers a viable replacement for existing 747-100s and -200s. The change to the airframe involves Boeing's customary fore and aft fuselage plugs adding over thirty feet to the aircraft's length. The 650,000 lb. weight of the new twin jet demanded new engines and this requirement has been met by Rolls-Royce with the Trent 892 and Pratt & Whitney with the PW4098. Operating economics of the '777-300 are expected to be outstanding with fuel and maintenance costs per passenger down by more than a third compared with the aircraft it replaces.

Production Details

All post-war Boeing aircraft carry a construction number in an overall Boeing sequence. Construction numbers ('c/ns') are allocated when an aircraft is placed on confirmed order, but if an order is cancelled the c/n is not reallocated to a new customer. It will be clear that, because of this, there are some gaps in the overall Boeing serial number sequence

Boeing 737-4YO, HL7254

caused by cancelled orders. The construction numbers cover all the models in production at any time but Boeing also uses a system of Line Numbers for each model which indicate the sequential position of each aircraft on the production line for that type. There is no relationship between the two numbering systems and, indeed, an aircraft with a late construction number can be built before a much earlier aircraft – but it will have an earlier line number. If an order is cancelled the delivery position (identified by the line number) is reassigned to a new aircraft. Some aircraft may have an early serial number but a late line number if the customer specifies a long-lead delivery date.

Two different sequences of construction numbers have been used by the two principal Boeing plants – at Seattle and Wichita. The Wichita production line used its own series of 75-prefixed serials for Stearman biplane production, 20-prefixed serials for the YL-15 and serials starting at c/n 450001 for B-47 production. However, since no airliners have been completed at Wichita (although major sections, particularly for the Model 737 have been made there) the serial system is not relevant. The Seattle serial numbers had reached approximately 8480 when the first XC-97s were built but large numbers of B-29s and B-50s used up the serial blocks from c/n 8487 to c/n 15921. Thereafter, Boeing allocated fairly large batches of serial numbers to individual types but in recent years the batches have been much smaller. The general ranges of serial number allocations from the start of Stratocruiser production has been as follows:

Type	Dates Built	Number Built	First c/n	Last c/n
367 – C-97	1947–1950	888	15712	17149
377 Stratocruiser	1947–1950	56	15922	15979
367-80	1954	1	17158	
707, 720	1957–1979	915	17586	21956
E-3, E-6	1975–1991	90	20518	24510
717 – C-135/KC-135	1956–1974	814	17234	20519
727	1963–1983	1,832	18252	23052
737	1967–current	2,946	19013	29804
747	1969–current	1,157	19637	29168
757	1982–current	592	22172	29115
767	1981–current	525	21862	29693
777	1994–current	123	26916	30250

Model Information

Details of all postwar Boeing transport types to date are as follows:

Type No.	Name	No. Built	Notes
367-1-1	XC-97	1	Heavy military transport using B-29 wings, engine nacelles, undercarriage and tail unit married to double curvature fuselage with lower cargo deck and main pressurised upper passenger/cargo section with rear loading under-fuselage doors. Six square cabin windows each side. Powered by four 2325 hp. Wright R-3350-57A radial piston engines. Prototype, s/n 43-27470 (c/n 8481) FF. 9 Nov. 1944.
367-1-2	XC-97	2	Second and third prototype XC-97s.
367-5-5	YC-97	6	Pre-production XC-97 with modified engine nacelles with separate lower air intake, improved electrical system and increased fuel capacity.

Type No.	Name	No. Built	Notes
367-4-6	YC-97A	3	YC-97 with enlarged folding vertical tail, strengthened structure, thermal de-ice system and Pratt & Whitney R-4360-35A engines.
367-4-7	YC-97B	1	YC-97A equipped as 80-passenger transport with deluxe interior, porthole windows, no rear loading doors. s/n 45-59596 (c/n 15721). Became C-97B.
367-4-19	C-97A	50	Production YC-97A with radome under nose, forward cargo door, Hamilton Standard hydromatic props and additional fuel capacity. Three conv. to KC-97A tankers and one conv. to VIP VC-97D.
367-4-29	C-97C	14	C-97A with strengthened cargo floor, new radios etc. Some conv. to MC-97C for aeromedical work.
367-4-29	KC-97E	60	C-97C aerial tanker with flying boom refuelling unit under rear fuselage, four internal fuel tanks and R-4360-35C engines.
367-76-29	KC-97F	159	KC-97E with R-4360-59B engines.
367-76-66	KC-97G	592	KC-97F as convertible passenger/tanker with external underwing fuel tanks. Some converted to all-passenger C-97G or HC-97G search and rescue. Also KC-97L upgrade with J47 jet engines mounted in place of external fuel tanks. Some civilianised as water bombers.
367-86-542	YC-97J	2	Conversion of KC-97G with four Pratt & Whitney YT34-P-5 turboprop engines.
377-10	Stratocruiser	56	Commercial 100-passenger model similar to YC-97B with four 3500 h.p. Pratt & Whitney R-4360-35A Wasp Major engines, full set of round or square passenger windows, no chin radome (except 377-10-30) lower deck lounge and customer-specified interior. See later details of customer model numbers. Prot. Model 377-10-19, NX90700 (c/n 15922) FF. 8 Jul. 1947.

Boeing 747SP-44, 3B-NAJ

Type No.	Name	No. Built	Notes
377M			Unofficial designation given to 3 Stratocruisers converted to military freight configuration by Israel Aircraft Industries with rear ventral loading doors.
377-PG	Pregnant Guppy		Model 377-10 converted for carriage of oversize loads by On-Mark Engineering with lengthened fuselage, new 20-ft high upper lobe structure and removable rear fuselage for loading. One aircraft N1024V (c/n 15924) FF. as 377-PG on 16 Sep. 1962.
377-MG	Mini Guppy		Model 377-10-26 converted by Aero Spacelines as oversize freighter with smaller upper lobe than 377-PG and with hinged swing tail. One aircraft, N1037V (c/n 15937) FF. 24 May 1967.
101	Mini Guppy		Model 377-MG built from several existing Stratocruisers with four 4680 shp Allison 501 turboprops and swing nose for loading. Two aircraft, N111AS (c/n 0001) FF. 1 May 1970 and N112AS (c/n 0002).
377-SG	Super Guppy		Wider and longer version of 377PG built by Aero Spacelines with four 5700 shp Pratt & Whitney T-43-PWA turboprops and swing-nose for loading. One aircraft, N1038V (c/n 15938) FF. 31 Aug. 1965.
201	Super Guppy		Model 377-SG for Airbus Industrie. Two built by Aero Spacelines (c/n 0001 and 0002) and two by UTA – Aeromaritime (c/n 0003 and 0004).
367-80		1	Intercontinental military/civil jet transport with four 10,000 lb.s.t. Pratt & Whitney JT3 engines in underslung wing pods. Fitted with swept wing incorporating complex flap and speed brake system. Used to develop Boeing 707 and later for various Boeing test programmes including in-flight refuelling. Prot. N70700 (c/n 17158) FF. 15 Jul. 1954.

Boeing 747-409, B-161

Type No.	Name	No. Built	Notes
707-100		56	Production civil version of Model 367-80 with longer fuselage and wingspan, full set of rectangular cabin windows, four 12,500 lb.s.t. JT3C-6 turbojets, 257,000 lb. TOGW, max 179-pax. seating. Later aircraft fitted with taller tail and some with ventral fin. First aircraft N708PA (c/n 17586) FF. 20 Dec. 1957.
707-138		13	707-100 for Qantas with 10ft. shorter rear fuselage and increased range. Later converted/built as -138B with JT3D turbofans.
707-100B		72	707-100 with 18,000 lb.s.t. JT3D-3 engines, modified wing inboard leading edge, extra leading edge slats and enlarged tailplane. First aircraft N7526A (c/n 18054) FF. 22 Jun. 1960. Many converted from 707-100.
707-200		5	707-100 with four 15,800 lb.s.t. Pratt & Whitney JT4A-3 turbojets. Built for Braniff as 707-227 for hot and high operations.
707-300	Intercontinental	69	707-100 with 100-in. fuselage stretch giving max 189-pax seating, longer wing with increased inboard area, increased fuel and 1600 mile increased range, four 15,800 lb.s.t. Pratt & Whitney JT4A-3 turbojets. 316,000 lb. TOGW. First aircraft N714PA (c/n 17592) FF. 11 Jan. 1958.
707-300B		175	707-300 with additional leading edge slats, longer wingtips and modified flaps. 335,000 lb. TOGW. Powered by four 18,000 lb.s.t. JT3D-3 turbofans.
707-300BA			707-300B Advanced conversions with 707-300C wing leading edge and no ventral fin.
707-300C		335	707-300B with modified leading edge slats and convertible pax/freight configuration with strengthened floor and forward port side cargo door.
707-300CH			707-300C with 336,000 lb. TOGW and JT3D-7 turbofans.

Boeing 757-23A, N916AW

Type No.	Name	No. Built	Notes
707-400		37	707-300 with 17,500 lb.s.t. Rolls-Royce Conway 50B turbofans.
707-700		1	707-300 fitted with CFM56 turbofan engines. N707QT (c/n 21956) FF. 27 Nov. 1979.
720		64	707 with 9ft. shorter fuselage, four 12,000 lb.s.t. Pratt & Whitney JT3C-7 turbojets (JT3C-12 on 720-025), increased sweep inboard wing section, modified leading edge slats, reduced fuel capacity, max 165-pax capacity and max 230,000 lb. TOGW. Prot. N7201U (c/n 17907) FF. 23.11.59. Also known as 720-020 and 707-000.
720B		88	720 with 17,000 lb.s.t. JT3D-1, JT3D-1-MC6 turbofans and 235,000 lb. max TOGW.
717-100A	Stratotanker KC-135A	29	Initial designation for USAF KC-135A aerial refueller based on commercial Model 707-120 with lower gauge skinning and other structural mods. Later batches designated Model 717-146 and 717-148.
717-146	KC-135A	68	Later production batch of KC-135A
717-148	KC-135A	635	Later production batch of KC-135A
717-157	C-135A	15	126-seat cargo/passenger version of KC-135A without cabin windows powered by four 13,750 lb.s.t. Pratt & Whitney J57-P-59W turbojets.
717-158	C-135B	30	C-135A with 18,000 lb.s.t. TF33-P-5 turbofans and wide-span tailplane.
717-165	C-135F	6	For French Air Force.
717-166	KC-135B	17	Aerial refuelling tanker version of C-135B.
717-200			Designation for McDonnell Douglas MD-95-30 following takeover by Boeing in 1997.
717-100			Boeing designation for McDonnell Douglas MD-95-20.
717-300			Boeing designation for McDonnell Douglas MD-95-50.

Boeing 767-204, G-BKPW

Type No.	Name	No. Built	Notes
739			Designation for various military 707 variants.
727-100		411	Medium-range airliner with T-tail, swept wing, ventral rear airstair, three 13,200 lb.s.t. JT8D-1 turbojet engines mounted in two rear fuselage pods and base of the tailfin, max 131-pax capacity. Later models with 14,000 lb.s.t. JT8D-7 or 14,500 lb.s.t. JT8D-9. Max 169,000 lb. TOGW. Prot. N9001U (c/n 18293) FF. 9 Feb. 1963. Some aircraft converted as freighters as 727-100F. Military C-22A/B ex airline aircraft for USAF. 727-100QF conversions with three Rolls-Royce Tay 651/54 turbofans.
727-100C		163	727-100 in convertible pax/freight configuration with strengthened floor and forward port side cargo door. Also 727-100QC quick change version with palletised pax seating.
727-200		1,243	727-100 with two 10ft. fuselage sections added in front of and behind wing to give max 189-pax seating. 172,000 lb. TOGW. Optional 15,000 lb.s.t. JT8D-11 engines. Prot. N7270L (c/n 19536) FF. 27 Jul. 1967.
727-200 Adv.			Advanced 727-200 with strengthened airframe and max 209,500 lb. TOGW, new thrust reversers, automatic braking and spoilers, noise-reducing nacelles, GPWS and fuel in centre section.
727-200F		15	727-200 Advanced freight variant with 16,000 lb.s.t. JT8D-17A engines, no cabin windows and port side forward freight door. Many standard -200 aircraft converted.
727-UDF			Experimental Boeing test aircraft with General Electric unducted turbofan engine mounted on starboard rear engine pylon. N32720 (c/n 19846).

Boeing 747-121, LX-GCV

Type No.	Name	No. Built	Notes
737-100		30	Short/medium range airliner with two 14,000 lb.s.t. Pratt & Whitney JT8D-7 turbojets mounted in underwing nacelles. Optional 14,000 lb. JT8D-9 or 15,500 lb. JT8D-15 engines. Max 124-pax. seating and max 110,000 lb. TOGW. Some fitted as all-cargo or combi aircraft with forward freight door and cargo floor. Prot. N73700 (c/n 19437) FF. 9 Apl. 1967.
737-200		996	737-100 with 78in. fuselage stretch and max 136-pax. seating. max 115,500 lb. TOGW.
737-200C		96	Freight version as 737-100.
737-200QC		2	Quick change Combi version as 737-100.
737-200Adv			Advanced development of 737-200 with modified slats and flaps, additional rear belly fuel tank, thrust reversers, automatic braking, and extended engine pods. Max. 128,100 lb. TOGW.
737-200	T-43A		U.S. military version of Boeing 737-200 for navigation training or as CT-43A transport with reduced number of cabin windows and hardened interior.
737-300		1,025	737-200 with fuselage extensions of 44in. forward and 60in. aft of the wing, extended wingtips, improved flight deck instrumentation, fin leading edge extension, max 149-pax seating, powered by two 22,100 lb.s.t. CFM56-3B-2 turbofans in oval-section nacelles set forward of wing on small pylons. Prot. N73700 (c/n 22950) FF. 24 Feb. 1984.
737-400		440	737-300 with fuselage extensions of 66in. forward and 48in. aft of wing and tail skid. Max 168-pax capacity, 138,520 lb. TOGW. Alternative engine option is 23,500 lb.s.t. CFM56-3C. Prot. N73700 (c/n 23886) FF. 3 Feb. 1988.
737-400HGW			737-400 with structural improvements and 150,000 lb. TOGW.
737-500		355	737-200 with extended wingtips, improved flight deck instrumentation, fin leading edge extension etc. similar to 737-300. 108-pax capacity. Prot N73700 (c/n 24178) FF. 30 Jun. 1989.
737-600			'Next Generation' development of 737-500 with improved wing of 16ft. 5in. increased span and increased chord, enlarged tailplane and fin, greater fuel capacity, 6-screen EFIS and FDCDS, new emergency exit hatches, improved 'wide-body' cabin design, 132-seat capacity, 124,000 lb. TOGW and two 22,000 lb.s.t. CFM56-7 turbofans. Prot. FF. 22 Jan. 1998.
737-600HGW			737-600 with structural modification for 143,500 lb. TOGW.
737-700		1	'Next Generation' development of 737-300 with 133,000 lb. TOGW, 149 seats and improvements as 737-600. Prot. 'NG' (Model 737-7H4) N737X (c/n 27841) FF. 9 Feb. 1997.

Type No.	Name	No. Built	Notes
737-700IGW	Boeing BBJ		737-700 with centre section, u/c and wing of 737-800 and 153,000 lb. TOGW. Corporate Boeing Business Jet (BBJ). Prot. N737BJ (c/n 29102) FF. 4 Sep. 1998.
737-800			'Next Generation' development of 737-400 with 108in. fuselage extension giving 189-pax capacity, strengthened wings and landing gear, CFM56-7 engines, 155,500 lb. TOGW and improvements as 737-600.
737-800HGW			737-800 with structural modification for 172,500 lb. TOGW.
737-900			Proposed development of 737-800 with fuselage stretch of 5ft 2in forward and 3ft 6in aft of wing and 189-pax capacity (or 207 with additional emergency exits).
747-100		165	Very large wide body intercontinental airliner with max 550-pax seats. Layout consists of main deck, underfloor cargo hold and upper deck containing cockpit and small passenger cabin. Fitted with swept wings with complex slats, flaps and speed brakes and large 8-wheel bogie main u/c units. Max. 735,000 lb. TOGW. Powered by four under-wing pylon mounted 43,000 lb.s.t. Pratt & Whitney JT9D turbofans. Prot. N7470 (c/n 20235) FF. 9 Feb. 1969.
747-100SP		52	Long-range version of 747-100 with 48ft shorter fuselage, larger tailplane and modified flap system. 700,000 lb TOGW and max 440-pax seats. Powered by four 46,500 lb.s.t. Pratt & Whitney JT9D-7A, 50,100 lb.s.t. Rolls-Royce RB.211-524B2 or 46,500 lb.s.t. General Electric CF6.-45A2 turbofans. Prot. N747SP (c/n 21022) FF. 4 Jul, 1975.
747-100SR		25	747-100 for short-range operations with strengthened undercarriage and airframe.
747-100B		11	747-100 with higher gross weight structure of -200B and 753,000 lb. TOGW. Fitted with customer-specified engines including Pratt & Whitney JT9D, Rolls-Royce RB.211 and General Electric CF6.
747-100BSR			747-100SR with upgraded 747B airframe.
747-100SUD			747-100BSR with extended 747-300 upper deck.
747-200B		222	747-100 with strengthened airframe and max. 820,000 lb. TOGW and increased fuel capacity and range. Powered by four customer-specified engines including 54,750 lb.s.t. Pratt & Whitney JT9D-7R4-62, 51,600 lb.s.t. Rolls-Royce RB.211-524-02 or 50,100 lb.s.t. General Electric CF6-50E turbofans.
747-200B Combi		93	Combined passenger/freight version of 747-200B with rear fuselage port side freight door and provision for palletised loads.
747-200M			Alternative designation for 747-200B Combi.

Type No.	Name	No. Built	Notes
747-200F		73	All-cargo version of 747-200B with upward-opening nose cargo door and rear port side rear fuselage hatch and no main cabin windows.
747-200C			Convertible passenger/freight version of 747-200F with cabin windows.
747-300		58	747-200 with stretched upper deck and max 630-pax seats. Max. 833,000 lb. TOGW. Powered by four 54,750 lb.s.t. Pratt & Whitney JT9D-7R4-G2, 53,000 lb.s.t. Rolls-Royce RB.211-524-D4 or 55,640 lb.s.t. General Electric CF6-80C2B1 turbofans.
747-300BC		18	Combined passenger/freight ('Combi') version of 747-300.
747-300SR		4	747-300 for short range operations with strengthened undercarriage and airframe.
747-400		345	Long-range 747-300 with lighter weight structure, wingtip winglets, modernised flight deck with 5-tube EFIS, tailplane fuel tanks, max 870,000 lb. TOGW. Powered by four customer-specified engines including 56,000 lb.s.t. Pratt & Whitney 4256, 57,900 lb.s.t. Rolls-Royce RB.211-524G or 57,900 lb.s.t. General Electric CF6-80C2B1F turbofans.
747-400D		6	Short range 747-400 for Japan Air Lines without wingtip winglets and strengthened airframe and undercarriage.
747-400 Combi		73	Convertible passenger/freight version of 747-400.
747-400F		12	All-cargo version of 747-400 with short (747-200) upper deck, upward-opening nose cargo door and rear port side rear fuselage hatch and no main cabin windows.
747-400IGW			747-400 with strengthened u/c and centre section, additional belly fuel tanks and 910,980 lb. TOGW.

Boeing 777-236, G-ZZZA

Type No.	Name	No. Built	Notes
757-200		517	Medium range narrow body airliner with max. 239-pax seating and 220,000 lb. TOGW. Powered by two 37,530 lb.s.t. Pratt & Whitney PW2037 or 36,720 lb.s.t. Rolls-Royce RB.211-535C engines forward-mounted beneath wings. Prot. N757A (c/n 22212) FF. 18 Feb. 1982. USAF C-32A.
757-200CB			Combi version of 757-200 with two 39,610 lb.s.t. Rolls-Royce RB.211-535E4 turbofans.
757-200PF		75	Package freighter version of 757-200 with no cabin windows, forward port upward-opening freight door, strengthened floor and forward internal cargo bulkhead and single forward crew entry door. Powered by two 37,530 lb.s.t. Pratt & Whitney PW2037 or 39,610 lb.s.t. Rolls-Royce RB.211-535E4 turbofans.
757-300			757-200 with fuselage stretch of 13ft 3in forward and 9ft 9in aft of wing, strengthened airframe and undercarriage, retracting tail bumper and upgraded systems. Prot. N757X (c/n 29016) FF. 2 Aug. 1998.
767-200		151	Short/medium range wide body airliner with max 290 seats, with conventional swept wing layout and two customer-selected turbofans forward-mounted beneath wings. Engines include 48,000 lb.s.t. P&W JT9D-7R4D, 50,200 lb.s.t. P&W PW4052, 58,000 lb.s.t. Rolls-Royce RB211-524G or 57,900 lb.s.t. General Electric CF6-80C2. Max TOGW 317,000 lb. Prot. N767BA (c/n 22233) FF. 26 Sept. 1981.
767-200ER		71	767-200 Extended Range variant with additional centre section fuel tanks and 388,000 lb. TOGW. Powered by two 50,200 lb.s.t. P&W PW4052 or 57,900 lb.s.t. General Electric CF6-80C2 turbofans.
767-300		79	767-200 with two fuselage extensions fore and aft of wing totalling 21ft. 1in. and max 360 seats, 350,000 lb. TOGW.

Boeing Super Guppy 201, F-BPPA

Type No.	Name	No. Built	Notes
767-300ER		224	767-300 Extended Range variant with additional centre section fuel tanks and 409,000 lb. TOGW.
767-400ER			767-300 with fuselage stretch of 11ft 1in forward and 10ft 1in aft of wing giving 304-pax capacity, taller u/c, wingtip extensions with winglets, upgraded 777-style flight deck, new cabin interior and General Electric CF6-80C2B7F engines. Prot. to fly Aug. 1999.
777-200		94	Medium/long-range wide body airliner resembling scaled-up Model 767 with 440-pax seats and powered by two General Electric GE90-95B, Pratt & Whitney PW4077 or Rolls-Royce Trent 877 turbofans. 545,100 lb. TOGW. Prot. N7771 (c/n 27116) FF. 12 June, 1994.
777-200IGW			777-200 with Gross Weight increased to 632,615 lb.
777-300		20	Model 777 with fuselage extensions of 17ft 5in forward and 15ft 8in aft of wing and max 550-pax seats. Ground positioning camera system. Powered by two General Electric GE90-92B, Pratt & Whitney PW4090/PW4098 or Rolls-Royce Trent 892 turbofans. 660,620 lb. TOGW. Prot. N5014K (c/n 27507) FF. 16 Oct. 1997.
777-300X			Stretched version of 777-300.

The designations for Boeing models also include additional suffixes identifying roles. The letter 'C' is added to indicate a convertible passenger/freight version – normally fitted with a fuselage side cargo door (e.g. 707-344C). The letter 'F' is used to indicate an all-freight configuration (e.g. 747-228F). 'ER' (e.g. 767-34HER) denotes extended range, 'Combi' is commonly used also to identify the convertible passenger/freighter and some aircraft are suffixed 'PF' (e.g. 757-24APF) to denote package freight configuration for carriers such as United Parcel Service.

As mentioned earlier, many of the earlier Boeing jetliners have been retrospectively fitted with hushkits or turbofan engines to meet Stage 3 noise regulations. Designations of aircraft so converted are generally not changed. Companies offering re-engining and other noise reduction modifications include Valsan Inc. (Boeing 727 'Super-27'), Quiet Technology Venture (Boeing 707), Dee Howard (Boeing 727QF), Burbank Aeronautical Corp. (Boeing 707/720) and Fedex Aviation Services (Boeing 727). Volpar Aircraft has also devised a twin-engined conversion of the Boeing 727 with two CFM56-5 turbofans although this has not yet flown.

Boeing Customer Codes

The designations of Boeing aircraft from the Stratocruiser onwards incorporated a numerical/alphanumerical code which identified the original customer for the aircraft. In practice, this specified the specific equipment and internal fit of the sub-model concerned. The requirements of individual customers could vary considerably, particularly in respect of seating configuration, galley specification, cargo arrangement and avionics – and the certificated gross weight of the aircraft. For example, Boeing 747-200Bs for Air France were specified at a gross weight of 785,130 lb. whereas the British Airways equivalent was 820,140 lb. The original seating specification has, of course, often changed since the original delivery. For instance, British Airways Boeing 747-236Bs may have either 356 seats or the high density 374 seats resulting from installing World Traveller seating on the upper deck.

COMMERCIAL AIRCRAFT AND AIRLINERS

The system of customer codes was introduced with the Model 377-10 Stratocruiser with an identifying number added after the basic model number. The prototype was the Boeing 377-10-19. Aircraft for the launch customer, Pan American, were Model 377-10-26, Transcontinental & Western (not built) were 377-10-27, SILA/SAS were 377-10-28, American Overseas were 377-10-29, Northeast were 377-10-30, BOAC were 377-10-32 and United were 377-10-34. Missing numbers were for carriers who were potential customers but did not place orders.

The system continued when the Boeing 707 was introduced and a new series of customer numbers was started. These same numbers have continued for all subsequent models. Thus, the British Airways customer code was '36'. As a result, Boeing 707-400s were Model 707-436, Boeing 737-200s were Model 737-236, Boeing 747-400s were Model 747-436, Boeing 757-200s were Model 757-236, Boeing 767-300ERs were Model 767-336ER and Boeing 777-200s were Model 777-236. As can be seen, the individual series number is shown before the customer number – so, the British Airways 747-200Bs were Model 747-236B and their 747-400s were Model 747-436. In the case of the early Boeing 727s, no series number was allocated with the result that the customer number had no prefix (e.g. aircraft for United Airlines were the Model 727-22). Subsequently, when the 727-200 was introduced the short fuselage '727 was designated 727-100 and the prefix '1' was included (e.g. 727-173).

After allocating the initial ninety-nine customer numbers, Boeing had to extend the system with a code containing a letter followed by a single digit (from 0 to 9). Thus, Indian Airlines was allocated code 'A8' and their Boeing 737-200s were model 737-2A8. Inevitably, this system also used up all the possible combinations, so Boeing went on to the current code system of a single digit followed by a letter. For example, the Boeing 737-500s ordered by Euralair (customer code '3C') are Model 737-53C. A list of all the customer codes allocated to date is as follows:

Code	Customer	Code	Customer	Code	Customer
1	Piedmont	20	Boeing	41	Varig
2	Wien Consolidated	21	Pan Am	42	Nordair
3	Caribair	22	United	43	Alitalia
4	Britannia Airways	23	American	44	South African AW
5	Braathens SAFE	24	Continental	45	Seaboard
6	KLM	25	Eastern	46	Japan Air Lines
7	W. German AF	26	Unknown	47	Western
8	Icelandair	27	Braniff	48	Aer Lingus
9	China Airlines	28	Air France	49	Flying Tiger/CP Air
10	Northern Consolidated	29	Sabena	50	Trek Airways
11	Wardair	30	Lufthansa	51	Northwest Orient
12	Singapore Airlines	31	TWA	52	Unknown
13	Ariana Afghan	32	Delta	53	USAF
14	Pacific Southwest	33	Air Canada	54	Mohawk
15	Lake Central	34	Transair Sweden	55	Executive Jet Aviation
16	LAN Chile	35	National	56	Iberia
17	CP Air	36	British Airways	57	Swissair
18	BEA	37	Air India	58	El Al
19	NZNAC/Air New Zealand	38	Qantas	59	Avianca
		39	Cubana	60	Ethiopian
		40	Pakistan Int.		

Code	Customer	Code	Customer	Code	Customer
61	FAA	A3	PLUNA	H9	Jugoslovenski AT
62	Pacific Northern	A4	Air Cal	J0	Air Jamaica
63	Faucett	A6	Essex Int./LTV	J1	Dominicana
64	Mexicana		Capital	J4	Sterling Airways
65	British Eagle	A7	Trans Caribbean	J6	CAAC
66	Egyptair		AW	J7	National Aircraft
67	Cathay Pacific	A8	Indian Airlines		Leasing
68	Saudia	A9	Transair, Canada	J8	Sudan Airways
69	Kuwait AW	B1	DETA,	J9	Imperial Iranian AF
70	Iraqi AW		Mozambique	K1	Tarom
71	Trans America/TIA	B2	Air Madagascar	K2	Transavia
72	Airlift Int.	B3	Aeromaritime/UTA	K3	Aviogenex
73	World Airways	B4	Middle East Airlines	K5	Hapag Lloyd
74	Not Used	B5	Korean Airlines	K6	SAHSA
75	Pacific Western	B6	Royal Air Maroc	K9	Bavaria Flug
76	Australian Airlines	B7	Allegheny Airlines	L4	American Capital
77	Ansett	C0	GATX		Av.
78	BWIA	C3	Cruzeiro do Sul	L5	Libyan Arab AL
79	Saturn	C9	Luxair	L6	Aviation Serv. &
80	Bankers Trust	D1	Universal		Support
81	All Nippon	D3	Alia Jordanian	L7	Air Nauru
82	TAP	D4	Ozark Airlines	L8	Yugoslavian Govt.
83	SAS	D6	Air Algerie	L9	Maersk Air
84	Olympic	D7	Thai International	M0	Aeroflot
85	LAN Chile	E1	Eastern Provincial	M1	Pelita Air Services
86	Iran Air/Iran Govt.	E3	Ladeco	M2	TAAG Angola
87	Aerolineas	E7	Arkia	M6	Royal Brunei
	Argentinas	F2	Turk Hava Yollari	M7	Hughes Airwest
88	Unknown	F5	Portuguese AF	M8	Trans European
89	Japan Domestic	F6	Philippine Airlines		AW
90	Alaska Airlines	F8	Royal Nepal	M9	Zambia AW
91	Frontier		Airlines	N0	Air Zimbabwe
92	Southern air	F9	Nigeria Airways	N1	Venezuelan AF
	Transport	G1	Saudi Arabian	N3	Brazilian AF
93	GATX/Air Cal		Govt.	N6	Nigerian Govt.
94	Syrianair	G4	U.S. Government	N7	Egyptian
95	Northeast	G5	Lufttransport Sud		Government
96	Quebecair	G7	America West	N8	Yemenia
97	Aloha	H2	ITT Corporation	N9	Niger Government
98	Air Zaire	H3	Tunis Air	P1	State of Qatar
99	Caledonian	H4	Southwest Airlines	P5	Thai Airways
A0	Lloyd Aero	H5	MeyAir	P6	Gulf Air/UAE
	Boliviano	H6	Malaysian Airlines		Govt.
A1	VASP	H7	Cameroon Airlines	Q2	Air Gabon

COMMERCIAL AIRCRAFT AND AIRLINERS

Code	Customer	Code	Customer	Code	Customer
Q3	Japan Southwest	W8	NOGA Import	4K	Air Nippon
Q4	Transbrazil	X2	Air Pacific	4N	China United
Q5	Air Liberia	X3	Air Charter International	4S	GB Airways
Q6	LACSA	X4	Supair	5A	Presidential Airways
Q8	ILFC	X6	Markair	5B	Germanair
Q9	ITEL	X8	Wistair	5C	Xiamen Airlines
R1	Govt. of Cameroon	X9	Indonesian AF	5D	LOT
R4	Alyemda	Y0	Guinness Peat Group	5E	Eva Airways
R6	Air Guinee			5F	GATX
R7	Cargolux	Y4	Rafiq Hariri	5H	C.Itoh Aerospace
R8	Air Tanzania	Y5	Air Malta	5S	CSA
S1	TACA	Y9	Air Malawi	6B	Novair International
S2	Federal Express	Z0	China Southwest		
S3	Air Europe	Z5	UA Emirates Govt.	6B	Cal Air
S4	Air Afrique	Z6	Royal Thai AF	6D	Shanghai AL
S5	Eldorado Av.	Z8	So. Korea AF	6E	Viva Air
S7	Republic Airlines	Z9	Lauda Air	6M	Virgin Express
S9	Maritime Inv. & Shipping	1A	Martin Air	6N	GECAS
T0	Texas Air/Continental AL	1B	China Southern	6P	Air Europa
		1B	China Southern	6Q	Bouillion Aviation
T2	Dome Petroleum	1C	Romanian Govt.	7A	Far East Air Transport
T3	Evergreen International	1H	Emirates Airways		
		1K	Airtours	7B	Air Holland
T4	CAAC/China Southwest	1L	Xinjiang Airlines	7C	Japanese Govt.
		1Q	Deutsche BA	7D	Air Seychelles
T5	Orion Airways	1R	Virgin Atlantic	7E	Aeromaritime Int.
T7	Monarch Airlines	2C	Air UK Leisure	7K	Zhongyuan AL
T8	Polaris Leasing	2K	Turkmenistan AL	7Q	Novel Lease Co.
T9	Boeing	2P	UA Emirates Govt.	8A	ILFC
U3	Garuda	2R	Pegasus AL	8B	Istanbul Airlines
U4	OSL	3A	Transpacific Enterprises	8E	Asiana
U5	Jordanian Govt.			8N	Chile AF
U8	Kenya AW	3B	Air Mauritius	9A	ARAVCO
U9	Polynesian Airlines	3C	Euralair	9D	Linjeflyg
V2	TAME	3N	American Trans Air	9H	ILFC
V5	Bahamasair	3P	Uzbekistan AW	9H	Leisure International
V6	Petrolair System AS	3Q	Boeing (BBJ)		
V8	Busy Bee	3R	Western Pacific AL	9J	Far Eastern AT
W0	Yunnan Provincial Av.	3V	Easy Jet	9K	Xinhua AL
		4A	United Parcel Service	9M	Austral
W2	Aerotour			9R	Pro Air
W6	Moroccan Govt.				

Military Type Numbers

Boeing transports have been used in considerable numbers by the U.S. military forces and overseas air arms. The principal military variants are included in the main model table. The following summary gives the U.S. military designations and limited details of numbers built. It should be noted that, in the case of many C-135s, aircraft have been converted several times from one variant to another.

U.S. Military Designation	Number Built	Notes
XC-97	3	Original military prototype 367-1-1 and -2 for evaluation.
YC-97	6	Service test version of XC-97 with increased fuel, higher-set engine nacelles and improved electrical system.
YC-97A	3	YC-97 with larger vertical tail, heavier gauge skinning, R-4360 engines etc. Became C-97A.
C-97A	50	Production C-97A with chin-mounted radar, cargo door and extra fuel capacity.
JC-97A		One C-97A used for experimental testing.
KC-97A		Three C-97A converted as tankers for testing.
YC-97B	1	Passenger version of YC-97A with cabin windows, lower deck lounge and 80-seat interior. Later became C-97B and VC-97B.
C-97C	14	C-97A with strengthened floor etc.
MC-97C		Medical evacuation.
VC-97D		C-97A as airborne command post.
C-97D		V-97B and two C-97A mod as airborne command post.
KC-97E	60	Tanker version of C-97C.
KC-97F	159	KC-97E with uprated engines.
KC-97G	592	Convertible passenger/tanker.
C-97G		135 KC-97G converted to passenger configuration.
EC-97G		C-97G converted for electronic systems tests.
HC-97G		29 KC-97G converted for Air-Sea Rescue role.
YC-97H		Initial designation for turboprop C-97. Became YC-97J.
KC-97H		One KC-97F fitted with probe and drogue refuelling system.

Boeing E-3D Sentry AEW.1, ZH102 (RAF)

U.S. Military Designation	Number Built	Notes
YC-97J		Turboprop powered KC-97G.
C-97K		27 conversions of KC-97G to passenger configuration.
KC-97L		82 KC-97G with additional jet engines.
KC-135A	29	Model 707-120 built as aerial refuelling tankers.
KC-135A	68	Second KC-135A batch.
KC-135A	627	Third KC-135A batch.
C-135A	18	126-pax cargo/passenger version.
EC-135A	6	Airborne command post/communications relay version.
JC-135A		Conversions for various test programmes.
JKC-135A		Conversions for various test programmes.
NC-135A	3	Conversions for nuclear test monitoring.
NKC-135A		Conversions for various test programmes including Naval fleet support with electronic jamming equipment.
RC-135A	4	KC-135A with refuelling equip deleted for mapping and photo-reconnaissance.
VC-135A		C-135A conversions to VIP and staff transport model.
C-135B	30	C-135A with 18,000 lb.s.t. TF33-P-5 turbofans and enlarged tailplane.
KC-135B	17	Aerial refuelling version of C-135B.
OC-135B	3	Open Skies arms treaty monitoring aircraft with forward belly radome.
RC-135B	10	C-135B for electronic surveillance.
TC-135B		Training aircraft for WC-135B crews.
VC-135B	11	VIP and staff transport model of C-135B.
WC-135B		11 C-135B converted for weather reconnaissance.
C-135C		WC-135B aircraft converted for passenger transport.
EC-135C	5	Looking Glass command post KC-135B with fuselage roof antenna bulge.
RC-135C	9	RC-135B converted with improved electronic equip and cheek fairings.
KC-135D	4	RC-135A aircraft converted as tankers.
RC-135D		KC-135A converted with long radar nose and additional electronic equipment and refuelling equipment removed.
C-135E		C-135A with 18,000 lb.s.t. TF33 (P&W JT3D-3B) turbofans and large tailplane.
KC-135E		KC-135A with TF33 turbofans.
NKC-135E		KC-135E for various test programmes.
EC-135E		Range support aircraft with large nose radome.
RC-135E	1	RC-135D with altered electronic equipment.
C-135F	12	KC-135B tankers for French Air Force.
C-135FR		C-135F with CFM56 engines and Adele RWR equipment.
EC-135G		EC-135A with altered electronic equipment.
EC-135H		KC-135A with modified equipment as Command posts.

U.S. Military Designation	Number Built	Notes
EC-135J	3	EC-135C converted as Airborne Command Posts.
EC-135K		KC-135A 'Head Dancer' with modified equipment as Command posts.
EC-135L		EC-135G communications relay stations with altered equipment.
RC-135M	6	VC-135B with CFM56 engines for electronic reconnaissance with rear fuselage fairings.
EC-135N	8	C-135A converted as satellite tracking stations with external ALOTS pods.
EC-135P	5	KC-135A with modified equipment as Command posts.
KC-135Q	56	KC-135A modified for refuelling of SR-71 aircraft.
KC-135R		KC-135A converted for secondary reconnaissance role.
KC-135RE		KC-135 retrofitted with four 22,000 lb.s.t. CFM.56 F108-CF-100 turbofans.
RC-135S	3	VC-135B for Cobra Ball overseas missile test monitoring tasks with long nose and forward external strake antennae and rear fuselage sensors.
TC-135S	1	RC-135S for electronic surveillance crew training.
KC-135T		KC-135Q refitted with CFM56 engines.
RC-135T	1	JKC-135A for special reconnaissance tasks.
RC-135U	3	RC-135C for Combat Sent special reconnaissance tasks with forward fuselage and chin electronic fairings and multiple belly antennae.
RC-135V	8	RC-135U for Rivet Joint special SIGINT tasks with long nose and forward and lower centre section antennae.
RC-135W		RC-135V with Pratt & Whitney TF33-P5 engines and thrust reversers.
TC-135W	1	Training version of WC-135W with reduced electronics fit.
WC-135W		Airborne nuclear pollution particle sampling aircraft.
RC-135X	1	One RC-135S fitted with missile surveillance cameras.
EC-135Y	1	NKC-135A converted as VIP aircraft with TF33 turbofans.
VC-137A	3	Model 707-153 for senior staff transport.
VC-137B		VC-137A re-engined with TF33 turbofans.
C-137B		Redesignation of VC-137B.
VC-137C	2	Model 707-353C for presidential transport.
C-137C	2	Model 707-300 commercial aircraft acquired as passenger transports.
EC-137D	2	Commercial 707-320B modified as prototype E-3 AWACS aircraft.
VC-138B		VC-137A refitted with Pratt & Whitney JT3D-3 turbofans.
C-18A		Eight Model 707-123B acquired from American Airlines as crew trainers.

U.S. Military Designation	Number Built	Notes
EC-18B		Three C-18A converted for use in ARIA range monitoring tasks with EC-135N nose radomes.
EC-18D		Model 707-123B acquired from American Airlines and fitted with APG63 radar for cruise missile control.
C-19A		Boeing 747 for Air National Guard. Designation not used.
C-22A		Ex-civil Boeing 727-30 for USAF.
C-22B		Ex-civil Boeing 727-35 for ANG.
C-22C		Ex-civil Boeing 727-212 for USAF.
VC-25A	2	Boeing 747-200B presidential transports.
C-32A	4	Boeing 757 for USAF general transport.
T-43A		Boeing 737-200 for navigation training with reduced cabin windows.
CT-43A		T-43A redesignated for alternative general transport role.
E-3A	58	Sentry AWACS version of C-135D with dorsal pylon mounted dish radome. Also E-3F for France and E-3D for RAF.
E-3B		E-3A upgraded with more capable surveillance systems.
E-3C	9	E-3A upgraded with extra crew stations and Have Quick communications.
E-4A		Boeing 747 NEACP strategic airborne command post.
E-4B	4	EA-4A upgraded with improved comms equipment and 52,500 lb.s.t. General Electric F103-GE-100 turbofans.
E-6A		Boeing 707 for TACAMO air to submarine communication link and command post duties.

Note: Many of the above types have been converted to other designations and as a consequence it is not possible to give complete production data.

Boeing 727-23, VR-BDJ

BOMBARDIER CANADA

Bombardier is a long-established Canadian industrial company which expanded into aerospace in the mid-1980s. In its early days, Bombardier was well known for its snowmobiles and the war years saw the company building a range of tracked vehicles for the military forces. After the war the company's focus shifted to producing equipment and products for the railway industry and had expanded overseas with businesses in Austria and Belgium engaged in manufacture of tramway equipment. The snowmobile business remained as an important activity and Bombardier continued to build military vehicles and various ranges of heavy equipment for the mining industry.

Today, Bombardier is a major aerospace manufacturer in a broad range of civil transport aircraft. This business results from the 1986 acquisition of Canadair followed by purchase of Shorts in October 1989, Learjet Corporation in June 1990 and De Havilland Canada in March, 1992. Bombardier has pursued a policy of separate development of each of these companies while establishing inter-company trading wherever this has been financially and operationally advantageous. One of the main cross-trading activities is production of the fuselage of the Learjet 45A by Shorts. The background and air transport activities of Canadair, De Havilland Canada and Shorts are described in the following sections. The product line of Learjet and more detailed information on the early De Havilland Canada designs and the Canadair CL.215/415 are included in the companion volume, *Airlife's General Aviation*.

CANADAIR

Canadair originated as the aircraft division of Canadian Vickers Ltd. which was established in 1922. The name was changed with the incorporation of Canadair on 3 October 1944 and in 1947 the company was acquired by the Electric Boat Company – an American company based at Groton, Connecticut. This eventually became General Dynamics through the amalgamation of Electric Boat, Canadair and Electro-Dynamics Inc. and the new group further expanded with the purchase of Consolidated Vultee in the following year. After a period of years during which the fortunes of Canadair fluctuated, General Dynamics sold their interest to the Canadian Government in January 1976. The next decade was a difficult time for Canadair which had to seek new production programmes and much time, energy and money was absorbed by the development of the Challenger business jet programme. The Government in the form of the CDIC (Canada Development Investment Corp.) eventually decided, in August 1986, to retire from ownership of Canadair which had absorbed substantial funds over the years and they accepted an offer from Bombardier.

Canadair C-4 Argonaut, G-ALHR

The original wartime business of Canadian Vickers involved production of some 369 Canso amphibians but peacetime conditions called for new production programmes. Initially, Canadair carried out a profitable conversion programme on tired wartime C-47s for civil operation. However, the needs of the newly established Trans Canada Airlines (TCA) and the Canadian Air Force brought the opportunity for the company to build an airliner suitable for domestic and international routes. A licence was set up with Douglas in February 1944 for production in Canada of an aircraft based on elements of the well established DC-4 and the projected DC-6. For RCAF requirements, the C-54GM was basically a C-54 airframe (in some cases using existing Douglas-manufactured fuselages) fitted with Rolls-Royce Merlin engines. TCA required the civil variant to be pressurised and Canadair created a hybrid version with the wings, tail and nose of a DC-4 married to a shortened version of the DC-6 centre fuselage and the strengthened DC-6 undercarriage. Canadair built a total of seventy-one aircraft, including the unique C-5 with Pratt & Whitney engines, and sold a large fleet of Argonauts to BOAC and four to Canadian Pacific Airlines. The Canadair 4 gave good service on domestic Canadian routes and on the transatlantic schedules operated by TCA and BOAC and once retired by these carriers the aircraft continued in service with operators such as Derby Airways, East African Airways Corporation and Flying Enterprise.

In 1954, the British aero-engine company N.D. Napier of Luton acquired a Convair 340 which they refitted with their new Eland turboprop engine. The aircraft (G-ANVP) was first flown in this form on 4 February 1956. Subsequently, Canadair took an interest in the programme and set up a plan to re-engine existing Convairs and to build new airframes as the Canadair 540. In the event, they received an order for ten aircraft from the Royal Canadian Air Force which were delivered between July 1960 and March 1961 as the CC-106. Three late airframes built as speculative aircraft at Convair's own production line in San Diego were also delivered to Canadair and two were sold as Canadair 540s to Quebecair. The Eland engine suffered from insufficient development and proved to be unreliable so the RCAF aircraft were subsequently re-engined with Allison 501 turbo-props becoming, essentially, Convair 580s.

During the 1950s, Canadair was heavily engaged on military production of the Canadair Sabre and the T-33 Silver Star but they also responded to an RCAF need for a maritime patrol aircraft by proposing a specially developed version of the Bristol Britannia. The Canadair CL-28 Argus used the Britannia tail and wings with a new fuselage which included two belly weapons bays, a radome for the search radar beneath the nose and a MAD stinger tail. The prototype was flown on 28 March 1957 and was followed by thirty-three production examples of the two versions of the Argus.

This production programme led to the 1957 announcement that Canadair was to build a 134-passenger military transport based on the Britannia for the RCAF. The CL-44 was, essentially, a Britannia Series 300 powered by Rolls-Royce Tyne engines and twelve were ordered by the Canadian Government as the CC-106 Yukon with the first aircraft flying in November 1959. The Yukon had a longer fuselage than the Britannia and was fitted with large cargo doors on the front and rear port fuselage. The final RCAF aircraft was delivered in March 1962.

Canadair, not unnaturally, were anxious to sell more than the small military batch and the civil CL-44 was launched in 1960 but it was only viable as a freighter and even then Canadair was unable to find a launch customer. As a result, the company reappraised the programme and developed the CL-44D which had a hinged tail unit to allow faster loading and unloading of commercial cargo. This version attracted orders from The Flying Tiger Line and Seaboard & Western Airlines totalling fifteen aircraft and further orders were gained to take CL-44D production to twenty-seven. The last delivery, of a stretched CL-44J, was made to the Icelandic carrier, Loftleidir in 1966. One of the CL-44s was converted by Conroy in 1970 as the Skymonster with a bulbous upper fuselage for carriage of Rolls-Royce RB.211 engines to the Lockheed factory for installation in TriStars. Once this task was completed, the Skymonster was used to transport outsized cargoes and has served with a number of carriers.

Canadair pursued a wide range of projects in the following years including the CL-215 amphibian which was aimed at firefighting agencies and served with units in Canada, France, Greece, Yugoslavia and other places where forest fires were a major problem. However, the company needed another major project as their lucrative military contracts for production of the F-104 and F-5 started to dry up in the late 1960s. In 1975 they became involved in the Learstar 600 business jet which was being designed by Bill Lear. The aircraft was a wide-bodied business jet with a pair of rear-mounted Lycoming ALF502D turbofans and a supercritical wing. Canadair obtained rights to the Learstar in early 1976 but they did some extensive redesign, including a change to T-tail configuration, before the prototype was built and flown two years later. The CL600 Challenger received its Canadian Type Certificate on 11 August 1980 and it quickly accumulated orders in competition with the Gulfstream G.III and G.IV.

The company saw the Challenger as being capable of further development and, in 1980, they carried out studies on the Challenger 'E' with a stretched fuselage. Although this was subsequently abandoned it did lay the basis for the fifty-seat Canadair Regional Jet which was based on the Challenger CL601-3A with a fuselage stretch. The prototype Canadair RJ was first flown in May 1991 and the first revenue flights by Lufthansa CityLine started in the third quarter of 1992. Over 260 Canadair RJs (CL600-2B19) had been ordered by the end of 1997 and operators include Delta Connection's partners, Comair, SkyWest and Atlantic Southeast Airlines together with European customers Lauda Air, Tyrolean Airways and BritAir. Production is shared between Canadair and Short Brothers plc. who

Canadair CL.44D4-2, N446T (prior to Skymonster conversion)

manufacture the centre fuselage and some of the control surfaces. Canadair has launched a stretched version of the aircraft titled the Canadair Regional Jet Series 700 which can carry up to seventy-four passengers and will enter service at the end of 2000.

Production details

Canadair has allocated straightforward consecutive serial numbers to each of its models. With the Challenger, Bombardier introduced a new four-digit serial with a prefix number indicating the model. For completeness, the following table gives details of all serial blocks including the non transport civil aircraft. It is believed that Bombardier is to incorporate the De Havilland Canada products into this system with the DHC-8 Dash 8Q Series 400 which has serial numbers commencing 4001.

Model	Serial Batch	Notes
C-54GM srs.	c/n 101 to 171	Includes Canadair C.5.
CL-66B	c/n 1 to 10	CL-66C have Convair c/ns 454, 462, 475.
CL-44	c/n 1 to 39	
CL.600 Challenger	c/n 1001 to 1085	
CL-215	c/n 1001 to 1125	
CL-415	c/n 2001 up	
CL.601 Challenger	c/n 3001 to 3066	
CL.601-3A/3R	c/n 5001 to 5194	
CRJ	c/n 7001 to 7269	
Global Express	c/n 9001 to 9006 up	
CRJ-700	c/n 10001 up	Not yet built.

Model Information

Details of all Canadair transport designs are as follows.

Type No.	Name	No. Built	Notes
C-54GM	North Star	18	Douglas C-54 built by Canadair with four 125 h.p. Rolls-Royce Merlin 620 engines. Prot. CF-TEN-X FF. 15 Jul. 1946. Also designated Canadair CL-2.
DC-4M1	North Star	6	C-54GM used by TCA and fitted with DC-6 undercarriage, rear passenger entry door and 1760 h.p. Merlin 622 engines.
DC-4M2-3	North Star	20	Civil airliner for TCA domestic ops. with max 62-pax seats. Developed from DC-4M1 with pressurised cabin using shortened DC-6 centre fuselage and square windows. 79,400 lb. TOGW.
DC-4M2-4	North Star		DC-4M2 for TCA transatlantic operations with 1760 h.p. Merlin 624 engines and 80,200 lb. TOGW.
C-4	Argonaut	22	DC-4M2-4 for BOAC with 1760 h.p. Merlin 626 engines, crew door and detail changes. 82,300 lb. TOGW. Also designated Canadair CL-4.
C-4-1	Canadair 4	4	C-4 for Canadian Pacific AL with 7950 lb. TOGW.

Type No.	Name	No. Built	Notes
C-5	Canadair C-5	1	DC-4M with 2100 h.p. Pratt & Whitney R-2800-CA15 engines. s/n 17524 (c/n 171).
CL-66A	Canadair 540		Intended new production civil version of Convair 440 powered by two 3500 shp Napier Eland NE.1 Mk. 504A turboprops. None built.
CL-66B	Cosmopolitan	10	CL-66 for RCAF as CC-109 Later re-engined with Allison 501-D36 engines.
CL-66C	Canadair 540	3	Convair-built CV-440 airframes completed as civil Canadair 540s.
CL-44-6	CC-106 Yukon	12	Licence-built military version of Bristol Britannia 300 with 12ft 4in fuselage stretch, port-side cargo doors fore and aft of wing, convertible freight or 134-pax interior and powered by four 5730 shp Rolls-Royce Tyne Mk. 515/10 turboprops. Prot. s/n 15501 (c/n 1) FF. 15 Nov. 1959.
CL-44D4-1		8	Freighter version of CL-44 with swing tail hinged on starboard side for tail loading. Prot. CF-MKP-X (c/n 9) FF. 16 Nov. 1960. Primarily for Seaboard World AL.
CL-44D4-2		13	CL-44D for Flying Tiger Line without cabin windows.
CL-44D4-6		4	CL-44D for Slick Airways without cabin windows.
CL-44D4-8		2	CL-44D for Loftleidir.
CL-44J			Four CL-44D converted to 160-passenger configuration for Loftleidir with cabin windows, fuselage stretched by 10ft 1in forward and 5ft 1in aft of wing and swing tail sealed off. Prot. CF-SEE-X (c/n 39) FF. 8 Nov. 1965.
CL-44-0	Skymonster		CL-44D-2 converted as oversize cargo carrier by Jack Conroy Aviation with bulbous upper fuselage. N447T (c/n 16) FF. 26 Nov. 1969.

Canadair RJ, N920CA

Type No.	Name	No. Built	Notes
RJ-100	CRJ	192	50-pax regional airliner based on Canadair Challenger with T-tail, enlarged low wing with winglets, fuselage stretched by 10ft 8in forward and 9ft 4in aft of wing, powered by two 9220 lb.s.t. General Electric CF34-3A1 turbofans in tail pods. Prot. C-FCRJ (c/n 7001) FF. 10 May 1991. 47,450 lb. TOGW. Also extended range RJ-100ER with increased range and 51,000 lb. TOGW and RJ-100LR with further range increase. SE corporate version.
RJ-200	CRJ	77	RJ-100 with CF34-3B1 engines. Also extended range -200ER and long range -200LR versions.
RJ-200B			RJ-200 for hot and high operations.
RJ-700			Developed CRJ-200 with 70-seats, fuselage stretched by 13ft forward and 2ft 5in aft of wing, two 12,670 lb.s.t. CF34-8C1 engines. To fly early 1999. To be produced as Srs. 700A and 700A-ER and 700B and 700B-ER with different weight and range.

DE HAVILLAND CANADA

The De Havilland Aircraft of Canada ('DHC') was established in April 1928 as a subsidiary of the British parent company and built a significant number of de Havilland designs during the 1930s and during World War II. The 1940s saw the company developing a number of new designs including the well known DHC-1 Chipmunk trainer which was built in Canada and by De Havilland in Britain. A Canadian-led demand for rugged bush aircraft gave DHC the opportunity to design the highly successful DHC-2 Beaver and its larger brother, the DHC-3 Otter – both of which designs continue in widespread service with small commercial aviation companies and have found a particular niche with floatplane operators.

As time passed, the aircraft built by DHC increased in size. The DHC-4 Caribou was

DHC-8 Dash Eight 200, A6-ADA

designed to fulfil a U.S. Army specification calling for a three-ton rear-loading tactical transport powered by two 1450 h.p. Pratt & Whitney R-2000-D5 piston engines. The first Caribou (CF-KTK-X c/n 1) was flown on 30 July 1958 and of the 253 examples built some 165 went to the U.S. Army and others were delivered to the air forces of Malaysia, Australia, Kenya, Zambia, India, Ghana and Canada. A fair number of ex-military Cariboux moved from their military owners to service with commercial companies as freight carriers in the more remote corners of the globe. One Caribou has been converted by Pen Turbo Aviation of Rio Grande, New Jersey to take 1420 shp Pratt & Whitney PT6A-67R turboprops but no further conversions have been carried out to date. A scaled-up turboprop-engined development of the Caribou, the DHC-5 Buffalo, was also developed for use by the U.S. Army but, while some 126 examples were completed, these were mainly delivered to other military users including the Canadian, Brazilian, Kenyan, Tanzanian and Peruvian air forces. The Buffalo was marketed to civil users as the forty-four-passenger DHC-5E Transporter but DHC failed to achieve any civil sales.

In 1963 DHC took the decision to build a twin-engined version of the Otter and this move was to provide an extremely valuable entry for the company into the commuter airline market. The DHC-6 Twin Otter was a strut-braced high-wing monoplane with a fixed tricycle undercarriage and two Pratt & Whitney PT6A turboprop engines. It entered production in 1965 following the first flight of the prototype, in May of that year. Initially, DHC focussed on the U.S. Army as the leading customer for the Twin Otter but this failed to materialise and commercial sales became essential. It was the relationships built up at this time which set the company on the course which was to establish its future direction. Early deliveries were made to Trans Australian Airlines, Air Wisconsin, Golden West and Pilgrim Airlines. Military sales also got underway with an order from the Chilean Air Force and the Twin Otter took on many utility roles including service with the British Antarctic Expedition. The initial model was the short-nosed Series 100 with 578 shp PT6A-20 engines and this was replaced in April 1968 by the Series 200 with a lengthened nose (though the floatplane continued with the short nose) and then the Series 300 with 652 shp PT6A-27 engines. The last of 844 Twin Otters was completed in December 1988.

Commuter airline demands led to the development of the DHC-7 'Dash Seven' high wing four-turboprop forty-eight-seat airliner which flew in prototype form in March 1975. The T-tailed Dash Seven employed large double-slotted flaps stretching over 80% of its wingspan and, while production only totalled 113 aircraft it became much sought after as a result of its fifty-seat capacity and STOL performance which allowed it to transport significant loads out of the more demanding airfields. In the early stages of operation of London's City Airport, the Dash Seven was the only aircraft capable of fulfilling the

DHC-6 Twin Otter, V2-LCO

DHC-7 Dash Seven, N905HA

stringent noise and glideslope conditions. The DHC-7 was widely exported and served with carriers such as Wideroes in Norway, Pelita Air Services in Indonesia and the Israeli airline, Arkia. In the United States, Rocky Mountain Airways had a six-aircraft fleet and other users included Golden West, Ransome and Henson Airlines. Many of the American operators of the Twin Otter and Dash Seven grew out of the explosive development of commuter airlines in the late 1970s, but DHC was not immune to the swings of fortune which brought several of these customers to the point of insolvency and it was with some corporate courage that the DHC-8 was announced in 1982 as a replacement for the Dash Seven.

DHC became the De Havilland Division of Boeing of Canada Ltd on 31 January 1986 but, in mid-1990 it became clear that the relationship between Boeing and de Havilland was not wholly satisfactory and negotiations were put in hand to sell the business. A proposed sale to Avions de Transport Regional (ATR) was frustrated by European monopoly regulations and, on 22nd January 1992, Boeing finally concluded a sale of DHC to Bombardier (51%) and the Province of Ontario (49%) with Bombardier becoming sole owner of the company in 1996.

Bombardier gained as the major asset the twin turboprop DHC-8 Dash Eight which was designed as a flexible airframe using the best features of the DHC-7 and capable of being stretched to meet various passenger loads. The first DHC-8, C-GDNK, first flew in the summer of 1983 and represented the initial Series 100 with a maximum of thirty-nine passenger seats. However, the airframe was intended to be stretched and DHC quickly introduced the Series 300 with up to fifty-six seats. As with the DHC-7, the aircraft quickly gained a reputation for its STOL operation which gave the Dash Eight an edge over the large number of competing medium capacity commuter airliners which were coming on the market.

Early users of the DHC-8 were found among the Canadian carriers including norOntair who received the first delivery in December 1984, the Air Canada commuter operators such as Air Nova, Air Alliance and Air Ontario, Canadian Pacific's associate Air Atlantic and City Express which operated the shuttle service between Toronto Island Airport and Ottawa and Montreal. The DHC-8 also established a reputation with the commuter carriers in the United States and the 500th aircraft was delivered in December 1997 to Horizon Air – a west coast operator which has ordered one of the largest fleets totalling forty-six aircraft. The latest version of the Dash Eight is the DHC-8-400 which is further stretched to provide up to seventy-eight seats and will go into service in mid-1999.

Production details

Model	Serial Batch	Notes
DHC-2 Beaver	c/n 1 to 1692	Includes 60 Turbo Beavers
DHC-3 Otter	c/n 1 to 466	Some converted to Turbo Otter
DHC-4 Caribou	c/n 1 to 303	DHC-4A from c/n 78
DHC-5 Buffalo	c/n 1 to 126	
DHC-6 Twin Otter	c/n 1 to 844	Srs. 100 c/n 1 to 115, Srs. 200 c/n 116 to 232, Srs. 300 c/n 233 to 844
DHC-7 Dash-Seven	c/n 1 to 113	
DHC-8 Dash-Eight	c/n 1 to 515 up	
DHC-8 Dash-8Q-400	c/n 4001 up	

Model Information

Details of the transport aircraft built by de Havilland Canada are as follows.

Type No.	Name	No. Built	Notes
DHC-4	Caribou	78	High wing military/civil utility aircraft with max 32-troop capacity, cruciform tail, upswept rear fuselage with ventral rear loading doors and retractable tricycle u/c. Powered by two 1450 h.p. Pratt & Whitney R-2000-7M2 radial piston engines. 26,000 lb. TOGW. Prot. CF-KTK-X (c/n 1) FF. 30 Jul. 1985. Military CV-2A.
DHC-4A	Caribou	225	DHC-4 with 28,500 lb. TOGW. Military C-7A (CV-2B).
DHC-5	Buffalo	59	Military utility aircraft based on DHC-4 with enlarged fuselage with rear loading ramp, T-tail and powered by two 2850 shp General Electric T64-GE-10 turboprops. Prot s/n 63-13686. FF. 9 Apl. 1964.

DHC-8 Dash Eight 300, C-BFHZ (D-BOBZ)

Type No.	Name	No. Built	Notes
DHC-5D	Buffalo	67	DHC-5 with new APU, anti-skid brakes and 2970 shp CT64-820-4 engines with beta control.
DHC-6-100	Twin Otter	115	High-wing utility and commuter aircraft with 20-pax seating, fixed tricycle u/c, cruciform tail and powered by two 579 shp Pratt & Whitney PT6A-20 turboprops. 11,579 lb. TOGW. Prot. CF-DHC-X (c/n 1) FF. 20 May 1965.
DHC-6-200	Twin Otter	117	DHC-6 with lengthened nose with baggage compartment and extended rear cabin baggage area. Seaplane may have short nose.
DHC-6-300	Twin Otter	613	DHC-6-200 with 652 shp PT6A-27 engines and 12,500 lb. TOGW. CAF Desig. CC-138, US Army UV-18A, USAF UV-18B.
DHC-7-100	Dash Seven	113	High-wing STOL 48-pax. commuter airliner with high wing, T-tail, retractable tricycle u/c and powered by four wing-mounted 1035 shp Pratt & Whitney PT6A-50 turboprops. Prot. C-GNBX (c/n 1) FF. 27 Mar. 1975. Srs. 101 is all-cargo version.
DHC-8-100	Dash Eight	294	High wing 40-pax commuter aircraft with T-tail and retractable tricycle u/c powered by two wing-mounted 1800 shp Pratt & Whitney PW120 turboprops driving 4-blade props. 33,000 lb. TOGW. Prot. C-GDNK (c/n 1) FF. 20 Jun. 1983.
DHC-8-101	Dash Eight		Production DHC-8 with 2000 shp PW120A engines.
DHC-8-102	Dash Eight		DHC-8-100 with 34,500 lb. TOGW.
DHC-8-103	Dash Eight		DHC-8-102 with PW121 engines.
DHC-8-100A	Dash Eight		Series 100 with 2000 shp PW120A engines, redesigned cabin interior with increased headroom and improved range.
DHC-8-100B	Dash Eight		DHC-8-100A with 2150 shp PW121A engines.
DHC8Q-100B	Dash Eight Q		DHC-8-100B with interior noise and vibration suppression system (NVS).
DHC-8M-100	Dash Eight M		Military version of Dash-Eight with hardened interior and customer-specified equipment. CC-142-passenger transport and CT-142 navigation trainer versions for Canadian A.F.
DHC-8-200	Dash Eight	69	DHC-8-100 with 2150 shp PW123C engines in DHC8-300 nacelles and 36,300 lb. TOGW.
DHC-8-200A	Dash Eight		Production DHC-8-200.
DHC-8-200B	Dash Eight		DHC-8-200A with improved hot and high performance.
DHC8Q-200B	Dash Eight Q		DHC-8-200B with NVS system.
DHC-8-300	Dash Eight	144	DHC-8-100 with 11ft 3in fuselage stretch for 56-pax capacity, extra starboard service door, enlarged galley and lavatory facilities, wingtip extensions and 2380 shp. PW123 engines. Prot. C-GDNK FF. 15 May 1987.

Type No.	Name	No. Built	Notes
DHC-8-301	Dash Eight		Production DHC-8-300.
DHC-8-311	Dash Eight		DHC-8-301 with 43,000 lb. TOGW.
DHC-8-300A	Dash Eight		DHC-8-300 with optional 43,000 lb. TOGW.
DHC-8-300B	Dash Eight		DHC-8-300 A with 43,000 lb. TOGW and improved airfield performance and takeoff power.
DHC8Q-300B	Dash Eight Q		DHC-8-300B with NVS system.
DHC-8-300E	Dash Eight		DHC-8-300 with improved hot and high performance.
DHC8Q-400	Dash Eight Q	8	DHC-8-300 with 22ft 4in centre fuselage stretch, longer wing centre section with larger fuel tanks, modified flaps and control surfaces, strengthened u/c, Sextant HFDS system, additional airstair entry door and two 5071 shp Pratt & Whitney PW150 turboprops with 6-blade props. Prot. C-FJJA (c/n 4001) FF. 31 Jan. 1998.

SHORT BROTHERS

Short Brothers plc has its origins in the long established company, Short Brothers & Harland Ltd which achieved a strong reputation before and during the war for flying-boat manufacture and for production of the Stirling heavy bomber. After the war, their first civil product was the Sealand light amphibian and this was followed by a number of experimental projects including the Sperrin bomber and the SC.1 vertical take-off aircraft.

Shorts' first major postwar civil production model was the SC.7 – a light freighter based on the design of the Miles Boxcar, rights to which were acquired in 1958. The resultant PD.36 (later christened the SC.7 Skyvan) retained the high-aspect-ratio wing of the Boxcar but was essentially a new design. The SC.7 had a square section fuselage with a rear loading ramp, fixed tricycle undercarriage and twin fins – and the prototype (G-ASCN c/n SH.1828), which flew on 17 January 1963, was powered by a pair of 390 h.p. Continental GTSIO-520 piston engines. In fact, Shorts had already concluded that turboprops should be used on the Skyvan and G-ASCN was soon re-engined with 554 shp Turbomeca Astazou IIs.

Short Skyvan, 9M-PIH

Short Belfast, G-BEPS

In its production form, with square windows and modified rudders and nosewheel, it became the 'Turbo Skyvan' (later Skyvan 2), fitted with the 637 shp Astazou X – and seventeen of this initial version were completed (c/n SH.1829 to SH.1845). The Astazou engine had certain shortcomings, however, and the Skyvan 3 (and its twenty-two-passenger equivalent, the Skyliner) was soon developed with 757 shp Garrett TPE331-201A engines. A total of 134 of this model (c/n SH.1846 to SH.1979) were built and ten of the Skyvan 2s were refitted with the Garrett powerplant to upgrade them to Series 3 standard. Skyvans have been operated as commuter transports by a number of airlines including British European Airways, Northern Consolidated, Wien Alaska, Loganair and Pelita Air Service.

The Skyvan gave Shorts an ideal entry into the light commuter aircraft market which was developing in the early 1970s and the design of the Skyliner was stretched to thirty-three-passenger capacity to become the SD.330. This also involved some alterations to the wings, a retractable undercarriage embodying external gear pods and installation of 1120 shp United Aircraft of Canada PT6A-45 turboprops. The SD.330 prototype (G-BSBH c/n SH.3000) made its maiden flight at Sydenham on 22 August 1974 and was followed by a production prototype (c/n SH.3001) in December 1975. Full production followed and the '330 achieved good acceptance in America with commuter carriers, with the United States Air Force who took delivery of a batch of eighteen C-23A Sherpa

Shorts 360, G-OAAS

freighters and with the Royal Thai Police who bought the '330UTT (Utility Tactical Transport). A basic batch of 123 production aircraft was built (c/n SH.3002 to SH.3124) the last of which was completed in May 1989. A new series of ten aircraft, commencing at c/n SH.3210 was initiated in 1990 to cover an order for additional Sherpas for the United States Air Force.

Shorts further developed the SD.330 into the thirty-six-passenger SD.360 with a longer fuselage, swept fin and 1327 shp PT6A-65R engines. The prototype SD.360 was G-BSBH (c/n SH.3600) which was first flown on 1 June 1981 and production ceased at c/n SH.3764. Again, the '330 and '360 were widely used on American commuter operations by the Allegheny Commuter participants and by other carriers such as Golden West, Command Airways, Mississippi Valley Airlines and Henson Airlines. A number of Shorts 360s were acquired in 1997 for conversion to '330 Sherpa standard with twin fins to meet an additional United States military requirement.

During 1987, Shorts released details of two advanced local service turboprop airliners, the NRA-90A and NRA-90B, which it was working on in co-operation with De Havilland Canada. One of these featured a large pusher turboprop in the tail, but this co-operation was limited and Shorts went on to develop the design of its FJX forty-eight-seat fanjet-powered regional airliner. As it turned out, in October 1989 Shorts was acquired by Bombardier Inc. This resulted in abandonment of the FJX project and Shorts became involved in production of the competitive Bombardier-Canadair 'RJ' Regional Jet.

Shorts SD.330, 43099 of Royal Thai Police

BRITISH AEROSPACE   UNITED KINGDOM

British Aerospace was formed on 29 April 1977 by the amalgamation of Hawker Siddeley Aviation Ltd, Hawker Siddeley Dynamics Ltd, Scottish Aviation Ltd, and British Aircraft Corporation (Holdings) Ltd. In turn, British Aircraft Corporation had been created through a merger of the Bristol Aeroplane Company, the English Electric Company and Vickers Ltd. The Hawker Siddeley Group had developed as a major aerospace group during the early 1960s, culminating in integration of Hawker, Blackburn, Folland, Avro, Armstrong Whitworth, Gloster and de Havilland under a restructuring carried out in July 1963. The air transports built by each of these companies are frequently referred to as British Aerospace models but are described under the separate companies which originally designed them.

AVRO

During World War II, Avro had built great quantities of the famous Lancaster bomber and this led to the Avro 685 York military transport which employed the Lancaster wing and tail unit married to a square-section fuselage. Many of the 256 Yorks produced were used on the Berlin Airlift and on commercial services and trooping flights in the

Avro Tudor 1, G-AGRH

immediate postwar period with operators such as Skyways and Hunting Clan. Avro were, however, also attracted to the postwar opportunities presented by the Brabazon Committee's blueprint for a range of new transport aircraft and experience with large aircraft led them to design a new airliner to operate long distance services including North Atlantic routes. The resultant Avro 688 Tudor was, essentially, based on the Lancaster/York wings and engines with a new circular section pressurised fuselage and a single tailfin.

The Tudor became the victim of constant modification and prevarication from its intended user, BOAC and from the Ministry of Supply and was unable to meet the trans-atlantic range and passenger-carrying requirement. The result was that the aircraft built did not enter service with BOAC and, in an attempt to salvage the programme, Avro came up with progressively stretched and modified versions. Tudors were operated for a while by British South American Airways on routes to Bermuda and ultimately the stretched 'Super Traders' of Air Charter gave useful service on long-distance freight routes. The Tudors also participated in the Berlin Airlift and four of the stretched Tudor Vs proved useful in carrying large quantities of petroleum. The Tudors were largely retired from service by 1956 as more efficient transports took their place. Details of the Tudor variants are as follows:

Type No.	No. Built	Notes
688 Tudor 1	10	All-metal pressurised 28-passenger low-wing transport with retractable tailwheel u/c and powered by four 1750 h.p. Rolls-Royce Merlin 102A piston engines in wing-mounted nacelles. 71,000 lb. TOGW. Prot. G-AGPF (c/n 1234) FF. 14 Jun. 1945.
689 Tudor 2	4	Tudor with increased fuselage width, 26ft 1in fuselage stretch and 60-pax. capacity. Powered by four 1770 h.p. Rolls-Royce Merlin 621 engines. Prot. G-AGSU (c/n 1235) FF. 10 Mar. 1946.
688 Tudor 3	2	9-pax VIP version of Tudor 1. Later modified as freighters.
688 Tudor 4	8	Tudor 1 with 6ft forward fuselage stretch and 32-pax capacity. 80,000 lb. TOGW. Most converted to Model 711 Trader with forward port cargo hatch and strengthened floor.
688 Tudor 4B		Five Tudor 1s converted to Tudor 4 standard but with 28-pax capacity and flight engineer's station.
689 Tudor 5	6	Tudor 2 with round windows and 44-pax capacity, powered by four 1770 h.p. Rolls-Royce Merlin 621 engines. Initially used as freighters.
689 Tudor 7	1	Tudor 2 equipped with four 1750 h.p. Bristol Hercules 120 engines. G-AGRX (c/n 1261) FF. 17 Apl. 1946.
688 Tudor 8		Tudor 1 converted with four Rolls-Royce Nene 5 turbojets in two underwing twin engine nacelles replacing four separate Merlin nacelles.
706 Ashton	6	Tudor 8 with strengthened structure, tricycle u/c and revised vertical tail. Used for military research.

The thirty-one completed Tudors were allocated Avro serial numbers c/n 1234 and 1235 (prototypes), 1249 and 1251 to 1270, 1341 to 1349, 1367 and 1368, 1417 to 1422. Many of the serials in these batches were unused as they were allocated to aircraft cancelled or not completed.

Among its largely military postwar aircraft programmes, Avro returned to the civil market in 1959 with an aircraft aimed at the short-haul 'Dakota replacement' class which had been successfully opened up by the Fokker Friendship. The Avro solution was

Hawker Siddeley Andover, 9Q-CYB

a low-wing aircraft of conventional layout with a pair of the well-proven Rolls-Royce Dart turboprops mounted in an over-centre position on the wings and with the main undercarriage legs contained in the lower part of the engine nacelles. The prototype was a forty-four-seater with four-abreast seating and it was not aimed at any single airline customer so as to maintain flexibility in the market.

The Avro 748 started to accumulate orders and the first deliveries were to Skyways Coach Air and BKS in 1962. Principal operators of the '748 included British Airways, Dan-Air, Indian Airlines, LIAT, Philippine Airlines, South African Airways and Varig. Avro also entered into a licence agreement with Hindustan Aeronautics in India under which twenty examples of the 748 Srs. 2M were built for the Indian Air Force. The '748 gained substantial orders from military users including the Brazilian, Colombian, Belgian and Australian air forces and this led to Avro developing the specialised Avro 780 Andover military freighter for the Royal Air Force. The Andover used the forward fuselage and wing structure of the 748 with an up-swept rear fuselage containing a ventral cargo loading ramp. Thirty-one Andovers were delivered to the RAF and ten of these were later sold to the Royal New Zealand Air Force. Many of these aircraft were subsequently released onto the civil market and operate as freighters around the world.

The '748 clearly offered the potential for growth and Avro had looked at an Avro 748E variant as early as 1961. This was revived in 1980 as the BAe.846 – which was later renamed 'ATP' (Advanced Turboprop). While the concept of the ATP was a simple stretch of the '748 the final configuration of the aircraft involved substantial structural change with incorporation of fuselage plugs fore and aft of the wing, new PW124 engines in redesigned nacelles and a redesigned vertical tail. The ATP also had a completely modernised electronic cockpit, new electrical system etc. The launch customer for the ATP was Airlines of Britain which received the first of sixteen aircraft for use by British Midland, Manx Airlines and Loganair in March 1988. The ATP was also sold to British Airways for Scottish services and to Air Wisconsin, Merpati, THT, LAR, SATA and Bangladesh Biman. The ATP was initially built at Woodford but British Aerospace formed Jetstream Aircraft in 1992 and transferred production to Prestwick where the ATP was to be built as the Jetstream 61. However, by that time orders had dried up and the line was closed down with a total of sixty-three aircraft completed.

While the aircraft was initially known as the Avro 748, the absorption of Avro into the Hawker Siddeley Group resulted in the designation HS.748 being adopted. The different variants of the '748 are as follows:

British Aerospace ATP, G-BTZG/PK-MTV

Type No.	No. Built	Notes
HS.748 Srs.1	20	Low-wing max. 52-pax short-range airliner with two 1740 shp Rolls-Royce Dart R.Da.6 Mk 514 turboprops. 35,800 lb. TOGW. Prot G-APZV (c/n 1534) FF. 24 Jun. 1960. Includes 4 built by Hindustan.
HS.748 Srs.2	153	Srs. 1 with two 1910 shp Rolls-Royce Dart R.Da.7 Mk 531 turboprops. 43,500 lb. TOGW. Includes 65 built by Hindustan.
HS.748 Srs.2A	120	Srs. 1 with two 2230 shp Rolls-Royce Dart R.Da.7 Mk 534-2 turboprops. 46,500 lb. TOGW. Some designated HS.748 Srs.2A/LFD with port-side forward freight door.
HS.748 Srs.2B Super 748	33	Srs.2A with 4ft wingspan increase and drag-reduction mods, improved flight deck and cabin interior design, optional port rear fuselage freight door and water-meth emergency engine injection system. Powered by two 2280 shp. Rolls-Royce Dart R.Da.7 Mk 536-2 turboprops. Some HS.748 Srs.2B/LFD with port-side forward freight door.
HS.748 Coastguarder		Maritime patrol version of Srs.2B with radar under forward fuselage and increased fuel.
HAL-748 Srs.2	69	Hindustan-built HS.748. First aircraft BH574 (c/n 500) FF. 1 Nov. 1961.
HS.748 Srs.2M/LFD	20	Srs.2B for military use with hardened interior and port-side forward freight door. Hindustan built.
HS.780/748MF		Military freighter based on HS.748 with new upswept rear fuselage incorporating ventral loading ramp, taller tail fin, kneeling u/c. HS.748 prot. G-APZV converted as 748MF Prot. G-ARRV (c/n 1548) FF. 21 Dec. 1963.

Hawker Siddeley HS.748-2B, V2-LCR

Type No.	No. Built	Notes
Andover C.1	31	HS.748MF production model for RAF.
ATP	63	HS.748 'Advanced Turboprop' with fuselage stretched by 16ft 6in, modified vertical fin, modified longer span wings, port-side rear and forward doors with airstairs, modernised cockpit, pointed nose and new engine nacelles mounting two 2653 shp Pratt & Whitney PW124A Turboprops with 6-blade Ham-Standard propellers. 64-pax accommodation. 50,550 lb. TOGW. Prot. G-MATP (c/n 2001) FF. 6 Aug. 1986.

Hawker Siddeley allocated customer numbers to the HS.748 which identified the exact equipment fit of each customer batch. In many cases several different numbers have been allocated to the same customer where there were a number of interior, cockpit or galley arrangements for separate aircraft ordered. The full designation of an individual aircraft consists of the series number and the customer number (e.g. a Series 2A for Bouraq Indonesia Airlines was designated HS.748 Srs.2A/216). This system was not continued with the ATP. Details of customer numbers, which are in the 100 series for Series 1 aircraft and the 200 series for Series 2 aircraft, are as follows:

Cust.No.	Customer	Cust.No.	Customer
201	Aden Airways	221,240	Argentine AF
104	Aerolineas Argentinas	226	Austrian AL
230	Aeromaya	225	Autair
212	Air Ceylon	245	Avianca
276	Air Gaspe	232,344,348	Bahamas AW
329	Air Liberia	288	Belgian AF
360,362	Air Madagascar	244	BFS
256	Air Malawi	102,106,108,214	BKS Air Transport
398,399	Air Niger	216,401,402	Bouraq
353	Air Senegal	204,205,281	Brazilian AF
400	AL of Marshall Is.	287,426	British AW
258	Amoco	310	Cameroun AF

Cust.No.	Customer	Cust.No.	Customer
435	Cameroun AL	259	SAESA
222	Channel AW	270,372	SATA
227	COPA	260,371	SATENA
378	DLT	101	Skyways
246,267,285	Ecuador AF	107	Smiths Industries
233	Fiji AW	272	South African AW
254	Ghana AW	278	TACV
333	Guinea-Bissau AL	282,314	Tanzania Govt.
309	Guyana AW	208	Thai AF
234	LAN Chile	207,243	Thai AW
215,283	LAV	334,335,347	Trinidad & Tobago AS
217,343,424	LIAT	351	Transkei AW
274	Merpati	238	UK Govt.
257	Midwest Av.	320,369	Upper Volta AF
242	Mount Cook AL	235	Varig
209	Philippine AL	223	Venezuelan AF
266	Polynesian AL	286	Williamsons Diamonds
228,229,268	RAAF/RAN	231,265	Zambia AF
206	RAF	263	Zambia AW
248	ROK AF		
264	Rousseau Av		
273	Royal Brunei AF		
253,352	Royal Nepal AL		

In addition, the Indian Air Force/Government used type numbers 203, 204, 218, 219, 220, 224 and 247. Hawker Siddeley/British Aerospace used type numbers 100, 200, 210, 239, 269, 271, 275, 301, 357 and 376.

The serial numbers allocated to Hawker Siddeley-built HS.748s ran from c/n 1534 to 1807. This batch included five Andovers and unused c/ns 1648 to 1655 which were allocated to a customer order which was subsequently cancelled. Hindustan-built HAL-748s used their own series of serials from c/n 500 to 588. The ATP had its own series of numbers running from c/n 2001 to c/n 2063.

ARMSTRONG WHITWORTH

The end of the war found Sir W.G. Armstrong Whitworth Aircraft Ltd in a similar situation to that of many other British aircraft companies. Expansion to meet wartime output of the Whitley, Albemarle and Avro Lancaster resulted in the company having a large factory at Baginton (Coventry). Despite a substantial order for Avro Lincolns, Armstrong Whitworth needed to plan for a peacetime product line. The pre-war success of the AW.27 Ensign airliners meant that the company turned its mind to a new airliner design which emerged as the beautifully streamlined AW.55 Apollo.

Designed to carry thirty passengers, the Apollo broke new ground in being powered by propeller-turbines which were just emerging as a means of propulsion. Armstrong Siddeley had designed the 1010 shp Mamba and the Apollo was powered by four of these set on its low wing. The prototype Apollo, carrying the military markings VX220, made its first flight on 10 April 1949. It was a thoroughly modern design with a tricycle undercarriage, pressurised cabin with air conditioning and thermally de-iced wings and tail. Regrettably, the Mamba engines suffered continual problems and only one further Apollo was built. The market for the Apollo went to the Vickers Viscount which had greater passenger capacity and used the much more reliable Dart engine.

It was the Dart which powered the next Armstrong Whitworth design – the AW.650 Argosy. Designed to a military specification for a general purpose freighter for the RAF, the Argosy had a high wing derived from the Avro Lincoln mounting four Darts, and twin booms. The main fuselage pod had a cockpit set on top so that loading doors could be positioned at the front and rear to allow roll-on roll-off handling of palletised and other cargo. Following the merger of Gloster and Armstrong Whitworth, the Argosy went into production and, while the main customer for the Argosy was the Royal Air Force, it also found favour with commercial operators. Riddle Airlines bought four Argosys for the 'Logair' supply operation which supported United States air bases and British European Airways bought three for freight operations.

In total, ten Series 100 were built as civil aircraft and fifty-six were delivered to the RAF as Argosy C.1s with a horizontally-split rear 'beaver tail' cargo door to permit parachute dropping. Some of these were sold for civil use after release by the RAF in 1975 although most were broken up for the value of their Dart engines. Gloster Whitworth also built six examples of the Series 222 with uprated Dart engines and an increased gross weight all of which went initially to BEA and thereafter found their way to Transair in Canada and, in a couple of cases, to IPEC Aviation in Australia. Argosy serial numbers ran from c/n 6651 (the prototype) to 6660 for the initial civil batch, c/n 6743 to 6798 for the RAF aircraft and c/n 6800 to 6805 for the Series 222. Details of the Argosy variants are as follows:

Type No.	No. Built	Notes
AW.650 Srs.100	10	All-metal twin-boomed freighter with tricycle u/c, high wing and through-loading fuselage with side-hinged front and rear loading doors. Powered by four 2020 shp Rolls-Royce Dart 526 turboprops. 88,000 lb. TOGW. Prot. G-AOZZ (c/n 6651) FF. 8 Jan. 1959. Aircraft referred to as Srs. 101 or Srs. 102 depending on fit.
AW.650 Srs.200	1	Srs. 100 with redesigned wing box spar structure and integral fuel tanks, 2-crew flight deck, modified loading door apertures and 90,000 lb. TOGW. Prot. G-ASKZ (c/n 6799) FF. 11 Mar. 1964.
AW.650 Srs.222	6	Srs. 200 with 2250 shp Dart 532 engines. 93,000 lb. TOGW.

Armstrong Whitworth Apollo, G-AIYN (APN)

AW.650 Argosy, N600Z

Type No.	No. Built	Notes
AW.660 Argosy C.1	56	Military version of Srs. 100 with bulged rear fuselage and beaver tail with horizontally-split clamshell doors, nose door deleted, strengthened wing with increased fuel capacity and 2470 shp Dart R.Da.8 turboprops. 97,000 lb. TOGW. Prot XN814 (c/n 6743) FF. 4 Mar. 1961.

BRISTOL AEROPLANE COMPANY

During the middle years of the war, the shape of post-war civil aviation was mapped out by the Brabazon Committee. A prime need was for a large passenger airliner to fly the North Atlantic routes and the Committee saw that there was a danger of the American aircraft industry dominating this sector since they were already developing a range of aircraft such as the Constellation and DC-4 which had the potential to fill the requirement. Proposals were sought from all the British aircraft companies and other unsolicited designs such as the Miles 'X' series were put forward but, eventually, the project was awarded to the Bristol Aeroplane Company who proposed the Bristol Type 167. This aircraft, named the Bristol Brabazon I, was massive by contemporary standards and could carry 100 passengers and twelve crew. The airframe design was conventional except that the outer wing leading edge had pronounced sweep. The eight Bristol Centaurus XX piston engines were mounted in coupled pairs in four engine nacelles set on the leading edges of the inboard wings.

The prototype Brabazon I, G-AGPW (c/n 12759) was first flown at Bristol-Filton on 4 September 1949 and was to be followed by a second aircraft (G-AIML c/n 12870) designated Brabazon I Mk.2 which would have been fitted with four double Proteus turboprops. Sadly, despite having excellent handling characteristics the Brabazon fell victim to government expenditure austerity after expenditure of £3 million (a substantial sum in those days). The prototype and incomplete second aircraft were broken up.

Bristol's principal product in the immediate post-war period was the highly successful Bristol 170 Freighter. Conceived as a general workhorse transport suitable for both civil and military applications, the Bristol 170 was a simple design using a development of the wing from the pre-war Bombay transport, powered by a pair of Bristol Hercules radial engines and fitted with clamshell nose doors for loading freight and vehicles as large as a three-ton army truck. This capability was to be a great asset to the Model 170 in its future use. An all-passenger version of the Freighter without the nose doors was known as the Wayfarer. The flight deck was mounted in the nose above the loading doors and, following the theme of simplicity, the Freighter had a fixed tailwheel undercarriage.

COMMERCIAL AIRCRAFT AND AIRLINERS

Following its first flight at the end of 1945, the Bristol 170's flight tests proceeded without incident and its certificate of airworthiness was awarded the following June. Orders came in steadily for the initial production batch with early customers including Aer Lingus, Indian National Airlines, Aviaco and Silver City Airways. Silver City became one of the most well-known operators of the Bristol Freighter through their car services across the English Channel and were the instigators of the development of the Freighter 32 (SuperFreighter)which had a longer nose to provide additional car capacity for the Channel air bridge. A large proportion of Bristol 170 deliveries went to military users, principally the Air Forces of Argentina, Pakistan, Iraq, New Zealand and Canada. The Bristol 170 specification was progressively improved as production advanced with increases in power and gross weight and many of the earlier production aircraft were subsequently upgraded to later marks. The last of 214 Bristol 170s was built in 1957 but examples of the type continued in operation late into the 1990s. Details of Bristol 170 variants are as follows:

Type No.	No. Built	Notes
170 Mk.I	6	All-metal freighter aircraft with high wing, fixed tailwheel u/c, clamshell nose loading doors and rear port-side pax door, powered by two 1675 h.p. Bristol Hercules 632 radial piston engines. 36,500 lb. TOGW. Prot. G-AGPV (c/n 12730) FF. 2 Dec. 1945.
170 Mk.IA	18	Mk.I for pax/freight operations with toilet and 16-pax seats in rear fuselage.
170 Mk.II	3	Wayfarer all-passenger model without nose doors.
170 Mk.IIA	13	Wayfarer with 32-pax seats, pax. toilet and galley.
170 Mk.IIB	1	Wayfarer Mk.IIA with additional passenger toilet.
170 Mk.IIC	2	Wayfarer with forward 20-pax cabin, rear toilet and baggage area.
170 Mk. XI	2	Mk.1 with 10ft longer wing with rounded tips, increased fuel capacity and. 39,000 lb. TOGW.
170 Mk. XIA	1	Mk.XI for mixed pax/freight operations.
170 Mk.21	21	Mk.XI with two 1690 h.p. Hercules 672 engines and 40,000 lb. TOGW.
170 Mk.21E	12	Mk.21 with convertible interior, 32 seats, cabin heating and sound insulation and removable freight compartment bulkhead.
170 Mk.21P	30	Mk.21 equipped for Pakistan Air Force.

Bristol 170 Mk.31E, EC-AHJ

Type No.	No. Built	Notes
170 Mk.31	17	Mk.21 with additional dorsal fin, 1980 h.p. Hercules 734 engines and 44,000 lb. TOGW.
170 Mk.31C	1	Mk.31 for RAF/A&AEE with special equipment.
170 Mk.31E	14	Mk.31 with 32-seat convertible interior similar to Mk.21E.
170 Mk.31M	62	Military version of Mk.31 for Pakistan and RCAF.
170 Mk.32	11	Mk.31E with 5ft nose extension and rear 23-pax cabin for car ferry operations.

Once again in search of the solution to the long-range needs of BOAC, Bristol received a contract in 1948 to develop its Type 175. This was initially intended to be a piston-engined aircraft using Bristol Centaurus engines but as the specification was refined the capacity of the aircraft grew from forty-four passengers to sixty-four and it was decided to fit the Britannia (as it was named) with four Bristol Proteus turboprops. Ultimately, the Britannia was designed to carry a maximum of ninety economy class passengers and the first prototype flew from Filton in August 1952.

Despite the loss of the second prototype which ditched in the River Severn following in-flight engine failure, the Britannia received its certificate of airworthiness on 30 December 1955 and the first two aircraft for BOAC were handed over on the same day. In the end, fifteen Series 100 aircraft were completed – all for BOAC – but the main production variant was the Series 300 which had a stretched fuselage and optional long-range fuel tanks. Twenty-five examples of the Series 300 were delivered to BOAC and other sales were made to El Al, Canadian Pacific, Cubana and British & Commonwealth. The Royal Air Force also received twenty-three Srs. 252 and 253 Britannias. Twelve of the 300 series aircraft were built under contract by Short Bros. & Harland at Belfast together with all the RAF aircraft. The last Britannia was completed in 1960. Once released from BOAC service, Britannias found their way into the inclusive tour market with various airlines including British Eagle, Donaldson, Caledonian Airways, BKS and British United. The Britannia airframe also formed the basis for the Canadair CL.44 and the military Canadair Argus (described under the Canadair entry).

The Britannia models were as follows:

Type No.	No. Built	Notes
Srs.100/101	1	Medium/long range pressurised passenger airliner with low wing, tricycle u/c and four Bristol Proteus 625 (later 3780 shp Proteus 705) turboprop engines. 130,000 lb. TOGW. 92-pax capacity. Prot G-ALBO (c/n 12873). FF. 12 Aug. 1952. Second prototype, Srs.101 (G-ALRX) with minor changes and 140,000 lb. TOGW.

Britannia 313, 5Y-ALT

103

Type No.	No. Built	Notes
Srs.102	15	Production Srs.100 for BOAC with 155,000 lb. TOGW, First a/c, G-ANBA FF. 15 Sep. 1954.
Srs.252	3	Srs.300 for RAF as mixed pax/cargo aircraft with strengthened forward cargo floor and forward port side cargo door. 139-pax capacity. Powered by 4450 shp Proteus 765 engines.
Srs.253	20	Srs.252 for RAF with full length strengthened floor for all-cargo operation.
Srs.301	1	Srs.100 with 10ft 3in fuselage stretch and max 100-pax capacity powered by four 4120 shp Proteus 755 turboprops. Prot. G-ANCA (c/n 12917). FF. 31 Jul. 1956.
Srs.302	2	Production Srs.300 for Aeronaves de Mexico with Proteus 762 engines. 165,000 lb. TOGW. Built by Short Bros.
Srs.305		Srs.300 ordered by Capital Airlines. Not delivered. Converted to Srs.308 and Srs.309.
Srs.306	1	Srs.300 ordered by Capital Airlines. Not delivered. Converted to Srs.307.
Srs.307	1	Srs.300 for Air Charter Ltd. with 100-pax. seating. Proteus 762 engines.
Srs.308	1	Srs.300 for Transcontinental SA. with 104-pax mixed seating. Proteus 762 engines.
Srs.309	1	Srs.300 for Ghana Airways.
Srs.310	1	Long-range version of Srs.300 with 4268 mile range. Prot. G-AOVA.
Srs.312	18	Srs.310 for BOAC with 4120 shp Proteus 755 engines.
Srs.313	4	Srs.310 for El Al with 4120 shp Proteus 755 engines.
Srs.314	6	Srs.310 for Canadian Pacific with 4400 shp Proteus 761 engines.
Srs.317	2	Srs.310 for Hunting Clan with 114 seats and Proteus 757 engines.
Srs.318	4	Srs.310 for Cubana with Proteus 765 engines.
Srs.324	2	Srs.310 for Canadian Pacific.

Production Details

Bristol serial numbers were issued in a single series covering all models. During the post-war period this embraced production of the Bristol Freighter, the Brabazons and the Britannia. Bristol Freighter serial numbers fell into batches and included c/n 12730 to 12834, c/n 12927 to 12937, c/n 13058 to 13061, c/n 13072 to 13081, c/n 13124 to 13143, c/n 13154 to 13193, c/n 13210 to 13219 and c/n 13249 to 13263. Britannias were c/n 12873 and 12874 (prototypes), c/n 12902 to 12926, c/n 13207 to 13208, c/n 13230 to 13238, c/n 13393 to 13400, c/n 13418 to 13437, c/n 13448 to 13457 and 13508 to 13517.

BRITISH AIRCRAFT CORPORATION

The late 1950s were years of political and business turmoil in the British aviation industry. In 1957 the government issued the Defence White Paper which established a new policy of replacing manned aircraft with ground-based missile systems and this threat of contraction in military procurement in turn put pressure on the independent aviation manufacturers to consolidate. In consequence, British Aircraft Corporation (BAC) was established on 1 July 1960 to bring together the aviation subsidiaries of Vickers Armstrongs, Bristol Aeroplane Company Ltd. and English Electric. BAC subsequently also acquired Hunting Aircraft Ltd.

With work on the Britannia, Viscount, VC-10 and Vanguard tailing off, BAC was left with contracts for the Lightning fighter and, consequently, needed a new project if it was to avoid massive contraction. Fortunately, Hunting Aircraft had been in the midst of designing a fifty-seat short/medium haul airliner designated H.107 and this formed the basis for the new BAC-111. Intended as a successor to the highly successful Viscount, the One-Eleven followed the design layout which was adopted by other manufacturers (such as Douglas) with a low wing, T-tail and rear fuselage mounted engines. The passenger capacity was increased to eighty (or eighty-nine in a high density configuration) and the basic Series 200 model was designed around a pair of 10,410 lb.s.t. Rolls-Royce RB.163 Spey 2 Mk. 506-14 turbofans.

At the time of its first flight in August 1963, the BAC-111 was in the fortunate position of having commitments for sixty aircraft from several airlines including British United Airways, Mohawk Airlines, Central African Airways Corporation, Aer Lingus and Braniff. There is no doubt that the good record of the Viscount contributed to this confidence – particularly with the American customers. BAC pressed forward with certification testing which brought the problem of deep stalls in aircraft of this configuration into sharp focus when the prototype was destroyed in October 1963. Design changes resolved the problem and the BAC-111 gained its type certificate of airworthiness on 9 April 1965.

While the basic version offered by BAC was the Series 200, they also configured a special version, the Series 400, for United States carriers who were gross weight restricted for two-crew operation and designed the Series 300 for longer range operations with an additional centre section fuel tank. Both of these variants were powered by higher thrust Spey 511 engines which used redesigned engine pods. The American market was of the greatest importance to BAC and they eventually gained orders for thirty aircraft for American Airlines, eighteen for Mohawk and fourteen for Braniff who had them painted in their multiple-colour livery. British United was the first airline to take delivery of its aircraft in April 1965.

Customer requirements soon dictated a stretched version of the One-Eleven and BAC launched the Series 500 which had fore and aft fuselage plugs totalling 13ft 6in. which allowed passenger capacity to be increased by four rows of five seats. The launch customer for the Series 500 was British European Airways who placed orders and options for twenty-four aircraft. BEA took delivery of its first One-Eleven in June 1969 and eventually operated forty-six aircraft, including those inherited from British Caledonian, on European and domestic United Kingdom routes. Other purchasers of the stretched

BAC-111-432FD, G-AXOX

One-Eleven included Austral, Court Line, Bahamasair, Philippine Airlines and Bavaria Fluggesellschaft.

British Aerospace finally closed the production line in 1981 after 264 aircraft had been completed at the Hurn factory. BAC had delivered three of these One-Elevens as pattern aircraft to Romania in connection with a licence production which was entered into with the IRMA factory in June 1979. It was intended that a full production line should be established at Baneasa to continue output after the Hurn factory ceased operations and components for some twenty-two aircraft together with jigs and tooling were transported to Romania in 1982. In the end, nine aircraft were completed commencing in September, 1982 for use by the Romanian national carrier, Tarom. However, ROMBAC (as the production company was titled) found it was necessary to offer a quieter re-engined version to meet the latest noise regulations. A project to offer the 'Airstar 2500' equipped with Rolls-Royce Tay 650 engines was undertaken with Dee Howard Co. but lack of funding and the political crisis in Romania resulted in the One-Eleven line being abandoned – although two airframes remain in an incomplete state at Baneasa.

A 1962 agreement between the British and French governments led to British Aircraft corporation becoming a partner with Aérospatiale in the joint supersonic Concorde airliner programme. This is described in more detail in the chapter on Aérospatiale; suffice to say that the British production line was established at Bristol (Filton) to build the seven Concordes ordered for British Airways. The first of these Series 102 aircraft was delivered in January 1976 and at the time of writing the British Airways fleet continues to operate daily transatlantic services together with numerous highly popular charter flights. The Concordes are expected to continue in service until at least 2020.

Production details

BAC allocated a simple serial number system to BAC-111s, starting with c/n 004 for the prototype and ending at c/n 277. The last nine aircraft (c/n 268 to 277) were reallocated with Romaero serials as c/n 401 to 409. A number of serial numbers were not allocated as a result of frustrated orders (e.g. c/n 036 to 038 which were intended for Bonanza Airlines).

Model Information

Type No.	No. Built	Notes
111-200		Short/medium haul jet airliner with T-tail, low wing and two rear fuselage mounted 10,410 lb.s.t. Rolls-Royce Spey 506-14 turbojets. Max 80-pax capacity. 79,000 lb. TOGW. Prot. G-ASHG (c/n 001) FF. 20 Aug. 1963.

BAC-Aérospatiale Concorde, G-BOAG

Type No.	No. Built	Notes
111-200AB	1	Definitive designation for BAC-111 prototype.
111-201AC	11	111-200 for British United. Spey 506-14A engines.
111-202AD		111-200 for Western Airlines (not taken up).
111-203AE	14	111-200 for Braniff. Spey 506-14D engines.
111-204AF	18	111-200 for Mohawk Airlines. Spey 506-14D engines.
111-206AH		111-200 for Bonanza Airlines (not taken up).
111-207AJ	2	111-200 for Central African AL (not taken up).
111-208AL	4	111-200 for Aer Lingus. Spey 506-14 engines.
111-211AH	1	111-200 for Helmut Horten (executive config.). Spey 506-14A engines.
111-212AR	2	111-200 for Tenneco (executive config.). Spey 506-14 engines.
111-215AU	3	111-200 for Aloha Airlines. Spey 506-14D engines.
111-217EA	2	111-200 for Royal Australian AF. Spey 511-14 engines.
111-300		BAC-111 with additional centre fuel tank to give increased range and 87,000 lb. TOGW. Powered by two 11,400 lb.s.t. Spey 511-14 engines.
111-301AG	3	111-300 for Kuwait Airways (not taken up).
111-304AX	2	111-300 for British Eagle.
111-320AZ	4	111-300 for Laker Airways.
111-400AM	1	BAC-111-300 for U.S. market with restricted gross weight of 79,500 lb. and Spey 511-14 engines or -14W (as shown). Some later upgraded to 87,500 lb. TOGW with increased payload/range.
111-401AK	30	111-400 for American Airlines
111-402AP	4	111-400 for Philippine AL.
111-407AW	2	111-400 for TACA. Spey 511-14W engines.
111-408EF	3	111-400 for Channel Airways
111-409AY	2	111-400 for LACSA. Spey 511-14W engines.
111-410AQ	1	111-400 for Victor Comptometer (executive config.).
111-412EB	1	111-400 for LANICA. Spey 511-14W engines.
111-413FA	1	111-400 for Bavaria Flug. Spey 511-14W engines.
111-414EG	4	111-400 for Bavaria Flug. Spey 511-14W engines.
111-416EK	4	111-400 for Autair.
111-419EP	1	111-400 for Page Airways.
111-420EL	4	111-400 for Austral. Spey 511-14W engines.
111-422EQ	2	111-400 for VASP. Spey 511-14W engines.
111-423ET	2	111-400 for Brazilian Air Force. Spey 511-14W engines.
111-424EU	6	111-400 for Tarom.
111-432FD	2	111-400 for Bahamas Airways. Spey 511-14W engines.
111-475		111-400 with Series 500 wings and Spey 512-14DW engines.
111-476FM	2	111-475 for Faucett.
111-479FU	2	111-475 for Air Pacific.
111-481FW	1	111-472 for Air Malawi.

Type No.	No. Built	Notes
111-485GD	3	111-475 for Oman Air Force.
111-487GK	1	111-475 for BAC/Tarom.
111-488GH	1	111-475 for Sheikh al Midani.
111-492GM	2	111-475 for McAlpine Aviation.
111-500		111-400 with fuselage stretched by 8ft 4in forward and 5ft 2in aft of wing, modified longer wing with new leading edge and flaps system. Powered by Spey 512-14DW engines except as shown. 106,500 lb. TOGW and 119-pax capacity. Available with optional long range tank in forward fuselage.
111-501EX	8	111-500 for British United.
111-509EW	4	111-500 for British Caledonian.
111-510ED	18	111-500 for British European Airways. Spey 512-14E engines.
111-515FB	4	111-500 for PanInternational.
111-516FP	1	111-500 for Aviateca.
111-517FE	3	111-500 for Bahamasair.
111-518FG	9	111-500 for Court Line.
111-520FN	3	111-500 for SADIA/TransBrazil.
111-521FH	3	111-500 for Austral.
111-523FJ	3	111-500 for British Midland.
111-524FF	4	111-500 for Germanair.
111-525FT	7	111-500 for Tarom.
111-527FK	5	111-500 for Philippine Airlines
111-528FL	3	111-500 for Bavaria Flug.
111-529FR	1	111-500 for Phoenix Airways.
111-530FX	1	111-500 for British Caledonian
111-531FS	3	111-500 for LACSA
111-537GF	3	111-500 for Cyprus Airways.
111-539GL	3	111-500 for British Airways.
111-560		111-500 built in Romania by Romaero. Also known as One-Eleven 2000.
111-561RC	9	111-560 for Tarom built by ROMBAC completely or from kits.

DE HAVILLAND

With a strong reputation for pre-war aviation design and production of aircraft such as the Dragon Rapide and DH.86 Express light transports, de Havilland moved into the post-war era with design of the DH.104 Dove all-metal twin-engined feeder liner. Doves for the airline industry were built to an eight/ten-seat specification but the company also gained a substantial RAF order for the Devon C.1 communications transport. Early Doves went into service in 1946 with West African Airways Corporation, South Africa Airways Corporation and to U.K. short-haul operators such as Morton Air Services and Olley Air Services. As commercial air transport expanded in the following years the Dove became too small for most routes and moved on to become business or air taxi aircraft. The following individual Dove models were built:

Model	Number Built	Notes
DH.104 Dove 1	207	Low wing 8/11 passenger transport with retractable tricycle u/c and two 305 h.p. D.H. Gipsy Queen 70 engines. Prot. G-AGPG (c/n 04000/P1). FF. 25 Sep. 1945.
DH.104 Dove 1B	15	Dove 1 with 340 h.p. Gipsy Queen 70-4 engines.
DH.104 Dove 2	35	Six-seat executive version of Dove 1.
DH.104 Dove 2A	84	Dove 2 for North American sale.
DH.104 Dove 2B	7	Six-seat executive version of Dove 1B.
DH.104 Dove 3		Proposed high altitude survey model. Not built.
DH.104 Dove 4	95	Military Devon C.1 derivative of Dove 1.
DH.104 Dove 5	33	Dove 1 with 380 h.p. Gipsy Queen 70-2 engines. Military Sea Devon C.20.
DH.104 Dove 6	25	Six-seat executive version of Dove 5.
DH.104 Dove 6A	16	Dove 6 for North American sale.
DH.104 Dove 7	9	Dove 5 with enlarged cockpit and raised cockpit roof with 400 h.p. Gipsy Queen Mk. 3 engines.
DH.104 Dove 8	15	Dove 7 for executive use.
DH.104 Dove 8A	3	Dove 8 for North American sale.
Riley Dove 400		Dove modified by Riley Aeronautics with two 400 h.p. Lyc. IO-720 engines, swept vertical tail, airstair door and new flight deck. 29 conversions inc. 5 by McAlpine Aviation, Luton. Prot. N1472V (c/n 04302).
Carstedt CJ-600A		Dove with 7ft 3in fuselage stretch, relocated fuel tanks, new flight deck and two 575 shp Garrett TPE-331 turboprops. 10,500 lb. TOGW. 6 conversions. Prot. N4921V (c/n 04284) FF. 18 Dec. 1966.

The Dove airframe offered scope for enlargement and de Havilland stretched the fuselage, lengthened the wings and fitted four engines to produce the DH.114 Heron. The early

DH.104 Riley Dove 400, VH-NBM

Heron 1 had a fixed tricycle undercarriage but the majority were built with retractable gear as used on the Dove. 149 Herons were delivered between 1952 and 1964 and the type became well known for its service with the Highlands and Islands air ambulance service operated by British European Airways. Other commercial operators included the Norwegian airline, Braathens SAFE, UAT-Aeromaritime, Ghana Airways and Jersey Airlines. A number of Herons were sold in the United States and many were re-engined with 290 h.p. Lycoming IO-540 engines by Riley Aeronautics Corporation. A rather more radical conversion was carried out in Canada as the stretched twin turboprop Saunders ST-27.

Model	Number Built	Notes
DH.114 Heron 1	1	Enlarged 17-passenger version of DH.104 with 10ft. fuselage stretch, fixed tricycle u/c, 12,500 lb. TOGW and four 250 h.p. Gipsy Queen 30 engines. Prot. G-ALZL (c/n 10903) FF. 10 May 1950.
DH.114 Heron 1B	50	Production version of DH.114 with 13,000 lb. TOGW.
DH.114 Heron 2	31	Heron 1 with retractable u/c. and 12,500 lb. TOGW. Prot. G-AMTS (c/n 14007) FF. 14 Dec. 1952.
DH.114 Heron 2A		Designation for North American deliveries.
DH.114 Heron 2B	20	Heron 2 with 13,000 lb. TOGW.
DH.114 Heron 2C	4	Heron 2B with fully feathering propellers and 13,150 lb. TOGW.
DH.114 Heron 2D	37	Executive Heron 2C with 13,500 lb. TOGW.
DH.114 Heron 2DA		Heron 2D for North America.
DH.114 Heron 2E	3	Heron 2D with dual executive/high density cabin.
DH.114 Heron 2X		Heron 2A with compressed rubber u/c dampers.
DH.114 Heron 3	3	Heron 2D for Queen's Flight (Heron C(VVIP)3).
DH.114 Heron 4	1	Heron 2D for RAF (Heron C.4).
Saunders ST-27	(13)	23-pax. version of Heron 2 with 8ft 4in fuselage stretch, forward starboard airstair door and two 715 shp PT6A-27 turboprops. Prot. CF-YBM-X FF. 18 May 1969.
Saunders ST-27A	(1)	Aerodynamic prototype for ST-27B. One aircraft, C-FYBM-X, FF. 18 Jul. 1974.
Saunders ST-27B	(1)	Redesigned low-cost version of ST-27. with PT6A-34 engines, larger vertical fin, larger windows.
Saunders ST-28	1	Revised designation for ST-27B. Prot. C-GYAP FF. 12 Dec. 1975. Fitted with enlarged cockpit and four-bladed propellers.

While the Dove and Heron were entering production, de Havilland was heading for a much more ambitious goal with the initiation of the DH.106 Comet project. Designed to meet the Type 4 requirement of the Brabazon Committee and specified to the requirements of BOAC, the Comet was a highly innovative four-jet transport with a 1750 mile range and capacity for thirty-six to forty-four passengers. De Havilland produced a streamlined low-wing design with four de Havilland Ghost turbines buried in wing root nacelles and at the time of its introduction it was as revolutionary as Concorde was to be two decades later. As it turned out, the engine installation was unique since world manu-

Saunders ST.27, CF-XOK

facturers decided to adopt externally mounted engines on subsequent airliner designs. It went into production at Hatfield in 1951 and entered service with BOAC in May 1952. It was ordered by Canadian Pacific, UAT, the RCAF and Air France but the catastrophic crashes of three BOAC Comets during 1953 and 1954 resulted in the grounding of Comet 1s.

The unprecedented investigation into the causes of the crashes and discovery that the skinning of the aircraft was too light for the high altitude pressure stresses, resulting in fatigue cracks, led to the subsequent Comet 2 being re-engineered. The Comet also had insufficient range for transatlantic operations and the Comet 4, built for BOAC was given a stretched fuselage and additional fuel capacity in which form it became a reasonably satisfactory aircraft. The shorter range (and further stretched) Comet 4B was developed for the needs of British European Airways and the hybrid Comet 4C with the long fuselage and long-range wings had some success with sales to Mexicana, United Arab Airlines, Kuwait Airways and Aerolineas Argentinas. Comet production finally ceased in 1964 with a total of 112 aircraft having been completed. Many Comets ended their days with the Royal Air Force where they served efficiently for a number of years and the Comet airframe formed the basis for the successful Nimrod anti-submarine patrol aircraft. However, the Comet never overcame the stigma of the early crashes which were, in reality, a learning experience for the worldwide air carrier aircraft industry.

The Comet variants were as follows:

DH.114 Heron 1B, JA6154

DH.106 Comet 4C, SU-AMV

Type No.	No. Built	Notes
Comet 1	11	Medium range pressurized jet airliner with swept low wing and powered by four 4450 lb.s.t. de Havilland Ghost 50/1 turbojets in buried wing root installations. 36-pax. capacity. 107,000 lb. TOGW. Prot. G-ALVG (c/n 06001) FF. 27 Jul. 1949.
Comet 1A	10	Comet 1 with 44-pax capacity, additional outer wing tanks and four 5000 lb.s.t. de Havilland Ghost 50/2 turbojets. 110,000 lb. TOGW.
Comet 1XB		Comet 1A re-engined with 5500 lb.s.t. Ghost 50/4 engines and re-engineered to resolve fuselage fatigue problems.
Comet 2	12	Comet 1A with strengthened fuselage structure, 36in fuselage stretch and powered by four 7300 lb.s.t. Rolls-Royce Avon 503 engines with modified offset jet pipes.
Comet C.2	4	Comet 2 for RAF use with four 7300 lb.s.t. Avon 117 engines.
Comet 2E		Two Comet 2s fitted with two Avon 504 and two Avon 524 engines.
Comet 3	1	Comet 2 with 5ft 6in fuselage stretch, 78 passenger seats and four 10,000 lb.s.t. Avon 502 (later Avon 523) engines. Prot. G-ANLO FF. 19 Jul. 1954. Later fitted with shorter span wing and thrust reversers as Comet 3B.
Comet 4	27	Comet 3 for transatlantic operations with wing leading edge fuel tanks, 10,500 lb.s.t. Avon 524 turbojets, max 81-pax capacity. 160,000 lb. TOGW.
Comet 4A		Proposed short/medium range Comet 4 with stretched fuselage. Not built.
Comet 4B	18	Short/medium range Comet 4 with 6ft 6in fuselage stretch and reduced span wings without leading edge fuel tanks. 99-pax capacity. 157,960 lb. TOGW. Prot. G-APMA (c/n 6421) FF. 27 Jun. 1959.
Comet 4C	24	Comet 4B with long-range Comet 4 wing and 10,500 lb.s.t. Avon 525B turbojets.
Comet C.4	5	Comet 4C for RAF with 10,500 lb.s.t. Avon 350 turbojets.

The Comet was followed on the drawing board by a short-range jet airliner whose design was initiated by British European Airways in 1956. De Havilland, in partnership with Fairey and Hunting under the title of 'Airco' designed the three-engined DH.121 Trident to meet the BEA need for a short-range airliner capable of operating from shorter runways. In tailoring the Trident for such a specific customer need, it transpired that the aircraft eventually lacked the market flexibility to be a substantial commercial success. Nevertheless, the first Trident (there being no prototype as such) flew in early 1962 and BEA took delivery of twenty-four examples of the Trident 1 following the award of the type certificate on 18 February 1964. This was followed by a further batch of Trident 2s with more powerful engines, increased seating and greater fuel capacity. Hawker Siddeley (which had absorbed de Havilland in 1960) also sold Trident 1s to Kuwait Airways, Iraqi Airways, Pakistan International and Channel Airways. The Trident 2 attracted a large order from the Chinese state airline, CAAC and thirty-three examples of the Trident 2E were delivered to China between November 1972 and June 1978.

In December, 1969, Hawker Siddeley flew the first stretched Trident 3 which provided an increase of thirty-one seats in passenger capacity and introduced a supplementary booster engine positioned in the base of the fin trailing edge to give added power for high gross weight take-offs. Again, BEA was the lead customer with an order for twenty-six aircraft but the only other airline user was CAAC which acquired the last two production aircraft in 1972. The following variants of the Trident were produced.

Type No.	No. Built	Notes
Trident 1C	26	Medium/short-range airliner with low wing, T-tail and three tail-mounted 9850 lb.s.t. Rolls-Royce RB.163/1 Spey 505/5 turbofans mounted in rear fuselage pods and base of tail fin. Max 103-pax. accom. 115,000 lb. TOGW. First aircraft G-ARPA (c/n 2101) FF. 9 Jan. 1962.
Trident 1E	8	Trident 1 with 5ft 2in wingspan increase and full-span leading edge slats, increased fuel capacity and 115-pax capacity. Powered by three 11,400 lb.s.t. RB.163-25 Spey 511-5 turbofans.
Trident 1E-140	5	Trident 1E with max 139-pax high density seating.
Trident 2E	50	Trident 1E with lengthened wingtips, strengthened u/c, Smiths autoland system, increased fuel capacity and 11,930 lb.s.t. RB.163-25 Spey 512W turbofans.
Trident 3B	26	Trident 2E with 16ft 6in fuselage stretch, increased wing chord and area, modified flaps and supplementary RB.162 turbojet mounted at base of rudder for operation on takeoff. 146-pax capacity. 150,000 lb. TOGW. Prot. G-AWYZ (c/n 2301) FF. 11 Dec. 1969.

HS.121 Trident 1E-140, G-AVYB

113

Type No.	No. Built	Notes
Trident 3B-104	2	Trident 3B for CAAC with strengthened structure, increased fuel and 158,000 lb. TOGW.

Production Details

Serial numbers allocated to de Havilland aircraft were comprised of six digits with the first two indicating the aircraft type number. The following four digits were a sequential individual aircraft serial commencing with 0001. This started to be modified with the Comet 4 which used a shortened version of the type number and individual numbers commencing with 4. A similar system was adopted for the Trident and details of serial numbers allocated are as follows:

Type	Serial numbers
DH.104 Dove	c/n 04000/P1 and 0400P2 (prototypes) and c/n 04001 to 04542
DH.114 Heron	c/n 10903 (prototype) and c/n 14001 to 14148
DH.106 Comet 1 and 2	c/n 06001 to 06037 (including static test c/n 06036)
DH.106 Comet 3	c/n 06100
DH.106 Comet 4 series	c/n 6401 to 6477 (last two converted to HS.801 Nimrod)
HS.121 Trident 1 and 2	c/n 2101 to 2189
HS.121 Trident 3B	c/n 2301 to 2328

SCOTTISH AVIATION

Scottish Aviation has been based at Prestwick since its formation in 1935. Shortly after the war Scottish Aviation moved into aircraft production with the five-seat high-wing Prestwick Pioneer the success of which encouraged the company to move on to a rather larger transport – the Twin Pioneer. This was a high-wing aircraft using the same high lift devices which had been adopted for the Pioneer to provide good short field performance, a fixed tailwheel undercarriage and sixteen passenger seats in its square-section fuselage. The prototype Series 1 (G-ANTP c/n 501) first flew at Prestwick on 25 June 1955 and was fitted with a pair of 570 h.p. Alvis Leonides 503/8 radial piston engines. Of the sixty-one Series 1 deliveries, some thirty-two were sold to the RAF as Twin Pioneer CC.1s.

Scottish Aviation followed this with the Series 2 which was fitted with 600 h.p. Pratt & Whitney R-1340 S3H1-G engines. The final Series 3 Twin Pioneer reverted to Alvis Leonides engines with the higher-powered 640 h.p. Leonides 531/8B and a number of Series 1 aircraft were subsequently upgraded. A further batch of seven aircraft for the RAF were to Series 3 standard and designated Twin Pioneer CC.2. Some eighty-six production aircraft were completed between 1956 and 1962 (with serial numbers c/n 502 to 590, excluding c/n 569, 585 and the static test c/n 506). Airline customers included the de Kroonduif subsidiary of KLM in the Netherlands Antilles and Philippine Airlines who received four (which were subsequently sold for clandestine Air America operations in South East Asia) and Borneo Airways.

In the mid-1960s, Scottish Aviation had obtained a contract for manufacture of wings for the Handley Page Jetstream. The pressurised eighteen/twenty seat HP.137 was powered by a pair of 850 shp Turboméca Astazou XIV.C constant speed turboprops and Handley Page flew the first Jetstream (G-ATXH c/n 198) at Radlett on 18 August 1967. Unfortunately, development and delay in the Jetstream programme brought Handley Page to a financial crisis in 1969. Following a series of attempts to salvage what remained of the programme, Scottish Aviation took over completion of an order for twenty-six Astazou-powered Jetstream T.1s for the RAF and, in February 1972, all production rights to the Jetstream were transferred to Scottish Aviation. The impetus of the RAF order

Scottish Aviation Twin Pioneer, G-APRS

allowed the company to develop the aircraft into the civil Jetstream 31 which used the wing designed for the abortive USAF version (the Jetstream 3M) with new environmental and electrical systems and 940 shp Garrett TPE331-1OUG-514H engines. The prototype Jetstream 31 (Model 3001) G-JSSD (c/n 227) was converted from an existing airframe purchased in the United States and it was first flown in its new form on 28 March 1980.

The CAA type certificate was awarded to the Jetstream 31 in June 1982 and production aircraft commenced with G-TALL (c/n 601). While a few corporate aircraft have been built, most Jetstream 31s have been sold to third level commuter carriers in the United States and large fleets have operated with the American Eagle contractors and with United Express, Trans World Express and Express Airlines I (for Northwest Airlink). Jetstream designations identify the country of delivery and include the following models:

3100	Various	3109	Italy
3101	United States	3110	Sweden
3102	United Kingdom	3111	Saudi Arabia (AF)
3103	Germany	3112	Canada
3104	United Kingdom	3113	not allocated
3105	not allocated	3114	not allocated
3106	France	3115	not allocated
3107	Australia	3116	Switzerland
3108	Netherlands	3117	Japan

British Aerospace introduced the Jetstream Super 31 (Model 3201) in 1987, the first production unit being c/n 790. The Super 31 has 1020 shp TPE331-12 engines with four-blade Rotol propellers, a redesigned wing, increased fuel capacity and an increase of 882 lb. in take-off weight. This was subsequently redesignated Jetstream 32 and an upgraded version with a number of detailed performance improvements is known as the Jetstream 32EP. The last standard Jetstream 31 was c/n 839. Jetstream 31 production was suspended in 1994 at c/n 984 with a total of 384 aircraft having been completed (c/n 601 to 984).

In 1989, Scottish Aviation followed up the standard Jetstream with the larger twenty-nine-seat Jetstream 41. This used the Jetstream 31 fuselage with the addition of fuselage plugs of 8ft 3in ahead of the wing and a 7ft 9in aft of the wing. The vertical tail was enlarged

SAL Jetstream 32, N301PX

with the tailplane set in the centre rather than mounted on the fuselage and the power-plants were upgraded to a pair of 1500 shp Garrett TPE331-14 engines. The prototype Jetstream 41 (G-GCJL c/n 41001) was first flown on 25 September 1991. Reorganisation of British Aerospace in 1992 into commercial business groups resulted in Jetstream coming under BAe. Regional Aircraft Ltd. This was followed, on 1 January 1996, by the establishment of the AI(R) organisation through a merger of the British Aerospace regional airliner subsidiaries, Jetstream and Avro and the ATR consortium. This brought the Jetstream 31, 41 and 61 (the former ATP) into the new marketing grouping with manu-facture of the aircraft being allocated to the British Aerospace Prestwick operation. However, with orders tailing off, it was decided to discontinue production of the Jetstream 41. The last unit completed was the 104th aircraft, c/n 41104 and the remaining two airframes under construction were scrapped and the line closed in early 1998. Jetstream 41s were delivered to many of the same users who had already taken the Jetstream 31. These included United Express and TW Express in the United states, Loganair and Manx Airlines in the U.K. and SA Airlink in South Africa. As with the Jetstream 31, separate geographical designations have been used as follows:

4100	United Kingdom
4101	United States
4102	Sweden
4112	Canada
4121	South Africa
4122	Thailand (Army)

VICKERS

With wartime experience of building heavy aircraft such as the Wellington and Warwick, Vickers started its peacetime activities with work on a new transport design, the VC.1, which would fulfil a similar role to that of the ever-capable DC-3 Dakota. The Vickers design used a development of the Wellington wing and a new unpressurised all-metal fuse-lage of stressed skin construction and was intended to meet immediate air transport needs in advance of the more radical designs envisaged by the Brabazon Committee. The Ministry of Supply issued a contract for the Viking, as it was titled, and a prototype was built rapidly and flown at the Vickers airfield at Wisley in June 1945.

SAL Jetstream 41, G-JMAC

The Viking proved to be satisfactory from the outset and moved into production with much less bureaucratic fuss than many of its contemporaries. Initial examples had a fabric covered wing but only twenty-four were built to this standard before the wing was changed to all-metal construction. It entered service with the British European Airways Division of BOAC in September 1946 with a fleet of forty aircraft finally being delivered. Such an endorsement by the national airline gave the Viking a valuable start and orders followed from Aer Lingus, DDL, South African Airways, Air India, Airwork and the Argentine Government who acquired Vikings for their Air Force.

Vikings also went into service with the King's Flight and were delivered to the RAF as the Valetta C Mk. 1. Vikings became well known as the backbone of the British inclusive tour holiday industry in the 1950s and were used by fringe airlines such as BlueAir, Independent Air Travel, Air Safaris, Air Kruise and more reputable operators such as Eagle Aircraft Services, Hunting-Clan and Channel Airways. A number of Vikings found their way into the German holiday market, serving with Deutsche Flugdienst, Condor Flugdienst and the enigmatic 'Dr Tigges Fahrten'. In total, 152 commercial production Vikings were built between 1945 and 1947 together with 251 Valettas for the RAF. Details of the different variants are as follow:

Type Number	Number Built	Notes
Viking 1A	24	19-pax airliner with low fabric-covered wing of geodetic construction and retractable tailwheel u/c, powered by two 1675 h.p. Bristol Hercules 130 radial piston engines. 33,500 lb. TOGW. Prot G-AGOK (c/n 101) FF. 22 Jun. 1945.
Viking 1	15	Viking 1A with modified wings of all-metal construction.
Viking 1B	113	Viking 1 with 2ft 2in forward fuselage stretch and 27-seat capacity, powered by two 1690 h.p. Bristol Hercules 634 engines.
Nene Viking	1	Viking 1 for jet engine research with piston engines replaced by two Rolls-Royce Nene turbojets in nacelles fitted beneath wing. One aircraft, VX856 (c/n 207) FF. 6 Apl. 1948. Type 618.
Valetta C.1	190	RAF version of Viking 1B with new fuel system, port side rear cargo doors, strengthened cabin floor, taller u/c and 1976 h.p. Bristol Hercules 230 engines.

Vickers Viking 3B, G-AJPH

Type Number	Number Built	Notes
Valetta C.2	21	Long-range passenger version of Valetta with 15 seats, additional fuel tankage and lengthened tail cone. King's Flight aircraft named *Viking*.
Valetta T.3	40	Navigation trainer version of Valetta C.2 with cabin roof astrodomes and internal navigator stations.
Valetta T.4		Valetta T.3s converted with thimble radar nose and deletion of cabin roof astrodomes for night fighter navigation training.
Varsity T.1	163	Type 668 Crew trainer developed from Valetta with tricycle u/c, increased wingspan, ventral pannier for bomb aimers.

The Viking introduced a system of Vickers model numbers which identified the particular specification of the aircraft for each customer. These type numbers and the original customers were:

Type No.	Customer	Type No.	Customer
491	Ministry of Supply (1st prot.)	626	RAF
495	Ministry of Supply (2nd prot.)	627	Airwork Services
496	BEA	628	DDL
498	BEA	632	Air India
604	Indian National AW	634	Aer Lingus
607	RAF (Prot. Valetta)	635	South African Airways
610	BEA	636	Vickers
614	BEA	637	RAF (Valetta C.1)
615	Argentine Government	639	Hunting Air Travel
616	CAA	641	Central African Airways
618	Vickers (Nene Viking prot.)	643	Suidair International
620	Argentine Government	644	Iraqi Airways
621	MoS/RAF	649	Pakistan Air Force
623	RAF/King's Flight	657	British West Indian Airways
624	RAF		

The success achieved by the Viking established Vickers as a manufacturer of transport aircraft and they moved on to design the VC.2 to meet another of the Brabazon specifications. The four-engined VC.2 was aimed, primarily, at a British European Airways requirement and through the familiar post-war planning process grew from a pressurised twenty-four-passenger aircraft to a forty-three-seater, being designed from the outset for propeller turbine power. An order for the equivalent capacity Airspeed Ambassador for BEA was a further complication. Nevertheless, the prototype Viscount 630 was flown in July 1948 and Vickers pressed forward with the stretched Viscount 700 as a private venture. In the event this was the salvation for the Viscount as it was by now intended to be flexible enough to appeal to a wide variety of airline customers rather than solely to the specialised requirements of BEA.

As it turned out, the first order came from BEA who placed an order for twenty of the forty-seven-seat Viscount 701s. Their first trunk route from London to Edinburgh could be flown by the Viscount in 100 minutes – which was a major breakthrough in 1953 compared with the Dakotas which had gone before. Vickers then sold Viscounts to Aer Lingus, Trans Canada, Air France and Trans-Australian Airlines. Certainly, the most significant order was from Capital Airlines in the United States who ordered forty Viscounts and this was followed by a fifteen-aircraft order from Continental Airlines. The Viscount, which was built in two main variants – the 700 Series and the stretched 800 Series – became accepted as a reliable performer and was made the more so by the excellence of the Rolls-Royce Dart turboprop engines.

The final Viscount, a Series 828 for All Nippon Airways, was delivered in February 1963. A total of 443 production Viscounts had been built and despite the arrival of pure jet replacements Viscounts are still in operation with a number of companies forty-five years after the first delivery. The Viscount variants were:

Type No.	No. Built	Notes
630	1	Short/medium range pressurised 32-seat airliner with low wing, tricycle u/c and powered by four 1380 shp. Rolls-Royce Dart R.Da. 1 Mk.502 turboprops in wing-mounted nacelles. 45,000 lb. TOGW. Prot. G-AHRF (c/n 1) FF. 16 Jul. 1948.
663	1	Type 630 second prototype used as engine testbed and fitted with two Rolls-Royce Tay turbojets in underwing nacelles. Prot. VX217 (c/n 2) FF. 15 Mar. 1950.
700 srs	290	Type 630 with 7ft 4in fuselage stretch and 5ft increased wingspan, max 53-pax seating, powered by four 1400 shp Rolls-Royce Dart R.Da.1 Mk.505/6 turboprops (or 1600 shp Mk 510) with inner engines positioned further out than on Type 630. Some fitted with wing leading edge slipper fuel tanks. 63,000 lb. TOGW. Prot. G-AMAV (c/n 3) FF. 28 Aug. 1950.
700D srs		Certain aircraft designations suffixed 'D' denoting 'developed'.
800 srs	67	Viscount 700 with 3ft 10in forward fuselage stretch and extended interior for max 71-pax., rectangular passenger entry doors and extra starboard rear service door, redesigned underfloor freight hold and 1600 shp Dart 510 turboprops in bulged engine cowlings. 64,500 lb. TOGW.
810 srs	86	Viscount 800 with strengthened structure, additional fuel capacity, 1800 shp Dart 525 (or 1850 shp Dart 541) engines with new props and synchrophasers and 72,500 lb. TOGW.

As with the Viking, Vickers allocated separate model numbers to each different customer specification aircraft. Certain aircraft were ordered but cancelled before delivery and the following table shows the customer numbers and the airline which actually took first delivery of the aircraft.

Type No.	Customer	Type No.	Customer
630	Ministry of Supply	755	Cubana
663	Ministry of Supply	756	Trans Australian A/L
700	Vickers	757	Trans Canada A/L
701	BEA	759	Hunting Clan
702	BWIA	760	Hong Kong A/W
707	Aer Lingus	761	Union of Burma A/W
708	Air France	763	TACA
720	Trans Australian A/L	764	U.S. Steel Corp. (exec)
723	Indian Air Force	765	Standard Oil (exec)
724	Trans Canada A/L	768	Indian Airlines
730	Indian Air Force (VIP)	769	PLUNA
732	Hunting Clan	772	BWIA
734	Pakistan Air Force	773	Iraqi A/W
735	Iraqi Airways	776	Kuwait Oil Co.
736	Fred Olsen Lines	779	Fred Olsen Lines
737	Canadian DoT	781	So. African Air Force
739	Misrair	782	Iranair
742	Brazilian Air Force	784	Philippine A/L
744	Capital Airlines	785	Alitalia-LAI
745	Capital Airlines	786	Lloyd Aero Colombiano
747	Butler Air Transport	789	Brazilian Air Force
748	Central African A/W	793	Royal Bank of Canada
749	LAV	794	Turk Hava Yollari
754	Middle East A/L	797	Canadian DoT

Vickers Viscount 806, G-BLOA

Type No.	Customer	Type No.	Customer
798	Northeast A/L	815	Pakistan Int. A/L
802	BEA	816	Trans Australian A/L
803	KLM	818	Cubana
804	Transair	827	VASP
805	Eagle Airways	828	All-Nippon A/W
806	BEA	831	Airwork
807	New Zealand NAC	832	Ansett/ANA
808	Aer Lingus	833	Hunting Clan
810	Vickers	837	Austrian A/L
812	Continental A/L	838	Ghana A/W
813	So. African A/W	839	Union Carbide/Iran Govt
814	Lufthansa	843	CAAC

The success of the Viscount in BEA service soon prompted the airline to look for a larger capacity aircraft for its trunk routes and, again, the aircraft which emerged was powered by four turboprop engines. The final Vickers 950 design had a two-lobe fuselage providing a main passenger deck and a large lower fuselage freight hold. The Vanguard was of generally conventional layout with a low wing mounting four 4985 shp Rolls-Royce Tyne 506 engines and a substantial tricycle undercarriage with twin wheels on all three legs.

In addition to BEA, Air Canada became an early customer but the Vanguard was in competition with the Lockheed Electra and with new pure-jet airliners and it had limited sales success with only forty-three aircraft being built for the two airlines. Eight Vanguards were converted as Merchantman freighters after their replacement in main line service. The type was not free from problems – particularly the resonance which plagued it for a large part of its life and resulted in the nickname 'Vickers Vibrator' – but Vanguards continued to operate with a number of airlines including Merpati, Europe Air Service, Invicta, Air Bridge Carriers and Air Gabon until the mid 1990s. The Vanguard variants were as follows:

Type No.	No. Built	Notes
950	1	Short-medium haul pressurised 126-pax airliner with low wing and powered by four 4985 shp Rolls-Royce Tyne R.Ty.1 Mk.506 turboprops. 135,000 lb. TOGW. Prot G-AOYW (c/n 703) FF. 20 Jan. 1959.
951	6	Type 950 for BEA with enlarged fin fairing and minor alterations.
952	23	Type 951 for TCA with 139 pax capacity, 141,000 lb. TOGW and four 5545 shp Tyne 512 turboprops.
953	14	Type 951 for BEA with increased fuel capacity and 141,000 lb. TOGW.
953C		Eight Vanguard 953s converted to all-freight Merchantman with windows deleted, forward freight door and strengthened floor.

So established had Vickers become as a manufacturer of transport aircraft for the British state airlines that, in 1951, the company was asked to prepare design proposals for a new long-range transport for the RAF and for BOAC. The result was the Vickers 1000 (VC.7) which would be able to carry 120 passengers over stage lengths of over 2000 miles. The

Vickers Vanguard 952, G-AXNT

aircraft, powered by four wing root-mounted Rolls-Royce Conway engines and derived in design from the Vickers Valiant bomber, showed great promise and construction of a prototype was initiated. Sadly, the project was cancelled by the government in 1955 even though the Vickers 1000 would have had a great opportunity for major commercial orders.

In 1957, Vickers revisited the concept of a long-range airliner. The VC-10 design which emerged embodied many structural features of the Vickers 1000 but the most significant difference was the installation of two pairs of Rolls-Royce Conway engines mounted in tail pods rather than the wing root installations of the earlier design and the advantages of this arrangement included a much lower cabin noise level. The VC-10 had a low-set swept wing and a T-tail and with its first customer being BOAC the design was crafted to meet their particular requirements for a medium-range aircraft. Initially, it was aimed at African and Far East routes but it was given transatlantic capability before the prototype made its first flight on 29 June 1962.

Following issue of the Certificate of Airworthiness on 23 April 1964, the VC-10 joined BOAC and became popular with passengers due to its smooth ride and cabin size incorporating six-abreast seating for economy class. Small orders were also placed by Ghana Airways, Middle East Airlines and by British United Airways which specified an upward-opening freight door in the forward fuselage. The standard VC-10 was also ordered by the RAF and fourteen were delivered between April 1967 and August 1968 with convertible high-density 150-passenger seating. Most of the RAF VC-10s were equipped with aerial refuelling probes.

In May 1964, Vickers flew the first Super VC-10 which had a stretched fuselage giving capacity for an additional twenty-eight seats and additional fuel tanks in the vertical fin. The Super VC-10 also benefited from uprated Conway R Co.43 engines. The principal customer was, again, BOAC who ordered twenty-five aircraft (but only took delivery of seventeen) but five Super VC-10s were sold to East African Airways and the last of these (which was the last production aircraft) was delivered in February 1970. After service with BOAC most Super VC-10s were sold to the RAF together with some of the standard VC-10s. Twenty of these were converted as dedicated or convertible flight refuelling tankers. Details of individual VC-10 models are as follows.

Type No.	No. Built	Notes
1100	1	Medium/long range 135-passenger jet transport with low wing, T-tail, tricycle u/c with main 4-wheel bogies and powered by four rear-fuselage mounted 21,000 lb.s.t. Rolls-Royce Conway R.Co.42 turbojets. 312,000 lb. TOGW. Prot. G-ARTA (c/n 803) FF. 29 Jun. 1962.

Vickers Super VC-10, G-ASGP (AHS)

Type No.	No. Built	Notes
1101	12	VC-10 for BOAC.
1102	2	VC-10 for Ghana Airways.
1103	3	VC-10 for British United with port side forward freight door and hardened floor.
1106	14	VC-10 Mk.1 for RAF with freight door, additional fin fuel tank and 22,500 lb.s.t. Conway R.Co.43 engines.
1109		Prototype VC-10 reconfigured for Middle East Airlines.
1151	17	Super VC-10 for BOAC with 13ft fuselage stretch giving 163 seats, additional fin fuel tank, and 22,500 lb.s.t. R.Co.43 engines. 335,000 lb. TOGW. Prot. G-ASGA (c/n 851) FF. 7 May 1964.
1154	5	Super VC-10 for East African Airways.

Production Details

The serial number batches allocated to commercial Vickers aircraft were as follows:

Type	Number Built	Serial number range
Viking	198	c/n 101 to 298 (incl. 21 Valettas)
Viscount	443	c/n 1 to 459 (excl. c/n 367, c/n 338, c/n 390, c/n 313 to 315, c/n 404 to 411, c/n 420)
Vanguard	44	c/n 703 to 746 (c/n 701 & 702 for static tests)
VC-10	32	c/n 803 to 839 (excl. c/n 816 to 818 and c/n 821, 822)
Super VC-10	22	c/n 851 to 867, c/n 881 to 885

BRITISH AEROSPACE

The first commercial aircraft initiated under the British Aerospace organisation was the BAe. 146 local service jet airliner. In fact, the '146 design already had a long and turbulent development history prior to its official launch by British Aerospace in July 1978. It had its origins in the DH.123 turboprop 'Dakota replacement' of 1959 and the later Hawker Siddeley HS.144 twin jet feederliner. Hawker Siddeley were unable to find suitable engines for the HS.144 and eventually settled on a high wing design with four small Lycoming ALF502 turbofans mounted on underwing pylons. The withdrawal of government funding in October 1974 resulted in the HS.146 being abandoned but the project was revived once Hawker Siddeley was merged into British Aerospace.

The BAe. 146 was designed with a wide fuselage cross section capable of accommodating six seats abreast with a central aisle for high density operation. Two variants were planned from the outset – the short fuselage Series 100 and the stretched Series 200 with maximum seating for ninety-three and 109 passengers respectively which were to be built at the former de Havilland factory at Hatfield. The prototype BAe. 146-100 was flown in September 1981 and certification was awarded on 20 May 1983. The launch customer was Dan Air which eventually operated a fleet of ten aircraft and early deliveries were also made to the American carriers Air Wisconsin, Pacific Southwest and Air Cal and to Ansett in Australia. The '146 was particularly valuable on the highly noise sensitive routes in Southern California where the low decibel reading of the Avco-Lycoming engines allowed Pacific Southwest's operation into Orange County Airport and other restricted destinations. In 1986, the Series 300 was announced. This was a further stretched version of the Series 200 with 122 passenger capacity and the first customer was, again, Air Wisconsin who received their first aircraft in December 1988.

British Aerospace was anxious to explore different markets for the '146 and launched the 146-200 Freighter (also known as the 'QT' or Quiet Trader) which was handled as a conversion by Hayes International at Dothan, Alabama. To date, fourteen Series 200 aircraft, one Series 100 and nine Series 300s have been converted to QT standard. The largest operator is TNT in Europe who had a fleet of seventeen assorted BAe. 146 freighters in operation at the end of 1997. British Aerospace also tried to market a military freighter version but have not yet obtained any customers. They also converted four Series 200s to BAe. 146-200QC convertible passenger/freight models.

Avro RJ70, RJ85 and RJ100

In the summer of 1990, the BAe. 146 range was extensively upgraded to higher gross weights and useful load and offered with a completely revised flightdeck and more powerful Textron Lycoming LF507 turbofans. This was followed by the announcement of new 'Regional Jet' versions of the range which would relaunch the '146 programme and would have improved operating costs. The new versions were the RJ70 (based on the Series 100), the RJ85 (based on the Series 200) and the RJ100 and RJ115 (based on the Series 300 but with standard 100-seat or high density 115-seat interiors). The new models did result in additional orders from important airline customers such as Lufthansa, Crossair, Air Malta and Sabena. This relaunch was followed in 1993 by British Aerospace resurrecting the old Avro name and forming a new subsidiary, Avro International Aerospace to build the BAe. 146 line with marketing being handled out of the AI(R) joint venture with ATR. With the collapse of AI(R), Avro has taken back responsibility for sales of the RJ models but an agreement signed in late-1997 with the Malaysian company, Kazanah Nasional Berhad is expected to result in that company taking a share of up to 50% in Avro and establishing production of RJ-series sub-assemblies in Malaysia.

Production Details

British Aerospace has allocated serial numbers consisting of the prefix 'E' followed by '1', '2' or '3' to identify the relevant Type Series and a chronological individual number starting at 001 (the prototype). These serial numbers commenced at c/n E1001 and had reached approximately c/n E2346 (i.e. the 346th aircraft) by the end of 1998.

Model information

The various models of British Aerospace BAe. 146 have been as follows:

Type No.	No. Built	Notes
BAe-146-100	34	Medium/short haul passenger airliner with T-tail and high wing mounting four 6700 shp Lycoming ALF502R-3 turbofans on underslung pylons. 80,750 lb. TOGW. Also -100QC and -100QT convertible, combi and freight variants. Prot. G-SSSH (c/n E1001) FF. 3 Sep. 1981.
BAe-146-200	97	BAe. 146-100 with 7ft 10in fuselage stretch for max 109-pax. capacity and increased fuel capacity. 89,500 lb. TOGW. Prot. G-WISC (c/n E2008) FF. 1 Aug. 1982.
BAe-146-200QT	14	Freight conversion of 146-200 by Hayes International with rear port fuselage freight door, most cabin windows blanked off and strengthened floor with pallet handling system.
BAe-146-100QT	1	Freight conversion of 146-100 similar to '146-200QT.
BAe-146-200QC	4	Convertible pax/freight or combi version of -200 similar to -200QT.
BA3-146-300	60	146-100 with fuselage stretch of 8ft 1in forward and 7ft 8in aft of the wing to give lower density 100-pax capacity. Prot. G-LUXE (c/n E3001, formerly c/n E1001) FF. 1 May, 1987. Also -300QC and -300QT convertible, combi and freight variants.
BAe-146-300QT	9	Freight conversion of 146-300 similar to '146-200QT.
BAe-146STA		Proposed tactical military troop transport/freighter based on 146QT.
BAe-146MSL		Proposed tactical military freighter based on 146QT.

Type No.	No. Built	Notes
BAe-146MT		Proposed military aerial refueller based on 146QT.
BAe RJ70	12	Revised version of 146-100 with 82-pax capacity.
BAe RJ70ER		RJ70 with increased fuel capacity and range.
BAe RJ85	55	Revised version of 146-200 with 100-pax capacity.
BAe RJ100	39	Revised version of 146-300 with 112-pax capacity.
BAe RJ115		Revised version of 146-300 with high density 116-pax capacity.

British Aerospace BAe. 146-300, B-1775

Avro York, G-AMGK (AHS)

CASA   SPAIN

Construcciones Aeronauticas S.A. (CASA) was originally founded in March 1923 with its first factory being established at Getafe to the south of Madrid. Its aircraft output until the mid-1940s was largely based on licence production of various German aircraft, starting with the Dornier Wal flying boat and progressing through to 170 examples of the Junkers Ju.52/3M trimotor transport (CASA 352-L), the Heinkel He.111 (CASA 2.111-D1) and the Bücker Jungmann biplane trainer (CASA 1-131H). Further production plants were built at Seville-Tablada and at Cadiz. CASA is now the dominant Spanish national manufacturer having taken over Hispano Aviacion in 1972 and Empresa Nacional de Motores de Aviacion in 1973. In addition to building its own indigenous C.212 and CN.235 it is a large subcontractor and partner in other manufacturers' programmes such as the Dassault Mercure. CASA is a 4.2% participant in the Airbus programme and currently manufactures tailplanes and some non-structural parts.

The first aircraft models designed and built by CASA were a range of military transport aircraft which were delivered to the Spanish Air Force during the immediate post-war period. The CASA.201 Alcotan was designed as a general purpose transport with up to ten passenger seats and alternative roles as a navigation or bombing trainer. It was a conventional low-wing twin-engined aircraft with a tailwheel undercarriage which was initially plagued by engine problems due to the development troubles of its ENMA Sirio powerplant and initial examples were delivered with other engines. CASA also built a

CASA Azor, T7-20

slightly larger version, the Halcon, with a tricycle undercarriage and the more reliable ENMA Beta engines. This design was then further enlarged to become the CASA.207 Azor which served until the early 1980s as the standard transport of the Ejercito del Aire.

1969 saw the start of design work on a new light STOL utility transport aimed at a Spanish Air Force requirement for a C-47 replacement. CASA's C.212 was a rugged high-wing turboprop aircraft intended to offer low maintenance and cost of operation. From the outset it maintained design simplicity with a fixed undercarriage and the ability to load both passengers and freight directly at ground level. It was equipped with a retractable rear ramp for loading small vehicles or freight and in its passenger version, fitted with nineteen seats in a 2+1 layout, it could use the retractable ramp for a baggage container. CASA adopted a pair of the reliable Garrett TPE331 turboprop engines to power the aircraft which was named 'Aviocar' at the time of its first flight in March 1971. Production got under way at Getafe with the first examples being delivered to the Spanish Air Force in October 1974.

The Aviocar has progressed through further variants – the Series 200 certificated in March 1979 and the Series 300 certificated in December 1987. These had increased gross weights and an increase in power and production from the Spanish factory had exceeded 320 examples at the end of 1997. Many of these have been delivered to military users including the air arms of Portugal, Chile, Nicaragua, Mexico, Angola and South Africa. Civil certification was awarded in June 1975 and the first nineteen-seat passenger aircraft was delivered to Pelita in Indonesia later that year. The airliner variant has seen service with a number of American commuter carriers including Bar Harbor, Gull Air, Simmons Airlines (Allegheny Commuter), and other commercial applications have included geodetic survey and package freight operations with Bader Express and other carriers.

In 1974, the Indonesian state oil company, Pertamina and its transport subsidiary, Pelita Air Service, represented by Dr B.J. Habibie entered discussions with CASA, for licence production of the C.212 in Indonesia. This led, in August 1976, to the establishment of IPTN (Industri Pesawat Terbang Nusantara) – otherwise known as Nurtanio which commenced production of the C.212 at the former Lipnur factory at Bandung. The initial fourteen Aviocars were built from CASA-supplied kits but, thereafter Nurtanio became self-sufficient and completed 108 examples by the time the line was closed in 1997.

CASA C-212-300M, PA-61 & PA-62

In 1979, CASA and Nurtanio launched a design programme for a larger version of the C.212 and established a joint design group entitled PT Aircraft Technology Industries ('Airtech'). The CN.235 emerged as a completely new design although it followed the C.212's high-wing twin turboprop layout and still had an upswept rear fuselage with a retractable loading ramp. The circular-section fuselage can accommodate four-abreast seating for forty-four passengers or the CN.235 can be delivered in commercial utility or military configuration with a hardened interior capable of carrying five LD2 containers. Two prototypes were built – one at Madrid and one at Bandung, both being rolled out on 10 September 1983 and FAA certification was gained in December 1986.

Two production lines have been operated and over 100 have been delivered by CASA and approximately forty by Nurtanio. The first commercial operator of the CN.235 was the Canary Isles carrier, Binter Canarias who received four and the CN.235 is also operated by Austral in Argentina. Nurtanio has delivered fifteen to Merpati Nusantara but the bulk of CN.235 orders have been for military aircraft for various forces including those of Saudi Arabia, Malaysia, South Korea – and for Turkey which will receive locally-built examples. CASA has also announced plans for a stretched version of the CN.235 – the CN.295. Intended, initially, as a military variant with increased payload, the CN.295 has been conceived unilaterally by CASA in response to a Spanish Air Force requirement and will be powered by Pratt & Whitney PW127 engines with new technology six-bladed propellers.

Production Details

CASA has used a complex serial number system for the C212. This includes the customer identity and is in a common series with Nurtanio. A typical serial number is C212-CB16-1-125 which is broken down into the aircraft type (C212), the Customer number (CB16 for Korean Air), the sequential number for that customer (the first aircraft) and the overall serial number in the C212 production run (125). A typical serial number for an Indonesian-built aircraft is C212-A4-19-136/22N which follows the same system with the additional /22N indicating that this is the twenty-second aircraft from the Nurtanio production line. In the case of Nurtanio-built aircraft the Customer number always contains the digit '4' (e.g. A4, AB4, CC4). The two prototype C212s were c/n C212-P1 and C212-P2 and production commenced at c/n C212-B-1-1 (for the Spanish Air Force) and had reached C212-AB10-2-455 (for the Chilean Army) by mid-1997 including 123 aircraft built by Nurtanio (i.e. up to c/n C212-4-448/123N), and excluding c/n 155 and 156 which were not built and c/n 299 used for static testing.

CASA CN.235, ECT-135

CN-235 serial numbers are allocated separately for Spanish and Indonesian production. Spanish serials run from c/n C001 to, currently, approximately C112 with aircraft being manufactured in Turkey at Tusas Aerospace (to meet an order for forty-seven for the Turkish Air Force) having serials in the main sequence. Indonesian aircraft have serials from 001N to, currently, 039N.

Model Information

The transport aircraft types built by CASA since the war are as follows:

Type No.	Name	No. Built	Notes
CASA.201B	Alcotan	112	Low-wing 10-pax. military transport with retractable tailwheel u/c and powered by two 500 h.p. ENMA Sirio-VIIA radial piston engines (or Cheetah 27, Alvis Leonides, Elizade 9C-29-750 or P&W Wasp Juniors). Prot. FF. 11 Feb. 1949. Spanish AF designation T.5. Also Model C.201F navigation trainer and C.201G bombing trainer.
CASA.202	Halcon	21	Developed C.201 with retractable tricycle u/c, 34ft longer fuselage with 14-pax seating, larger wing and two 775 h.p. ENMA Beta 9C-29-750 radial engines. Prot. FF. May 1952.
CASA.202B	Halcon	1	C.202 with lengthened fuselage, 8-seat executive interior, angular vertical tail and two 1300 Wright R-1820-56 engines.
CASA.207A	Azor	22	Military transport derived from C.202 with enlarged airframe for 36-pax and powered by two 2040 h.p. Bristol Hercules 730 radial engines. Prot. FF. 28 Sep. 1955. Spanish AF designation T.7.
CASA.401			Proposed high-wing STOL 55-pax. transport developed with Dassault and MBB with ventral tail loading ramp and powered by four Lycoming T.5321A turboprops. Not built.
C212-100	Aviocar	122	High-wing light tactical military of 19-pax. civil transport with fixed tricycle u/c, ventral rear loading ramp and powered by two 715 shp Garrett TPE331-5 turboprops. 14,330 lb. TOGW. Prot. XT.12-1 FF. 26 Mar. 1971. Spanish military C.212A (T.12B), C.212AV (T.12C) VIP model, C.212B (TR.12A) survey aircraft and C.212E (TE.12B) trainer.
NC-212-100	Aviocar	28	C.212-100 built by IPTN (Nurtanio) in Indonesia.
C212-200	Aviocar	153	C.212-100 powered by two 900 shp TPE331-10 engines and max 17,640 lb. TOGW. Military D.3B SAR aircraft with large nose radome and TR.12D ECM trainers.
NC-212-200	Aviocar	61	C.212-200 built by IPTN (Nurtanio) in Indonesia.

Type No.	Name	No. Built	Notes
C212-300	Aviocar	52	C.212-200 with wingtip winglets, extended nose with baggage compartment, optional deletion of rear loading ramp, increased useful load and TPE331-10R-513C engines with new prop synchrophasers. Airliner has 26-pax 4-abreast seating.
C212-300DE	Aviocar		Specialised military ELINT version with nose radome and tail sensors.
C212-300M	Aviocar		Military general purpose transport with optional underwing fuel tanks and offensive equipment hardpoints.
C212-300MP	Patrullero		Maritime patrol version with search radars etc.
C212-300P	Aviocar		C212-300 powered by 1100 shp Pratt & Whitney PT6A-65 turboprops.
CN-212-300	Aviocar	7	C.212-300 built by IPTN (Nurtanio) in Indonesia.
C212-400	Aviocar		C-212 with Allied Signal TPE331-12 engines and increase gross weight and useful load.
CN235-10		13	High-wing 44-passenger or general utility transport with retractable tricycle u/c and upswept rear fuselage with retractable loading ramp. Powered by two 1700 shp General Electric CT7-7A turboprops. 33,289 lb. TOGW. Prototypes ECT-100 (c/n 991/P1) FF. 11 Nov. 1983 and PK-XNC (c/n 992/01N) FF. 30 Dec. 1983. Military version referred to as CN235-10M.
CN235-10	Tetuko	17	Nurtanio-built version of CN235-10.
CN235-100		4	CN235 with 1750 shp CT7-9C engines.
CN235-110		21	Nurtanio-built version of CN235-100.
CN235-100M		88	Military version of CN235-100.
CN235-100MPA	Persuader	2	Maritime reconnaissance version with nose mounted radar, FLIR and external anti-shipping missile hardpoints.
CN235-200		8	CN235 with strengthened airframe, increased fuel capacity, modified wing and 34,833 lb. TOGW.
CN235-220		2	Nurtanio-built version of CN235-200.
C295		1	Proposed military development of CN.235 with 9ft 8in fuselage stretch, new u/c and Pratt & Whitney PW127G engines with six-blade Hamilton Standard propellers. Prot. FF 28 Nov. 1997

EMBRAER   BRAZIL

Embraer (The Empresa Brasileira de Aeronáutica S.A.) was formed on 19 August 1969 at São José dos Campos near São Paulo. Its first product was the EMB-110 Bandeirante which was developed from the experimental IPD-6504 design created in 1965 by a team led by Max Holste at the Centro Tecnico Aerospacial ('CTA'). The production version of the low-wing turboprop Bandeirante had a larger fuselage than the original concept prototype. The first EMB-110 was flown in August 1972 and civil certification was received in April of the following year although first deliveries were military-standard aircraft for the Brazilian Air Force.

The Bandeirante was built in a number of variants and with effective marketing and good financing programmes Embraer was able to deliver a large proportion of the 496 production examples to commuter airlines in the United States who found them cost effective and efficient. They were widely used by the affiliates of the major airlines – United Express, Allegheny Commuter and Northwest Airlink and by independent local service carriers such as Royale Airlines, Provincetown-Boston, Pilgrim and Wright Air Lines. In Europe they provided services with Air UK, Jersey European, Loganair and Air Littoral.

EMB-145, PT-ZJD

A good number were also sold to military users around the world including the air forces of Chile, Uruguay, Gabon, and Colombia. A specialised patrol version is designated EMB-111 and known as the P-95 Bandeirulha in FAB service.

Production of the Bandeirante was completed at the end of 1989 and it was succeeded on the production line by the Brasilia. Embraer had seen that Bandeirante customers would require a larger pressurised aircraft in the thirty to forty passenger category as their routes grew. This prompted a design study which defined the EMB-12X as a family of related aircraft with an aerodynamically very clean airframe with a circular section fuselage and T-tail. The basic fuselage and wing design first resulted in the Xingu executive aircraft of which 111 examples were built between 1979 and 1987. Embraer also planned the twenty-seat EMB-120 Araguaia and the smaller EMB-123 Tapajos but both of these were shelved in favour of a much larger version which became the thirty-passenger EMB-120 Brasilia with power provided by a pair of Pratt & Whitney PW118 turboprops. Full scale Brasilia development started in 1979 and the first of three flying prototypes took to the air in July 1983 with Brazilian certification following in May 1985. The launch customer was Atlantic Southeast Airlines which eventually received over sixty aircraft and other early deliveries were made to Skywest, DLT, Air Littoral and Rio Sul. Over 300 examples were in airline service by the end of 1997.

Embraer further developed the Brasilia into the CBA-123 Vector nineteen-seater which was also aimed at the corporate user and was to be built as a co-operative development by Embraer and FAMA (Argentina). The Vector was powered by a pair of pusher Garrett TFE731-20 turboprops mounted on the rear fuselage. The first of two prototypes (PT-ZVE) was flown on 18 July 1990 but the programme was abandoned after Embraer concluded that there was an insufficient market for this category of aircraft. Embraer was also facing major financial pressures during 1991 when the Vector project was in full swing and had to choose between it and the EMB-145.

The EMB-145, initially named 'Amazon', was a logical development of the EMB-12X family and was Embraer's response to the sector which was becoming dominated by the Canadair RJ. Essentially, the EMB-145 was a Brasilia airframe with two fuselage plugs fore and aft of the wing, a newly-designed supercritical wing and a modified tail. Two Allison AE3007A turbofans were to be used in underwing pylon-mounted pods but a series of revisions to the design changed these to rear fuselage mountings. The EMB-145 was laid out to carry fifty passengers and to have a 3000 nautical mile maximum range – largely to reduce frequency of refuelling on multi-sector routes. Despite Embraer's financial pressures, the first aircraft was flown in August 1995 and certification was accelerated so that the initial delivery to Continental Express took place just over a year later. Embraer has been fortunate in gaining large orders from AMR-Eagle and Continental Express which, alone will account for over 250 aircraft and would take the EMB-145 to its commercial break-even point. The expansion of business meant that, in mid-1998, Embraer was considering moving from its private status to a public flotation. A shorter thirty-seven-seat version of the EMB-145 was under development in mid-1998 as the EMB-135 using the prototype EMB-145 modified with a shorter fuselage. It is to be expected that the design will continue to be stretched to create further variants, possibly including the EMB-170 with a wider fuselage and seventy-passenger capacity. In late-1997 the aircraft were redesignated ERJ-145 and ERJ-135.

Production Details

Embraer transport aircraft serial numbers are prefixed with the model number which is followed by a three-digit individual serial. Details are as follows.

Model	Serial Batches	Notes
EMB-110	c/n 110001 to 110500	Plus prots. c/n 01, 02, 03
EMB-120	cn 120001 to 120345 up	c/n 120002 static test airframe
EMB-145	c/n 145001 to 145099 up	c/n 145001 converted to prot EMB-135

Model Information

Embraer has built the following individual transport aircraft models.

Type No.	Name	No. Built	Notes
IPD/PAR-650 4		1	Low-wing 10-pax military transport and commuter aircraft with retractable tricycle u/c, circular cabin windows and powered by two 550 shp Pratt & Whitney PT6A-20 turboprops. Prot. s/n 2130 (c/n 01) FF. 22 Oct. 1968.
EMB-100		2	Developed IPD-6504 with extra cabin windows, modified u/c and improved systems.
EMB-110	Bandeirante	57	Production 12-pax EMB-100 with rectangular cabin windows, 2ft 6in fuselage stretch. Military C-95.
EMB-110A	Bandeirante	2	EMB-110 for airways navaid calibration. Military EC-95.
EMB-110AN	Bandeirante	2	EMB-110A for Chilean Navy.
EMB-110B	Bandeirante	6	EMB-110 for aerial mapping and survey. Braz. military R-95.
EMB-110B1	Bandeirante	2	Convertible commercial EMB-110B with alternative Passenger/executive/air taxi interior.
EMB-110C	Bandeirante	30	15-pax commercial commuter airliner.
EMB-110CN	Bandeirante	3	Transport variant for Chilean Navy.
EMB-110E	Bandeirante	15	Executive transport with 7-pax interior and galley. Also EMB-110EJ with alternative interior fit.
EMB-110F	Bandeirante	1	All-cargo version.
EMB-110K1	Bandeirante	21	EMB-110 with 2ft 9in forward fuselage stretch, ventral fin and port rear cargo door for military cargo operations as Braz.AF C-95A.

EMB-120RT Brasilia, N210AS

EMB-110P1, XC-DUA

Type No.	Name	No. Built	Notes
EMB-110P	Bandeirante	25	Commercial 18-pax commuter aircraft developed from EMB-110C with PT6A-27 engines.
EMB-110P1	Bandeirante	193	Commercial pax/cargo version of EMB-110K1.
EMB-110P1A	Bandeirante	31	EMB-110P1 with increased tailplane dihedral, improved cabin trim and soundproofing and modified control surfaces.
EMB-110P1K	Bandeirante	55	Military cargo, utility and SAR version of EMB-110P as Braz. military C-95B, EC-95B, C-95C, SC-95B.
EMB-110P2	Bandeirante	37	High-density commuter airliner version of EMB-110P1 with 21-pax capacity. EMB-110P2/41 with 13,010 lb. TOGW and FAR Part 41 certification.
EMB-110P2A	Bandeirante		EMB-110P2 with increased tailplane dihedral, improved cabin trim and soundproofing and modified control surfaces.
EMB-110P3	Bandeirante		EMB-110P with pressurized fuselage, T-tail and 1173 shp PT6A-65 engines. Not built.
EMB-110S1	Bandeirante	1	Survey version with increased fuel capacity, 750 shp PT6A-34 turboprops, tail magnetometer and wingtip tanks.
EMB-111A	Bandeirante	19	Maritime patrol version of EMB-110 with radar nose and search equipment. Braz. military P-95B.

Type No.	Name	No. Built	Notes
EMB-120	Brasilia	3	Pressurised low-wing 30-pax. commuter aircraft with T-tail, retractable tricycle u/c and two 1500 shp Pratt & Whitney PW115 turboprops. Prot. PT-ZBA (c/n 120001) FF. 27 Jul. 1983.
EMB-120RT	Brasilia	275	EMB-120 with two 1800 shp PW118 or PW118A engines. Also EMB-120 QC convertible version.
EMB-120ER	Brasilia	52	EMB-120RT with additional fuel capacity/range and increased takeoff weight.
ERJ-145		100	50-pax regional jet airliner based on EMB-120 with 30ft 2in fuselage stretch, new swept wing, new u/c and powered by two 7040 lb.s.t. Allison AE3007A turbofans in pods on rear fuselage. Prot. PT-ZJA (c/n 145001) FF. 11 Aug. 1995.
ERJ-145LR			Long-range version of ERJ-145 with additional fuel capacity.
ERJ-135		3	37-pax. version of EMB-145 with fuselage shortened by 11ft 7in. and AE3007A3 turbofans. For certification June 1999.
ERJ-135LR			Long range version of ERJ-135 with additional fuel capacity and derated Allison AE3007A1 engines.
EMB-170			Proposed 70-pax development of EMB-145 with stretched and enlarged fuselage, bigger wing and new engines.

Embraer EMB-111A (P-95), 2262 of FAB

FAIRCHILD-DORNIER   USA/GERMANY

After a wartime of production of two-seat training aircraft, Fairchild Engine & Airplane Corporation faced a major challenge in 1944 with the first flight of its XC-82 prototype. One of the most unusual aircraft of its time, the twin-boomed C-82 Packet military cargo transport and its subsequent C-119 derivative became the mainstay of the military transport fleets of the USAF and many other NATO nations. The rear clamshell doors of the Packet allowed the U.S. Army to load most of its wheeled and tracked vehicles directly into the aircraft's hold and the cargo compartment was set at truck bed height which made it simple to achieve rapid movement of cargo or air dropping of palletised loads. The Packet was not widely used by commercial operators although TWA and Cruzeiro do Sul did use the C-82 for transportation of aero engines and general freighting and a number of C-119s, often equipped with auxiliary jet engines, were taken over by Aero Union and other operators for fire bombing missions in the 1970s and 1980s.

Fairchild followed the C-119 with the Chase-designed C-123 Provider. The Provider was a conventional aircraft with a high wing and twin piston engines which was fitted at a later date with a pair of podded auxiliary jet engines. Again, this was designed to a military requirement and embodied a sharply upswept rear fuselage providing a rear loading ramp. Extensively employed during the Vietnam war, the C-123 was not sold to commercial users although a number of surplus aircraft have served as freighters in the United States.

In 1952, Fairchild became involved in close co-operation with Fokker and took out a general licence to build Fokker types in the United States. Attention was focussed on a DC-3 replacement and Fokker's F-27 was seen as fitting the requirements of many local service airlines. The licence production agreement under which the F-27 would be built at Fairchild's Hagerstown, Maryland plant was formalised in April 1965 and Fairchild soon obtained orders from Bonanza Airlines, Piedmont and West Coast Airlines. Fairchild's version of the F-27 was virtually the same as the Fokker model except for provision of a forward cargo door and a longer radar nose. Their prototype was flown on 12 April 1958 and the F-27 gained its FAA type certificate on 27 March 1959. The first customer delivery was made to West Coast Airlines on 24 July 1958 and over forty aircraft were delivered during the following year to the launch customers and to other airlines such as Northern Consolidated, Quebecair, AVENSA and Aloha. Fairchild also developed useful orders for the executive version from business aircraft users such as Ideal Cement, Continental Can, Kimberley-Clark and Champion Spark Plug Co.

Fairchild (which became Fairchild-Hiller in September 1964) progressively improved the F-27 with increased gross weights and engine improvements. In June, 1966 they obtained type approval for the stretched FH-227 which increased passenger capacity to fifty-two seats and this replaced the F-27 on the production line from the 130th aircraft. Fairchild-Hiller eventually completed seventy-eight examples of the FH-227, many of which were sold to existing F-27 operators. More than half of the production FH-227s were delivered to Mohawk Airlines who acquired twenty-three and Ozark Airlines who received twenty-one. The FH-227 line was finally closed at the end of 1968.

Since 1968, Fairchild-Hiller had been in co-operation with Swearingen Aircraft on the joint development of a twenty-two-seat turboprop commuter airliner. This was named the Metro and the prototype was first flown in the summer of 1969. It employed virtually the same nose, engines and tail unit as Swearingen's Merlin III business turboprop but had a new circular section centre fuselage which would accommodate nineteen passengers seated either side of a centre aisle. First deliveries started in 1970 and Swearingen also took the opportunity to gain certification for the very similar Merlin IV for sale to corporate buyers.

Having co-operated on Metro development, it was arranged that a substantial amount of Metro sub-assembly would be done by Fairchild at Hagerstown, Md. The Metro programme also meant that Swearingen's financial and organisational resources were being stretched and eventually, on 2 November 1971, it was announced that Fairchild would take over Swearingen's assets. A new company, Swearingen Aviation Corporation, was formed by Fairchild to build the Merlin and Metro. On 5 January 1981 the name was again changed – to Fairchild Swearingen Corporation – and in October 1987 the company was sold to GMF Investments by Fairchild Industries. Fairchild Aircraft declared Chapter 11 bankruptcy on 1 February 1990 but this was resolved when the company was acquired by Fairchild Acquisition Inc. in September 1990.

Both the Merlin III and Merlin IV/Metro have undergone numerous model changes aimed at improving performance. In particular, the introduction of new airworthiness regulations SFAR-41 and SFAR-41B allowed Fairchild to bring in versions of the Metro and Merlin III with a 12,500 lb zero-fuel weight instead of the previous FAR-23 gross weight at this level. The Metro was attractive to many of the smaller commuter airlines as a result of its high cruise performance and good operating economics – even though the cabin was smaller than most of the competitors. Large fleets were operated by Air Midwest, Air Wisconsin, Skywest and the American Eagle carriers. In Europe, Metros flew with the Swiss operator, Crossair and with Battenfeld in Germany – and the Australian Airline, Kendall Airlines used the Metro alongside its fleet of Saab 340s. In its Expediter all-freight version, the Metro went into service with DHL. Fairchild launched several military variants including the Metro III Sentry and the MMSA with a belly-mounted surveillance pod, and six aircraft for the Swedish Air Force are equipped with an Ericsson PS-890 Erieye system with a Saab 340AEW a/c SLAR antenna mounted on pylons above the roof. The company has not been particularly successful in sales of the

Fairchild C.82, N9701F (AHS)

military variants but several air forces have Metros for personnel transport and the U.S. Air Force received a fleet of sixty-seven C-26s for operation with the Air National Guard.

In 1979, Fairchild joined with Saab to design a new pressurised local service airliner of larger capacity than the Metro. The low-wing Saab-Fairchild SF.340, powered by two General Electric CT7 turboprops was designed to seat thirty-five passengers and was first flown in January 1983. Following the award of the FAA Type Certificate on 29 June 1984, the SF.340 went into production with wings, engine nacelles and tail units being built by Fairchild and the fuselage, undercarriage and final assembly handled by Saab at Linkoping.

Early success was recorded with sales to Air Midwest, Crossair and Comair with deliveries commencing in 1984. However, not long after commencement of production, Saab and Fairchild announced that the whole programme was being handed over to Saab and by late 1987 manufacture of wings and tail units had been passed over to the Swedish factory and Fairchild retained no further involvement with the programme.

Production Details

Fairchild's production of the F-27 series used a simple serial number system with production standard F-27s allocated c/n 1 to 128 and the later FH-227 being c/n 501 to 579. In its acquisition of the Metro line, Fairchild inherited the somewhat complex serial number system created by Swearingen which involved separate serial sequences for each model. Shortly after Fairchild took over the line, an integrated serial system was introduced covering both the Metro and the Merlin business aircraft. This commenced at c/n 340 and the different models were identified by a two letter prefix. The commercial transport aircraft had prefixes with a 'C' as the second letter (e.g. TC, AC, PC) and the business aircraft had 'T' as the second letter (e.g. AT).

In the early production stages, the company changed from one model to another on the production line (for instance from Merlin IV to Metro) or inserted a priority order. Rather than bringing these into the normal serial sequence they allocated 'Extra' serial numbers consisting of the line number at the point of insertion with the letter 'E' as a suffix (e.g. T205E). In some cases, several extra aircraft were introduced and this led to more than one letter 'E' being added. The most notable occasion was a batch of four additional Metros which became c/n TC211E, TC211EE, TC211EEE and TC211EEEE. There were also examples of aircraft being given new serial numbers with the result that there are gaps in the number sequences and in some cases the prefix letters change. Fairchild have also given an 'A' suffix to the Merlin IIIC to FAR Part 23 standard (e.g. N3067W which was given c/n TT-486A). Metro III aircraft with heavy duty landing gear have a 'B' suffix (e.g. AC-650B) and the SA.227DC delivered as C-26As to the U.S. Air Force have the suffix 'M' (e.g. DC-836M).

The initial Swearingen production of Metros used the dedicated serial number batch from c/n TC201 to TC339 (together with the 'extra' serials mentioned above). The latest production has been of the SA.227DC Metro 23 with the highest recorded serial at the end of 1998 being c/n DC904B. Details of the Metro serial allocations in the integrated series are as follows:

Model	Range of c/ns in integrated series
226TC	TC340 to TC419
227AC	AC422 to AC788B
227PC	PC436 and PC562
227BC	BC762 to BC789B
227CC	CC827B to CC844B
227DC	DC791B to DC904B+ (Metro 23)
SA227DC	DC748M to DC836M (C-26A)

Fairchild SA227-AC Metro 111, N343AE

Model Information

Details of production of the Swearingen and Fairchild Merlin business aircraft are contained in the companion volume *Airlife's General Aviation*. Details of the Fairchild F-27 and the different Metro variants are as follows:

Type No.	Name	No. Built	Notes
F-27		40	F-27 built by Fairchild with heavier skinning, single u/c doors, improved electrical and air conditioning systems, modified cockpit, radar nose etc. Powered by two 1670 shp R.Da-7 Mk.514-7 engines. 40,500 lb. TOGW. First aircraft, N1027 (c/n 1) FF. 12 Apl. 1958.
F-27A		17	Fairchild F-27 with 1870 shp R.Da-7 Mk.528-7E engines and 42,000 lb. TOGW.
F-27B		3	Fairchild F-27 with forward port-side cargo door.
F-27F		31	F-27A for corporate executive use with deluxe interior and customised avionics and optional long-range tanks.
F-27G			F-27A modified with forward cargo door, strengthened cabin cargo floor and movable passenger compartment bulkhead for combi operations.
F-27J		35	F-27A with 1990 shp R.Da-7 Mk.532-7 engines.
F-27M		2	F-27J with larger diameter propellers for high altitude operation.
FH-227		1	F-27J with forward fuselage stretch of 6ft 6in, 43,500 lb. TOGW and 52-pax capacity.
FH-227B		54	FH-227 with strengthened structure, heavier landing gear, larger diameter propellers and 56-pax capacity.
FH-227C		7	FH-227 with larger propellers as used on FH-227B.
FH-227D		11	FH-227B with 2040 shp R.Da-7 Mk.532-7L engines and improved anti-skid brakes.

Type No.	Name	No. Built	Notes
FH-227E		6	FH-227C with 2040 shp R.Da-7 Mk.532-7L engines.
SA226-TC	Metro	197	19-seat commuter airliner similar to Merlin IV. Prot. N226TC (c/n TC200) FF. 26 Aug. 1969.
SA226-TC	Metro II		Metro with minor changes to flight deck, modified fuel system and rectangular windows instead of portholes.
SA226-TC	Metro IIA		Metro to SFAR-41 standard. Replaced by Metro III.
SA227-AC	Metro III	273	Metro II to SFAR-41 standard with TPE331-11U-601G engines, 4-blade Dowty props, improved u/c doors and increased wingspan. Offered as Metro III-41 and Metro III-41B. Military C-26A. Also Metro III Sentry for military surveillance.
SA227-BC	Metro III	18	SA227-AC with TPE331-12 engines.
SA227-PC	Metro IIIA	2	Metro III with 14,500 lb. TOGW and PT6A-45R turboprops for both commuter and executive use.
SA228-AE	Metro V		Proposed Metro III with T-tail, deeper cabin, heavier landing gear, stronger wing, 5-blade props and 1100 shp Garrett TPE331-12UA-701G engines. Not built.
SA227-CC	Metro 23	5	Initial designation for civil Metro 23.
SA227-DC	Metro 23	99	Metro with 1100 shp TPE331-12UAR engines, 16,500 lb. TOGW. certificated to FAR.23 (Amdt. 34). Initially known as 'Metro IV'. Expediter 23 is all-cargo version. Military version designated C-26B.
SA227	Metro IV		Proposed higher-powered Metro V. Not built.
SA227	Metro 25		Proposed Metro III with belly baggage compartment, 25 seats and TPE331-12 turboprops. Project discontinued.
SA227	MMSA		Multi-mission surveillance type based on any Metro model, fitted with belly-mounted multi-sensor surveillance pod and Mitsubishi IRM.500 FLIR in nose.

On 5 June 1996, Fairchild Aircraft acquired an 80% holding in Dornier and the new company operates as Fairchild Dornier. Dornier is a name famous from pre-war days as the builder of the Dornier Wal and other giant flying-boats and for its wartime bomber production. The original Dornier concern collapsed at the end of the war but was reformed in 1954 to develop the Do.25 high-wing light aircraft and its derivative, the Do.27 which was delivered in large numbers to the West German forces as an army liaison aircraft. A twin engined version, the Do.28 followed and Dornier GmbH then produced the enlarged Do.28D Skyservant, which was a light utility aircraft with a square-section fuselage and two Lycoming IGSO-540 engines mounted on stub wings. From the outset, the Do.28D established itself with the German forces and the first examples were delivered to the Luftwaffe in 1970. A small number of civil Skyservants were sold, including thirteen aircraft delivered to the United States and some of these were used in air taxi and low density commuter work.

The Do.28D formed the basis for a new group of commuter airliners – the Do.228 series. In the late 1970s Dornier carried out extensive research into new technology wing design

Dornier Do.328, VT-VIF

and converted a Do.28D into its 'TNT' prototype for the advanced 'Tragsflugels Neuer Technologie' programme. The Do.228 (originally known as the Do.28E) was fitted with this wing and has been built in both standard and stretched fuselage versions. The Do.228 fuselage incorporated sections of Do.28D structure but was, essentially, a new design and the aircraft received its German type certificate on 18 December 1981 with the first delivery, to A/S Norving taking place on 3 March 1982. The Do. 228 has also been built in India by Hindustan for the Indian Navy and commercial customers with over twenty having been completed to date. Production is due to cease at Dornier's Oberpfaffenhofen factory with the 243rd example at which point Hindustan at Kanpur will assume full responsibility for future Do.228 output. HAL may also be contracted to build the wing of the Dornier 328.

In December 1991, Dornier flew the prototype of the new Do.328 which offered greater capacity and passenger comfort than the Do.228 with substantially better performance. The Do.328 was, essentially, a new aircraft with a wing based on the TNT wing of the '228 but with a pressurised circular section fuselage providing a stand-up cabin for thirty-three passengers in a 2+1 seating configuration. With a maximum cruise speed in excess of 400 m.p.h., the Do.328 was able to come close to the regional jets in block time performance while retaining the flexibility of turboprop engines. The Do.328 is assembled at Oberpfaffenhofen but the fuselage is built by Aermacchi and OGMA. The launch customer was Horizon Air of Seattle, Washington to whom the first of an initial twelve-aircraft order was delivered in November 1993 following JAR certification in the previous month. Other early customers have been Air Engiadina, Lone Star and Mountain Air Express while PSA Airlines have taken a large batch for operation of USAir Express routes.

Dornier was acquired by Daimler-Benz in 1985 and then became part of Deutsche Aerospace and, subsequently, Daimler-Benz Aerospace who eventually disposed of the company to Fairchild. Its latest venture is the Fairchild–Dornier 328JET which is a straightforward modification of the Do.328 airframe with two Pratt & Whitney PW306/9 turbofans fitted in underwing pods replacing the standard Do.328 turboprop installation. The second Do.328 prototype was converted as the development aircraft for the '328JET and made its first flight in January 1998 at which time orders had been placed for seventeen aircraft. Fairchild–Dornier has also launched the '428JET project and seventy-seat '728JET and ninety-seat '928JET. Executive versions of the 328JET, 428JET and 728JET, launched in October 1998 are named Envoy 3, Envoy 4 and Envoy 7 respectively.

Production Details

Dornier serial numbers started at c/n 101 for the Do.27 and were allocated in blocks to the various models built including the military Fiat G-91. Export Do.27s had serials in the 2000 range (e.g. c/n 2034), Do.28s were in the 3000 range and the Do.28D was in the 4000 range. The Dornier Do.228 started at c/n 7001 but, while a common individual aircraft serial sequence was used, Do.228-100s had 7000 series numbers (e.g. c/n 7039) and Do.228-200s had 8000 series prefixes (e.g. c/n 8110). Hindustan allocated its own serial numbers in batches and the early aircraft which were built from Dornier kits also had a Dornier number. The Do.328, rather surprisingly has serials starting at c/n 3001.

Model	Serial Batch	Notes
Do-228-100	c/n 7001 to 7116	Common c/n series with Srs.200 but with 7 prefix.
Do-228-200	c/n 8002 to 8243	Common c/n series with Srs.100 but with 8 prefix.
HAL 228-201	c/n HAL1001 to HAL 1007, c/n HAL2008 to HAL2017 c/n 81-3018 to 81-3027 c/n 81-4028 to 81-4040	Batch system. Aircraft up to HAL2017 also have a Dornier c/n (e.g. 8052/HAL1007).
Do-328	c/n 3001 to 3097 up	

Model Information

Type No.	No. Built	Notes
Do.28E TNT	1	Do.28D fitted with high technology wing. Prot. D-IFNT (c/n 4330). FF. 14 Jun. 1979.
228-100	13	15/16-seat commuter aircraft, originally designated Do.28E-1, with TNT wing, two 715 shp Garrett TPE331-5 turboprops, stretched fuselage and retractable tricycle u/c. 12,566 lb. TOGW Prot. D-IFNS (c/n 4358). FF. 28 Mar. 1981.
228-101	22	228-100 with 13,184 lb. TOGW and increased fuel.
HAL.228-101	10	228-101 built by Hindustan.

Dornier Do.228-201, D-IDBG

Type No.	No. Built	Notes
228-200	19	19/20 seat 228-100 (formerly Do.28E-2) with 5ft fuselage stretch and 776 shp TPE331-5A engines. Prot. D-ICDO (c/n 4539) FF. 9 May 1981.
228-201	53	228-200 with 13,184 lb. TOGW and increased payload.
HAL.228-201	12	228-201 built by Hindustan.
228-202	38	228-200 with 13,668 lb. TOGW and increased fuel.
228-202K	24	228-202 with the ventral strakes of the 228-212.
228-202F	5	Freight conversion of Do.228-202 under Dornier Aviation (NA) STC.
228-212	65	228-202 with 14,110 lb. TOGW, ventral rear fuselage strakes, strengthened u/c and brakes, improved systems, better short field performance and TPE331-10 engines.
328-100	35	33-seat high wing pressurised commuter airliner with retractable tricycle u/c, T-tail and two Pratt & Whitney PW119B turboprops with 6-blade props. 30,070 lb. TOGW. Prot. D-CHIC (c/n 3001) FF. 6 Dec. 1991.
328-110	46	328-100 with larger tail, spoilers, larger propellers, increased flap deflection and 30,840 lb. TOGW.
328-120	5	328-110 with PW119C engines and improved performance.
328JET	3	328 fitted with two 6100 lb.s.t. PW306/9 turbofans in underwing pods. Prot. D-BJET (c/n 3002). FF. 20 Jan. 1998. Corporate Envoy 3.
328-300		Certificated designation for 328JET.
428JET		Proposed stretched 42-44 seat version of 328JET with larger wing and 7900 lb.s.t. PW308 turbofans. Prot. to fly mid-1999. Corporate Envoy 4.
528JET		Proposed new 50-seat airliner with low-set swept wing and underwing pylon-mounted General Electric CF34-8D turbofans. Corporate Envoy 5.
728JET		Proposed stretched 70-seat version of 528JET. Corporate Envoy 7.
928JET		Proposed stretched 90-seat version of 528JET. Corporate Envoy 9.

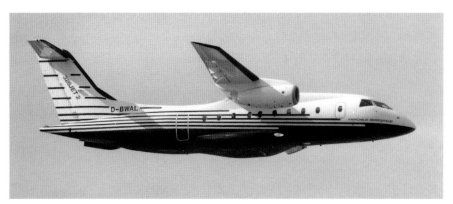

Fairchild Dornier 328JET, D-BWAL

FOKKER

THE NETHERLANDS

The end of the war found the Dutch economy emerging from occupation and the ravages of war. In February 1947 the aircraft industry was reconstituted with state funding based on an amalgamation of De Scheldt, Aviolanda and Fokker under the overall Fokker banner. As the manufacturing capability of Fokker grew, largely through military manufacturing programmes, an introduction to airliner manufacture materialised through a licence to construct a batch of six SAAB Scandias. Fokker had already considered civil transport opportunities with the F.26 Phantom project for a seventeen-passenger aircraft with twin jet engines fitted under the fuselage. However, this fairly radical project was abandoned. The Scandia was one of the plethora of 'DC-3 replacements' which appeared in this period and it prompted Fokker to reconsider the commercial market and design an airliner of their own which would serve regional airline routes.

Fokker's F.27 was a modern pressurised twin-turboprop airliner with a circular section fuselage and a high wing which resulted in an almost unobstructed cabin for thirty-six passengers. The penalty was a fairly tall main undercarriage although this was minimised by the depth of the engine nacelles. The design incorporated a number of fibreglass components and high impact thermal metal-to-metal resin bonding – both of which were advanced concepts at the time. Fokker had, initially, attempted to progress the F.27 in co-operation with another manufacturer and both Canadair and Boeing had been involved in talks. However these contacts were not fruitful although Fokker did come to agreement with Fairchild Engine and Airplane Corporation (later Fairchild-Hiller) for possible future licence production in the United States. Accordingly, the prototype F.27 Friendship was built at the Schiphol factory as a solely Fokker project and made its maiden flight on 24 November 1955. The second and subsequent aircraft were lengthened by three feet ahead of the wings to give forty-two seats.

Production of the F.27 got underway to meet orders which totalled 140 by early 1958 and the first delivery, to Aer Lingus took place on 23 March of that year. Fokker sub-contracted production of F.27 fuselages to Breguet who built a number at their Biarritz factory. Several United States carriers, including Bonanza, Piedmont, West Coast and Northern Consolidated had ordered the F.27 as a result of which the Fairchild agreement was activated and a production line opened up at Hagerstown, Maryland. The Fairchild F.27 varied in detail from the Dutch-built model and had a number of different features including a heavier gauge skin, nose weather radar, modified air conditioning and single main undercarriage doors. A significant number of orders were received for executive aircraft from corporate operators including the Champion Spark Plug Company who acquired two, Gates Rubber, Exxon, Kimberley-Clark and Olin Mathieson who acquired five aircraft. Fairchild did not sell any military aircraft, that market being reserved by Fokker, but they did develop the FH-227 with a stretched forward fuselage – a variant

Fokker F.28-1000, VH-ATG

which was not duplicated in the Fokker product line – and this took over from the standard F.27 in 1966. Fairchild–Hiller finally completed the last of 206 aircraft in December, 1968.

Despite a temporary lull in orders, Friendship production advanced steadily and new variants of the aircraft were developed with increased power and higher gross weights. Inevitably, the F.27 experienced a fuselage stretch with the Mk.500 which allowed the aircraft to take up to sixty passengers in high density configuration. The aircraft experienced its fair share of unusual applications including Conair's fire bombing conversions with a belly-mounted drop door pannier and their oil pollution dispersal system with underwing spraybars and two large internal dispersant tanks. Fokker announced the Fokker Sentinel border surveillance model in 1984 which was equipped with a Motorola AN/APS135 SLAMMR SLAR system and the F.27 Maritime was introduced as a coastal reconnaissance aircraft with external long range tanks and an under-fuselage radome and ESM equipment and a FLIR system. The Dutch Government was an early customer for this model, replacing Lockheed Neptunes in the Netherlands Antilles and deliveries were also made to the Spanish Air Force, the Philippines and the Peruvian Navy. The Maritime Enforcer was an enhanced version with anti-submarine warfare capability including up to six torpedoes or four AM.39 Exocet or AGM-84-A Harpoon missiles.

A commercial passenger/freight 'combi' variant was launched which featured a strengthened cargo floor and forward cargo loading hatch together with a military variant named 'Troopship'. Military orders were received from the Dutch air force and from the military forces of other countries including Argentina (sixteen), Iran (forty-four), Indonesia (eight), The Philippines (ten) and Nigeria (six). The aircraft could also be fitted with underwing long-range tanks if required.

By 1983, F.27 orders had slowed down and it was clear that the design needed refreshing. Fokker came out with a wide-ranging upgrade designated Fokker 50. While externally similar to the F-27, the Fokker 50 was redesigned to use composite materials in many parts of the structure and the systems were modernised. The faithful Dart engines were replaced by the Pratt & Whitney PW125 and Fokker took the opportunity to change the cabin windows from the familiar oval style to a smaller rectangular shape and give the cabin interior a more modern design. The Fokker 50 brought in a new flow of orders including some military aircraft. The company launched a number of specialised military designs and equipped new customers, such as the Singaporean Navy, with the maritime surveillance Enforcer. However, orders for the Fokker 50 started to tail off again in the late 1980s as regional airlines moved towards the light jet commuter airliners such as the Canadair

RJ. Following the collapse of Fokker in 1996, Hindustan Aeronautics expressed an interest in taking over rights to the Fokker 50 but this did not progress beyond initial discussions.

In 1969 Fokker had merged with the German company, VFW to form VFW–Fokker with the intention of launching an expanded line of transport aircraft. This included the VFW.614 airliner which turned out to be unsuccessful and absorbed considerable development funds. In the end, it was decided to merge VFW into the newly created Messerschmitt–Bölkow–Blohm group and consequently, in 1980, Fokker returned to being an independent Dutch public company.

Fokker had initiated the design and development of a new jet airliner in 1962. The F.28 Fellowship started as a fifty-seater but grew during design development to sixty-five-passenger capacity and became one of the principal products of VFW–Fokker. The prototype was flown in the spring of 1967 and the first production delivery took place at about the same time as the original merger with VFW was affected. The F.28 was an entirely new design owing little to the Friendship and was aimed at the lower capacity segment of the market which was being addressed by the DC-9 and the BAC-111. It adopted a very similar low-wing layout with rear-mounted engines and a T-tail and was powered by Rolls-Royce Spey 555-15P turbofans. The launch customer, to which initial deliveries were made immediately following award of the type certificate on 24 February 1969, was Lufttransport Unternehmen (LTU) and the subsequent customers included Braathens SAFE, Itavia, Iberia and the Australian carrier, MacRobertson-Miller Airlines. These airlines all received the basic Mk. 1000 variant and customers were also offered a combi version with a forward upward-opening port side cargo door.

Fokker subsequently stretched the fuselage of the F.28 to create the seventy-nine-seat Mk. 2000 which was limited on fuel load with a full passenger complement since it was certificated at the same gross weight as the Mk. 1000. As a result, the Mk. 2000 was further improved as the Mk. 4000 with longer span wings and improved Spey 555-15H engines which gave it an optional eight-five-passenger high density seating layout and better overall performance and range. Fokker also sold the Mk. 3000 which combined the short fuselage of the Mk. 1000 with the wings, engines and other improvements of the Mk. 4000. The Mk. 4000 was the most popular version of the F.28 and 112 were built between 1976 and closure of the F.28 line in 1987. The Mk. 4000 was sold to a wide variety of operators including Garuda, Linjeflyg, NLM Cityhopper and Nigeria airways. A few military orders were obtained, notably from Argentina, Ecuador, Colombia and Peru. In January 1997, Fokker Services announced a programme for modifying early Fokker F.28s to Fokker F.28RE standard with a forward fuselage plug, modified wings and new Tay 620 engines.

During the late 1970s, Fokker looked at further developments of the F.28 and developed the F.29 project which was a growth variant of the F.28 with wing-mounted engines and substantially greater passenger capacity. Fokker also explored a joint project with McDonnell Douglas entitled MDF.100 but this was abandoned and Fokker eventually decided on a fairly conventional stretch of the F.28 fuselage to seat 107 passengers and adoption of a new wing, Rolls-Royce Tay engines and an upgraded glass cockpit. With the airline industry coming out of recession, Fokker was able to capture early orders for twenty-eight of the new Fokker 100s for KLM, Swissair and, significantly, USAir. This important U.S. sale was followed later by an order from American Airlines for seventy-five (with seventy-five options). The Fokker 100 was also adopted by the leasing company, GPA which had a requirement for up to 100 aircraft.

The prototype Fokker 100 was flown at Schiphol in November 1986 and it gained Dutch type certification one year later on 20 November 1987. Final assembly of the production aircraft was carried out at Schiphol but Fokker brought in production partners including Shorts who were tasked with building the wing and MBB who had responsibility for the tail and fuselage centre section. Swissair was the first customer to take delivery in February 1988 and other early operators included Sempati Air Transport in Indonesia, the Brazilian airline, TAM and Air Europe which used the F.100 briefly before it went out of business in 1991. Over 270 Fokker 100s were in use at the end of 1997 with American Airlines as the largest fleet operator with seventy-five aircraft in service. Fokker also launched the Fokker 70 which was, essentially, a Fokker 100 with a shorter fuselage and seventy-nine seats and the first of these started to be delivered in 1994.

Fokker's ownership history became increasingly complex during the 1990s. Having demerged from VFW in 1980 the company returned to the German fold in 1993 when DASA acquired a 51% interest. DASA subsequently increased its stake to 78% by acquiring part of the Dutch Government's interest. Much reorganisation took place at Fokker as a result of a slow down in business – largely due to poor sales of the Fokker 50 and Fokker 100 and a shortage of capital to launch new products. In January 1996, DASA decided to withdraw its investment in Fokker and this was followed by the company going into receivership on 15 March 1996. A number of other aircraft manufacturers expressed interest including Yakovlev, Samsung and a Malaysian industrial group and the production line was kept open by the receivers. However, the rescue plans foundered and Shorts, who had been manufacturing wings, closed down their production line and the Fokker factory ceased operation in May 1997.

Production details

Fokker started a new series of serial numbers for the F-27, all commencing with '10'. The F-28 had serials commencing with '11' and Fairchild-built aircraft had their own consecutive numbering systems for the F-27 and the FH-227. Details are as follows:

Type	Serial Number Batch	Notes
Fokker F-27	c/n 10101 to 10692	c/n 10685 and 10688 prots for Fokker 50. c/n 10103 & 10104 static test. Not built: c/n 10117, 10128, 10129, 10130, 10685, 10688
Fokker 50 and 60	c/n 20103 to 20335	Not built: c/n 30139, 20140 and c/n 20289 to 20292.
Fairchild F-27	c/n 01, c/n 1 to 128	
Fairchild FH-227	c/n 501 to 579	
Fokker F-28	c/n 11001 to 11241 c/n 11991 to 11994	c/n 11005 and 11007 for static test. c/n 11991 to 11994 intended for Fairchild
Fokker 100 & 70	c/n 11242 to 11583	Some from c/n 11508 on not completed.

Fokker 50, V8-RBI

Model List

The following list gives details of Fokker's F.27 and F.28 series together with the versions built by Fairchild (also shown separately in the Fairchild chapter).

Type No.	Name	No. Built	Notes
F-27	Friendship	2	High-wing 36-pax regional airliner with pressurised cabin incorporating oval windows, retractable tricycle u/c and powered by two 1600 shp Rolls-Royce Dart Da-6 Mk.511 turboprops. 34,200 lb. TOGW. Prot PH-NIV (c/n 10101) FF. 24 Nov. 1955. Second Prot. (PH-NVF, c/n 10102) and subsequent aircraft with 3ft forward fuselage stretch and 40-pax capacity.
F-27-100	Friendship	70	40-pax production short range F-27 with two 1670 shp RR Dart Da-6 Mk.514-7 turboprops, 40,500 lb. TOGW.
F-27-100MAR	Maritime	1	F-27-100 for maritime patrol with external overload tank fittings, observation windows, search radar with radome under forward fuselage, flare chute etc. Prot. PH-FCX (c/n 10183) FF. 29 Feb. 1976.
F-27-200	Friendship	121	F-27-100 with increased fuel capacity, up to 48 pax seats, 45,000 lb. TOGW, radar nose and two 1870 shp Dart R.Da-7 Mk. 528 (later Mk.536-7R) engines. Prot PH-FBA (c/n 10133) FF. 20 Sep. 1959.
F-27-200MAR	Maritime	15	F-27-200 with similar configuration to F-27-100MAR.
F-27-200MPA		1	Maritime patrol version of F-27-200. PH-FGA (c/n 10262).
F-27-300	Combiplane	5	Pax/freight F27-100 with forward cargo hatch, strengthened floor, R.Da-6 Mk.514-7E engines, increased (1357 USG) fuel, 44-pax and 39,000 lb. TOGW.
F-27-300M	Troopship	9	Military version of -300 with hardened interior, military equipment and twin rear fuselage parachute doors, 40,500 lb. TOGW.
F-27-400	Friendship	21	F-27-300 with 2140 shp R.Da-7 Mk.536-7R engines.
F-27-400M	Troopship	77	F-27-300M upgraded to F-27-400 standard.
F-27-400MAR	Maritime	2	F-27-400 with similar configuration to F-27-100MAR.
F-27-500	Friendship	95	F-27-400 with 5 ft. fuselage stretch, 56-pax capacity, one extra cabin window each side, longer-stroke u/c.
F-27-500F	Friendship	8	F-27-500 with modified cargo door.

Type No.	Name	No. Built	Notes
F-27-500RF	Friendship	21	F-27-500 with strengthened rough field u/c and larger engine nacelles and modified nose gear well.
F-27-600	Friendship	131	F-27-400 with forward cargo door but standard floor.
F-27-600RF	Friendship	6	F-27-600 with mods as on F-27-500RF.
F-27-700	Friendship	1	F-27-100 fitted with large forward cargo hatch. One aircraft PH-FCP (c/n 10176).
F-27		40	F-27 built by Fairchild with heavier skinning, single u/c doors, improved electrical and air conditioning systems, modified cockpit, radar nose etc. Powered by two 1670 shp R.Da-7 Mk.514-7 engines. 40,500 lb. TOGW. First aircraft, N1027 (c/n 1) FF. 12 Apl. 1958.
F-27A		17	Fairchild F-27 with 1870 shp R.Da-7 Mk.528-7E engines and 42,000 lb. TOGW.
F-27B		3	Fairchild F-27 with forward port-side cargo door.
F-27F		31	F-27A for corporate executive use with deluxe interior and customised avionics and optional long range tanks.
F-27G			F-27A modified with forward cargo door, strengthened cabin cargo floor and movable passenger compartment bulkhead for combi operations.
F-27J		35	F-27A with 1990 shp R.Da-7 Mk.532-7 engines.
F-27M		2	F-27J with larger diameter propellers for high altitude operation.

Fokker 100, PH-EZE (CS-TPB)

Type No.	Name	No. Built	Notes
FH-227		1	F-27J with forward fuselage stretch of 6ft 6in, 43,500 lb. TOGW and 52-pax capacity.
FH-227B		54	FH-227 with strengthened structure, heavier landing gear, larger diameter propellers and 56-pax capacity.
FH-227C		7	FH-227 with larger propellers as used on FH-227B.
FH-227D		11	FH-227B with 2040 shp R.Da-7 Mk.532-7L engines and improved anti-skid brakes.
FH-227E		6	FH-227C with 2040 shp R.Da-7 Mk.532-7L engines.
50-100		220	F-27-500 for max 58-pax with re-engineered fuselage incorporating more square cabin windows, longer radar nose, four fuselage doors, EFIS-equipped cockpit, twin wheel nose gear and two 2160 shp Pratt & Whitney PW124 turboprops with 6-blade props. 41,865 lb. TOGW. Prot. PH-OSO (c/n 10685) FF. 28 Dec. 1985.
50-100	Special Mission		Military special missions variants of 50-100 including Kingbird 2 AEW version with Ericsson Erieye SLAR on top of fuselage, Maritime Enforcer 2 armed maritime patrol, Sentinel 2 border reconnaissance model and Black Crow 2 electronic intelligence aircraft.
50-100 (502)	Troopship 3	2	Military transport based on 50-100 with forward fuselage stretch of 2ft 11in and starboard forward freight door.
50-120			50-100 without port rear service door.
50-300			50-100 for hot and high operations with 2500 shp PW127A turboprops.
50-320			50-300 without port rear service door.
60/604	Utility	4	Military Fokker 50-100 with 8ft 3in forward fuselage stretch and large cargo door.
F-28-1000	Fellowship	98	Medium haul max 65-pax regional airliner with low wing, T-tail and two 9750 lb.s.t. Rolls-Royce Spey Mk.555-15 turbofans mounted in rear fuselage pods. 56,700 lb. TOGW. Prot. PH-JHG (c/n 11001) FF. 9 May, 1967.
F-28-1000C		2	F-28-1000 combi with upward-opening cargo door in forward port-side fuselage and strengthened cabin floor.
F-28-2000		10	F-28 with 7ft 3in fuselage stretch to give 79-pax max capacity. Engines and TOGW unchanged. Prot. PH-JHG (c/n 11001) FF. as Mk. 2000 on 28 Apl. 1971.

Type No.	Name	No. Built	Notes
F-28-3000		9	F-28-1000 with wing and powerplant changes of F-28-6000, wingtip extensions of the -4000 and redesigned passenger cabin. 70,998 lb. TOGW.
F-28-3000M		1	Military variant of -300 for Argentine Navy.
F-28-3000MC		1	Military variant with modified cargo door.
F-28-3000R		7	F-28-3000 with additional 872 USG centre tank.
F-28-3000C		1	F-28-3000 with forward cargo door.
F-28-4000		112	F-28-2000 with 5ft wingspan increase, 9900 lb.s.t. Spey Mk.555-15H turbofans, redesigned cabin and max 85-pax capacity.
F-28-6000		2	F-28-2000 with full-span leading edge slats, 70,800 lb. TOGW and two 9900 lb.s.t. spey Mk.555-15H turbofans. PH-JHG converted and first flown 27 Aug. 1973.
F-28RE			Fokker F-28 re-engined by Fokker Services with Rolls-Royce Tay 620 turbofans.
F-228			Proposed stretched version of F-28 for production by Fairchild. Planned in 1967 but not built.
70		45	Fokker 100 with fuselage shortened by 15ft 2in and max 80-pax capacity. Powered by two 13,850 lb.s.t. Tay 620 turbofans. 92,000 lb. Max TOGW. Prot. PH-MKC (c/n 11243) FF. 2 Apl. 1993. Also 30-pax Fokker Executive Jet 70.
70ER		1	Fokker 70 executive version with additional long-range tanks.

Fairchild F-27A, HC-BSL

Type No.	Name	No. Built	Notes
80			Proposed shortened Fokker 100 with 77-pax capacity. Not built.
100		280	F-28 with fuselage stretched by 18ft 10in for max 122-pax, redesigned wing with 9ft 10in additional span, integral fuel tanks, new flight deck with 6-tube EFIS and powered by two 13,850 lb.s.t. Rolls-Royce Tay Mk.620-15 or 15,100 lb.s.t. Tay Mk.650-15. 98,000 lb. TOGW. Prot. PH-MKH (c/n 11242) FF. 30 Nov. 1986. Also 40-pax Fokker Executive Jet 100.
130			Proposed stretched 130-pax Fokker 100 with new engines and redesigned wing.
F.29			Proposed 1980 project for 150-pax stretched development of F-28 with twin under-wing mounted turbofans. Not built.

Fokker 70, PH-EZW/OE-LFG

Fokker 60, U-03

GENERAL DYNAMICS
– CONVAIR

UNITED STATES

General Dynamics is rightly referred to by many observers as a 'conglomerate' in view of its growth through acquisition following its establishment in 1947. One of the principal components of the early General Dynamics was Convair which became part of the group on 29 April 1954. Convair itself was the product of a merger of Consolidated Aircraft Corporation and Vultee Aircraft Inc. which took place in March 1943 and Consolidated-Vultee (shortened to 'Convair') played a leading role in wartime production of the Liberator, Catalina, Vengeance, Privateer, Coronado and the Stinson light aircraft range.

With a specialisation in military aircraft, Convair was forced to explore the possibilities for commercial business as the war came to a close in 1945. The Liberator had been widely used as a transport during the war and an obvious solution was to develop an equivalent commercial airliner. The company followed a similar process to that used by Boeing for the Stratocruiser by designing a new forty-eight passenger fuselage which would be mated to the wings and tail of the PB4Y-2 Privateer. Convair constructed two prototypes of the Liberator-Liner but they were unable to strike up sufficient interest by the intended launch customer, American Airlines and the two aircraft were eventually scrapped.

One fruitful result of Convair's talks with American Airlines was the requirement for a DC-3 replacement. The company's design studies resulted in the Model 110 which was an unpressurised low-wing all-metal aircraft with a tricycle undercarriage and a slightly upswept rear fuselage which incorporated a retractable entry staircase in its underside. By the time the Convair 110 prototype flew in July 1946 it had become clear that airline needs were for a larger aircraft and that pressurisation was necessary, so the Model 110 enjoyed a fairly brief life as Convair advanced to a stretched version with forty seats which was designated Convair 240. American Airlines placed an order for 100 aircraft (later reduced to seventy-five) and this was quickly followed by orders from Pan American, Western and the Dutch airline, KLM.

The Model 240 was an attractive aircraft powered by two Pratt & Whitney Double Wasp engines installed so as to provide exhaust thrust augmentation. A variety of door options were available to customers including the ventral staircase prototyped on the Model 110, a forward starboard side main door with integral airstair, a starboard rear cargo door and service doors on the port or starboard forward fuselage. Convair's prototype flew in March 1947 and was certificated on 12 July 1948 by which time a number of aircraft had already been handed over to customers. The Convair-Liner became widely adopted by the United States airline industry although it faced some competition from the Martin 2-0-2 which was chosen by TWA even though it did not have a pressurised cabin. The first foreign delivery was made to Trans Australia Airlines in December 1948 and other overseas airlines to use the CV-240 included Aerolineas Argentinas, Orient Airways in Pakistan, KLM, Swissair and Sabena.

Convair completed civil production of the Model 240 in October 1950 with delivery of the 177th aircraft to Garuda but they also found a valuable customer in the United States Air Force. The T-29A crew trainer was an unpressurised version of the Convair 240 with four roof-mounted astrodomes and cabin consoles for fourteen navigation trainees. T-29s were widely used as VT-29A staff transports. The later T-29B was built with full pressurisation and the USAF also acquired the C-131A Samaritan casualty evacuation version and the C-131B general transport which was equipped with forty-eight seats and based on the later Convair 340. In total, 391 military Convairs were delivered and many were converted to alternative roles in service including the AT-29C and ET-29D for Airways calibration.

The Convair 240 was starting to show its age and Martin had introduced its much improved Martin 4-0-4. Consequently, Convair went into a major upgrade and produced the Model 340 which featured a four feet six inch fuselage stretch, allowing capacity to be increased to forty-four passengers. The '340 was fitted with a more logical arrangement of port-side entry doors and also had longer wings incorporating larger fuel tanks and more powerful engines. United and Braniff were the first major customers for the Convair 340 with the first aircraft being handed over in March 1952. Once again, there were military variants for the USAF and the U.S. Navy and Convair successfully exported significant numbers of the new model. In 1955, the '340 was replaced by the final and further improved variant – the Convair 440 Metropolitan which had modified engine exhausts incorporating rectangular noise suppressing outlets, a higher useful load and, in most cases, a lengthened radar nose. A number of Convair 340s were converted to '440 standard during their lives. The Metropolitan was adopted by many operators such as Lufthansa, Sabena, Swissair, Iberia, Alitalia, SAS and Cruzeiro do Sul. The last example of the Convair-Liner was completed in 1958 but many are still in operation in 1998.

Over a long period, Convair had been working with General Motors' Allison Division on turboprop power for the Convair-Liner. The Model 340 had reached the market at a time of transition from piston-engines to turboprops and it was an ideal candidate for upgrading. The Allison YT-56 was first installed in a pair of Convair 340s which became YC-131Cs and the Allison 501, which was the civil version of the T-56 provided the basis for the Convair 580. At about the same time Convair also pursued installation of the Rolls-Royce Dart 542-4 which resulted in the Convair 600 (based on the CV-240) and the Convair 640 (based on the CV-340 and CV-440) and, in the end, 33 Convair 240s

Convair 580, C-FARO

became CV.600s. 183 Convair 340s and 440s were converted to turboprop power. This represented over 55% of the later series civil aircraft built (excluding write-offs) and demonstrated how satisfactory the Convair-Liner was as a regional turboprop airliner in the market which became dominated by the Fokker F-27. The majority, a total of 155 airframes, became Convair 580s (ninety-seven converted from '340s and fifty-eight from '440s) and twenty-seven became Convair 640s (nineteen based on '340 airframes and eight using '440 airframes). In addition, Convair delivered three late model '440s to Canadair for completion as Canadair 540s and Canadair also built seven new aircraft for the RCAF which were subsequently converted to Convair 580 standard.

In the early 1950s the air transport industry was moving into the era of long-range four-jet transports and Boeing and Douglas were working on the '707 and the DC-8. Convair also started work on a four-jet design to meet the needs of TWA but it was not until 1956 that they were able to finalise the specification of the Model 22 Skylark 600. This aircraft, which became known as the Golden Arrow and then the Convair 880 was a medium range aircraft with a swept wing and accommodation for up to 124 economy passengers in five-abreast seating. TWA and Delta Air Lines both placed orders for a total of forty aircraft and Convair flew the prototype in January 1959. Type approval followed in May 1960. In reality, the Convair 880 was too rigidly tailored to the needs of TWA and had a narrow fuselage by comparison with the DC-8. Further orders were slow in coming and despite the introduction of a specialised '880M short-range variant, Convair only completed sixty-five aircraft. Other operators of the Convair 880 included Northeast Airlines, Swissair, Cathay Pacific and Japan Air Lines.

With a commercial disaster on their hands, Convair sought to put some life into the '880 and developed the Model 30 (otherwise known as the Model 600 and later Model 990 Coronado). The Model 880 fuselage was stretched by ten feet and new General Electric CJ805-21 turbofans were fitted. The Model 30 had a thinner section wing of increased area and was fitted with four distinctive shock bodies on the wing trailing edge. This resulted in increased cruise performance and range but further development delays resulted in a reduction of the launch order placed by American Airlines for twenty-five aircraft with twenty-five options and Swissair and American had to face restrictions on operation of the aircraft for a while after delivery. Only thirty-six Convair 990s were completed with other users including SAS, VARIG and Garuda. American only operated the 990 for five years and their aircraft were sold on to other operators such as Modern Air Transport, Middle East Airlines and Aerolineas Peruanas. After the Convair 880/990 débâcle, Convair abandoned the commercial aircraft business and General Dynamics concentrated on more lucrative production of military types.

Convair 990, OD-AFH (AHS)

Production Details

Simple serial number systems have been used for Convair aircraft and the types and serial batches are as follows:

Type	Serial Number Batch
240	c/n 1 to 178 (including 28 military aircraft)
240 (T-29A, T-29B, T-29C)	c/n 179 to 448
240 (T-29D, C-131A)	c/n 51-1 to 52-92 and c/n 53-1 to 53-26
340	c/n 1 to 239
340 (C-131B)	c/n 240 to 275
340 (R4Y-1)	c/n 276 to 311
440	c/n 312 to 510
Canadair 540 (CL-66B)	c/n 1 to 10
880	c/n 22-00-1 to 22-00-65
990	c/n 30-10-1 to 30-10-37 (excluding c/n 30-10-12)

Model Information

Details of all the Convair transport models are as follows.

Type No.	Name	No. Built	Notes
39	Liberator Liner	2	48-passenger medium haul airliner with tail and shoulder-set wing from Convair PB4Y-2 married to circular-section fuselage with tricycle u/c. Powered by four 1200 h.p. Pratt & Whitney R-1830-65 radial piston engines. Prot. Bu.09803 (later NX30039), FF. 15 Apl. 1944.
110		1	Low-wing unpressurised all-metal 30-seat airliner with ventral rear air stair and tricycle u/c, powered by two 2100 h.p. Pratt & Whitney R-2800-SC13G radial engines. Prot. NX90653 (c/n 1) FF. 8 Jul. 1946.
240	Convairliner	176	Convair Liner – enlarged pressurised development of Model 110 with 40-pax seating, square windows and optional arrangements of ventral air stair, fore or aft cargo doors, starboard rear or front pax doors and port or starboard service doors. Powered by two 2400 h.p. Pratt & Whitney R-2800-CA3 (or -CA15 or -CA18) radial engines. 42,500 lb. TOGW. Prot. N90849 (c/n 1) FF. 16 Mar. 1947.
240-17		31	Military unpressurised version of Convair 240 as T-29A navigation trainer with roof astrodomes, under-fuselage radar etc. Also CT-29A cargo version and VT-29A staff transport.
240-27		122	T-29B pressurised version of T-29A.
240-27		119	T-29C similar to T-29B with 2500 h.p. R-2800-99W engines. Also AT-29C, ET-29C for airways calibration and VT-29C staff transport.

Type No.	Name	No. Built	Notes
240-52		92	T-29D bomber training model without roof astrodomes and with revised interior. Also ET-29D and VT-29D conversions.
240-53		26	Military C-131A Samaritan 37-seat transport or MC-131A casualty evacuation aircraft with port rear cargo door and R-2800-99W engines. Also USCG HC-131A and VC-131A staff transport.
340	Convairliner	205	Convair 240 with fuselage stretch of 1ft 4in ahead of and 3ft 2in behind wing, 44-pax seating. 13ft 7in increase in wingspan with additional fuel tanks taller u/c, port-side passenger doors and 2400 h.p. Pratt & Whitney R-2800-CB16 (or -CB17) engines. 47,000 lb. TOGW. Prot. N3401 (c/n 1) FF. 5 Oct. 1951.
340-70		36	C-131B version of Model 240/340 as USAF 48-seat transport.
340-64			Two YC-131C conversions of Model 340 with two 3750 shp Allison 501D-13 turboprops. First a/c 53-7886 (c/n 91).
340-79		76	C-131D 44-seat transport based on Model 340 with two 2500 h.p. R-2800-52W engines. Also VC-131D (340-67) staff transport or US Navy R4Y-1/C-131F or R4Y-1Z/VC-131F 24-seat VIP transport.
440	Metropolitan	171	Convair 340 with longer engine nacelles and rectangular exhaust boxes, lengthened radar nose, 52-pax seating, 49,700 lb. TOGW.
440-72		22	Military Convair 440 as TC-131E electronic countermeasures trainer and US Navy/Marines R4Y-2/C-131G transport. Also photo survey RC-131F and airways checking RC-131G.
540	CL-66B Cosmopolitan	10	Convair 340 converted with two 3060 shp Napier Eland turboprops (later Eland 504 engines of 3412 shp). Prot G-ANVP (c/n 153) FF 4 Feb. 1956. 53,200 lb. TOGW. Subsequent production by Canadair as CC-109 for Canadian Armed Forces. First a/c CAF.11151 (c/n 1) FF. 7 Jan. 1960. Also four conversions of Model 340/440 as CL-66C. Eight CC-109s later converted to CV-580 standard.
580			Convair 340 and 440 converted by Pac-Aero with STC SA4-1100 spec. to 'Prop-Jet Super Convair' standard with two 3750 shp Allison 501-D13D turboprops with four-blade Aeroproducts props and larger vertical and horizontal tail. 58,156 lb. TOGW. First PacAero aircraft N5100 (c/n 33) FF. 19 Jan. 1960. 159 conversions. Military C-131H.

Type No.	Name	No. Built	Notes
600			Convair 240 converted with two 2559 shp Rolls-Royce Dart R.Da. 10/1 engines. Prot. conversion N94294 (c/n 178). 38 conversions.
640			Convair 340 and 440 converted with two 2559 shp Rolls-Royce Dart R.Da. 10/1 engines. Prot. conversion N73137 (c/n 88). 27 conversions. 53,200 lb. TOGW.
22	Convair 880	48	Transcontinental jet airliner with low swept wing and max 124-pax. seating. Powered by four 11,200 lb.s.t. General Electric CJ-805-3 turbojets in underslung wing pods. 184,500 lb. TOGW. Initially named 'Skylark 600' and 'Golden Arrow'. Prot. N801TW (c/n 880-22-1) FF. 10 Aug. 1959. Some later converted to cargo configuration.
22M	Convair 880M	17	880 with extra mid-section fuel tank, strengthened u/c, new wing leading edge slats, 11,650 lb.s.t. CJ-805-3B engines and taller fin. 192,700 lb. TOGW. One to US Navy as UC-880.
30	Convair 990 Coronado		880 with 10ft fuselage stretch and 121-pax capacity, new 16,100 lb.s.t. CJ-805-23 turbofans, four anti-shock fairings containing fuel tanks on wing trailing edges and modified leading edge slats and flaps. Prot. N5601G (c/n 30-10-1) FF. 24 Jan. 1961. Also known as Convair 600. All aircraft modified to 990A standard.
30A	Convair 990A Coronado	36	990 with repositioned and redesigned engine nacelles, inboard leading edge slats and other modifications.

Convair 240, N94278

COMMERCIAL AIRCRAFT AND AIRLINERS

Convair Customer Codes

The Convair airliners were allocated identifying code designations for each customer consisting of the Model number followed by a simple sequential identification code. Details for the Convairliner series are as follows.

Type	Customer	Type	Customer	Type	Customer
240-0	American	340-37	Pratt & Whitney	440-35	Continental
240-1	Western	340-38	Delta	440-38	Delta
240-2	Pan American	340-40	Aero OY	440-40	Aero OY
240-3	Continental	340-41		440-42	executive
240-4	KLM		Northeast/Alitalia	440-47	National
240-5	TAA			440-49	Garuda
240-6	Aerolineas Argentinas	340-42	Philippine AL	440-58	JAT
		340-47	National	440-59	Cruzeiro do Sul
240-7	Orient A/W	340-48	KLM	440-62	REAL
240-8	J. Pasquel (exec)	340-51	Aeronaves de Mexico	440-63	Union Oil of Cal.
240-9	Convair			440-71	US Navy (R4Y-2)
240-10	H. Vanderbilt	340-54	Pan American		
240-11	Swissair	340-57	Avensa	440-72	USAF (C-131E)
240-12	Sabena	340-58	JAT	440-75	SAS
240-13	Northeast	340-59	Cruzeiro do Sul	440-77	Convair
240-14	Central Air Transport	340-60	Pioneer AL	440-78	RAAF
		340-62	REAL	440-79	USAF (C-131D)
240-15	Hughes Tool Co.	340-63	Union Oil of Cal.	440-80	Iberia
240-17	USAF	340-64	Convair	440-81	Alitalia
240-19	Air fleets	340-66	US Navy (R4Y-1Z)	440-82	Union Carbide
240-21	General Motors			440-83	Gulf Oil
240-23	Garuda	340-67	USAF (VC-131D)	440-85	Trans America
240-24	Ford Motor	340-68	Saudi Arabian AL	440-86	Eastern
240-25	Ethiopian			440-86	Brooklyn Dodgers
240-26	American	340-69	executive		
240-27	USAF	340-70	C-131B	440-88	Lufthansa
240-29	USAF	340-71	US Navy (R4Y-1)	440-89	All Nippon
240-52	USAF			440-90	General dynamics
240-53	USAF	340-79	USAF (C-131D)		
340-30	Convair	440-0	Convair	440-94	Glenn L. Martin Co.
340-31	United	440-3	Bethlehem Steel		
340-32	Braniff	440-11	Swissair	440-95	US Industries
340-33	Arabian Amer. Oil	440-12	Sabena	440-96	Italian AF
340-34	Texaco	440-24	Ford Motor	440-97	Ansett
340-35	Continental	440-32	Braniff	440-98	Kar-Air
340-36	Hawaiian				

In a similar fashion, the Convair 880 and 990 also had individual customer numbers.

Model	Customer	Model	Customer
880-22-1	TWA	990-30A-6	Swissair
880-22-2	Delta Air Lines	990-30A-8	VARIG
880-22M-3	Swissair	880-22M-21	VIASA
880-22M-4	Civil Air Transport	880-22M-22	Japan Air Lines
9909-30A-5	Convair/American		

Convair 880, N8482H

Convair T-29C, 3464

HANDLEY PAGE

UNITED KINGDOM

Handley Page Ltd was one of the world's oldest aircraft companies, having been incorporated in June 1909 by Frederick (later Sir Frederick) Handley Page in order to develop powered aircraft. It was an important manufacturer in World War I, producing the O/100 and O/400 bombers and between the wars was a prolific producer of military bombers (such as the Heyford) and civil aircraft including the legendary HP.42 biplane airliner.

The Second World War took Handley Page back into bomber production, the most successful of which was the Halifax. The original design specification for the Halifax envisaged a secondary role as a military transport and in 1943 the company started design work which would allow the aircraft to be used either as a freighter or as a passenger transport. Several versions of the Halifax were produced with bomb-bay mounted freight panniers, the most effective of which was the HP.70 Halifax C.VIII which entered RAF service in late 1945. In 1948, when the Berlin Airlift got underway the RAF demobilised most of its Halifax C.8 fleet so that they could be used as freighters and tankers by commercial companies. The Halifax had also been produced as a paratroop transport under the designations Halifax A.III, A.VII and A.XI and a full airline passenger version, the Halton, was produced by Short Brothers & Harland as a conversion to the requirements of BOAC. The Halton had the belly pannier and a solid nose, providing baggage

Dart Herald, G-ATIG

stowage together with a twelve-passenger compartment in the rear fuselage with rectangular windows. Twelve Haltons were delivered to BOAC and eighty-two other civil conversions were carried out as freighters or passenger aircraft to bridge the post-war commercial transport gap.

While the Halifax freighter and Halton did meet an immediate need it was not a satisfactory transport for the RAF or for post-war civilian needs and Handley Page proposed a new aircraft using the tail and modified low-set wing of the Halifax married to a new circular-section fuselage. The tail was altered to a single fin/rudder in which form the aircraft became the HP.67 Hastings and its pressurised civil equivalent, the HP.68 Hermes. The prototype Hermes I was completed in December 1945 but suffered a fatal crash while taking off on its first flight from the company's Radlett base which resulted in the installation of a considerably enlarged tailplane on the second aircraft. It was some while before Handley Page finally resolved the problems of the tail design of the Hastings and Hermes.

Handley Page went on to build 145 production examples of the military Hastings for the RAF (together with four of the C.3 for the RNZAF). These replaced the Avro York in service with the RAF as the standard transport workhorse and were eventually replaced by the Argosy and then the Hercules in the late 1960s. By contrast, the Hermes must be counted as less than successful as a commercial transport. The second prototype Hermes was built with a longer fuselage and it was intended that the production Hermes would be the Hermes III with Theseus turboprops and a tricycle undercarriage. In the event, the version ordered for BOAC was the Hermes IV which had the tricycle undercarriage but was fitted with Bristol Hercules piston engines. Handley Page had considerable difficulty in making the Hermes IV meet the BOAC guaranteed specification but eventually they delivered twenty examples during 1949 and 1950. They were strictly an interim type because BOAC had ordered Canadair Argonauts and the turboprop Britannia. Consequently, by 1955 most of the Hermes IVs had passed on to other charter operators such as Airwork, Skyways and Britavia and by 1963 almost all of them had been retired from service.

1947 brought a new opportunity for Handley Page as a consequence of the sad demise of Miles Aircraft. Miles, based at Woodley near Reading had run into financial crisis during the harsh winter of 1946/47 at a time when it was grappling with a large range of new aircraft projects. One of these was the four-engined Miles M.60 Marathon fourteen-passenger aircraft which had flown in prototype form and was expected to receive a Ministry of Civil Aviation contract to meet a need for a regional light airliner. Handley Page (Reading) was established at Woodley to acquire the Miles assets and production commenced to meet a forty-aircraft requirement for BEA and the BOAC Associated Companies. In the event, BEA rejected the Marathon as being unsuitable as a replacement for the DH.89A Rapides which were in service on their Highlands and Islands routes and, while some of the completed aircraft went to overseas airlines such as Union of Burma Airways and WAAC, the majority were passed over to the RAF for use as navigation trainers. The twenty-eight Marathon T.11s were delivered in 1953 and continued until 1959 at which time a number of them found civil careers with Derby Aviation and other operators including the Royal Jordanian Air Force.

The Miles acquisition also brought with it the design of a larger version of the Marathon designated M.73 which was aimed at the elusive DC-3 replacement market. This high-wing aircraft was intended to use many parts from the Marathon including the outer wings and be powered by four Alvis Leonides piston engines. The redesign instituted by Handley Page resulted in a much modified pressurised fuselage and the twin fins of the M.73 were replaced by a single fin and rudder. The prototype HPR.3 Herald made its maiden flight from Woodley on 25 August 1955. At this stage, Handley Page retained the four Leonides engines even though the competitive Fokker F.27 was to be powered by two Rolls-Royce Dart turboprops but it was envisaged that the Herald would be powered by two Napier Eland engines which were expected to provide sufficient power when fully developed. However, it was then decided to re-engine the Herald with Darts and the prototype was modified with a pair of these engines and a lengthened forward fuselage.

Marathon, G-AMGW

As the HPR.7 Dart Herald this aircraft took over from the piston-engined version and went into production at Woodley in 1958 to meet an initial order for three machines for the BEA Scottish services. The majority of production Dart Heralds were the Series 200 version with a longer fuselage giving fifty-passenger seating and Handley Page eventually built forty-eight production aircraft which were sold to customers as diverse as Arkia, the Malaysian Air Force, Eastern Provincial Airways and Jersey Airlines. By 1997, the last three Dart Heralds were reaching the end of their useful lives in the hands of Channel Express and Aerovias in Guatemala.

In the parent Handley Page organisation at Radlett, the mid-1960s saw the tailing off of lucrative contracts for maintenance and support of the Victor bomber and Handley Page needed new production programmes to keep it in business. They saw an opportunity to build an aircraft to meet a growing need for small turboprop commuter aircraft – particularly for American local carriers. There was also the opportunity for such an aircraft to fit into the business executive market. The resulting pressurised eighteen/twenty-seat HP.137 Jetstream was powered by a pair of 850 shp Turbomeca Astazou XIV.C constant speed turboprops and Handley Page flew the prototype at Radlett on 18 August 1967. While it was a most attractive design and gained good advance orders from customers such as Cal-State Airlines (who required six aircraft) a great deal of re-engineering and weight reduction took place before Jetstreams could start to be delivered to users. Much time, cost and effort was also expended on development of the Garrett TPE331 powered C-10 Jetstream 3M to meet an initial USAF order for eleven aircraft.

By mid-1969, Handley Page was in the midst of a financial crisis. Cammell Laird, the parent company of Scottish Aviation, agreed to invest new working capital of some £1.25 million, but on 8 August 1969, Handley Page was forced to call in a receiver. Jetstream production was temporarily carried on by a new operating company named Handley Page Aircraft Ltd but the U.S. Air Force order was then cancelled. All the Mk.3M airframes which were in course of completion had to be abandoned and the financial rescue operation which was underway foundered. In addition to the Jetstream prototypes Handley Page had built forty complete aircraft and thirty-three incomplete airframes including the USAF order.

The Official Receiver had been called in at the end of February 1970 and the history of Handley Page came to an end. Later that year, all the stocks of Jetstream production components and design documentation were sold to Terravia Trading Services who formed Jetstream Aircraft Ltd. The intention was to build Mark 1 aircraft from existing components and the Mark 200 (powered by Astazou XVI engines) as a completely new model. Terravia was not able to establish the complex production facility necessary to meet future production demands but a contract was awarded for twenty-six Jetstream T.1

trainers for the RAF. In February 1972 all production rights were transferred to Scottish Aviation. The history of the Jetstream from this point on is described under the chapter on British Aerospace (Scottish Aviation).

Production Details

Model	Serial Batches	Notes
Halifax C.VIII	c/n 1301 to 1400	c/n 1309, 1311, 1316, 1320, 1358, 1380 not converted to civil. c/n 1308, 1310, 1312, 1318, 1341, 1342, 1350, 1370, 1372, 1376, 1377, 1378 converted to Halton.
Hermes IV	c/n HP.81/1 to HP.81/25	
Hermes V	c/n HP.82/1 and HP.81/2	
Marathon I	c/n 101 to 140	Also Miles prototypes c/n 6265 and 6430.
Herald/Dart Herald	c/n 147 to 197	c/n 193 static test airframe. c/n 252-257 not built.
Jetstream	c/n 198 to 251, c/n 258 to 262	c/n 219, 228, 232, 236, 239, 242, 244, 247, 250, 260 (all Jetstream 3M airframes) not completed. c/n 249, 251, 259, 261, 262 completed as Jetstream T.1 by Scottish Aviation.

Model Information

Handley Page aircraft were all allocated sequential design numbers which had reached HP.67 at the time the Hastings was conceived. The Reading factory which took over the Miles designs started its own new series of 'HPR' numbers covering the Marathon and the various Herald variants together with the abortive HPR.2 military trainer. Heralds were given type numbers which identified the original customer and these included Jersey Airlines (Srs.201), Nordair (202), Itavia (203), British United (204), Eastern Provincial (206), Royal Jordanian Air Force (207), Arkia (209), Globe Air (210), Maritime Central (211), Bavaria Fluggesellschaft (213), Sadia (214) and Air Manila (215). Details of all production postwar transport models are given in the following table.

HP.81 Hermes IV, G-ALDM

Type No.	Name	No. Built	Notes
HP.67	Hastings	2	Low wing unpressurised military transport with max 50-troop capacity, freight interior and port-side rear cargo door, retractable tailwheel u/c and powered by four Bristol Hercules 106 radial piston engines. Prot. TE580 FF. 7 May 1946.
HP.67	Hastings C.1	100	Production Hastings for RAF. Some C.1 converted to C1A with Hastings C.2 fuel tanks. 75,000 lb. TOGW. Some converted to Hastings Met.1 for weather reconnaissance.
HP.67	Hastings C.2	41	Hastings C.1 with tailplane lowered on fuselage and increased fuel capacity. 80,000 lb. TOGW.
HP.68	Hermes I	1	Low-wing commercial 50-pax transport designed for pressurisation with retractable tailwheel u/c and powered by four Bristol Hercules 100 radial piston engines. Prot. G-AGSS (c/n HP68/1) FF. 2 Dec. 1945 (crashed).
HP.74	Hermes II	1	Hermes I with (non-pressurised) fuselage stretch of 6ft 8in forward and 6ft 8in aft of wing and powered by four Bristol Hercules 130 engines. Prot. G-AGUB (c/n HP74/1) FF. 2 Sep. 1947.
HP.81	Hermes IV	25	Hermes II with 4ft 8in fuselage stretch, wing positioned further forward, retractable tricycle u/c and modified instrumentation and avionics. Prot. G-AKFP. FF. 5 Sep. 1948.
HP.82	Hermes V	2	Hermes IV with increased fuel capacity and powered by four Bristol Theseus turboprops. Prot. G-ALEU (c/n HP.82/1) FF. 23 Aug. 1949.
HP.94	Hastings C.4	4	Hastings C.2 VIP transport with deluxe interior and long-range tanks.
HP.95	Hastings C.3	4	Hastings C.2 for RNZAF with Hercules 737 engines and modified instruments and avionics.

Handley Page Hastings C1, TG621 (AHS)

Type No.	Name	No. Built	Notes
M.60	Marathon	42	High wing 18-pax local service airliner with three-fin tail unit, retractable tricycle u/c and powered by four 330 h.p. DH Gipsy Queen 71 piston engines. Prot. G-AGPD/U-10 (c/n 6265) FF. 19 May 1946.
M.69	Marathon II	1	Marathon fitted with two 1010 shp Armstrong Siddeley Mamba turboprops. Later re-engined with two Leonides Major radial piston engines. Prot. G-AHXU/VX231 (c/n 6544). FF. 23 Jul. 1949.
HPR.1	Marathon I		Revised designation for M.60.
HPR.3	Herald	2	High wing pressurised 36-pax regional airliner with retractable tricycle u/c and powered by four 870 h.p. Alvis Leonides Major 7011 radial piston engines. 37,500 lb. TOGW. Prot. G-AODE (c/n 147) FF. 25 Aug. 1955.
HPR.4	Herald		Proposed Herald with two Napier Eland turboprops. Not built.
HPR.5	Marathon II		Revised designation for M.69.
HPR.7	Dart Herald 100	3	HPR.3 with 1ft 7in fuselage stretch for 44-pax, improved pressurisation, dorsal fin and two 2105 shp Rolls-Royce Dart 527 turboprop engines. Prot. G-AODE FF. 11 Mar. 1958.
HPR.7	Dart Herald 200	36	Model 100 with 3ft 6in forward fuselage stretch and 56-pax cabin.
HPR.7	Dart Herald 401	8	Military Dart Herald for Malaysian AF with rear paratroop door.
HP.137	Jetstream 1	38	Low-wing pressurised 18-pax commuter airliner with retractable tricycle u/c and powered by two 850shp Turboméca Astazou XIV turboprops. 12,500 lb. TOGW Prot. G-ATXH (c/n 198) FF. 18 Aug. 1967.
HP.137	Jetstream 2	4	Jetstream 1 with Astazou XVI engines.
HP.137	Jetstream 3M	1	Jetstream for U.S. Air Force as C-10 with 895 shp Garrett TPE331 engines, rear cargo door and strengthened cargo floor. 14,500 lb. TOGW. Prot. G-AWBR (c/n 258) FF. 21 Nov. 1968. 10 airframes not completed.
HP.137	Jetstream T1	5	Jetstream 2 crew trainer for RAF with 14,000 lb. TOGW. Built by Scottish Aviation with initial batch of five from completed HP airframes, 14 using HP fuselages and five new-build.

ILYUSHIN   SOVIET UNION

Although he died in 1977, Sergei Ilyushin gave his name to one of the most famous Russian aircraft design bureaux and conceived transport aircraft which were to become the backbone of Aeroflot's fleet. In the early 1930s Ilyushin produced a series of bomber aircraft of advanced all-metal monocoque design which led to the famous Il-12 Shturmovik ground-attack aircraft of the Second World War.

With an eye to the needs of the Soviet Union under conditions of peace, Ilyushin turned his attention to fulfilling an official specification for a medium capacity transport aircraft. The resultant design was a very modern low-wing aircraft – the Il-12 – which was intended as a replacement for the Lisunov Li-2 (Russian DC-3) but differed from that aircraft in having a tricycle undercarriage. The Il-12 was a large aircraft and the design incorporated advanced features such as de-icing through heated wing leading edges. Unfortunately, the Il-12 was overweight and underpowered and, while originally intended to carry up to thirty-two passengers, it operated normally with a maximum of twenty-one seats. Despite this, the Il-12 became the principal equipment on Aeroflot's routes throughout the Soviet Union and was delivered to the Soviet Air Force in large numbers. Several were delivered to satellite countries of the USSR including batches for the Polish airline LOT and Ceskoslovenskie Aerolinie (CSA). A good number of the 600-odd Il-12s built at Tashkent were converted to freighters with the addition of large double cargo doors on the port side.

Ilyushin Il-12

Ilyushin Il-14, SP-LNN

The shortcomings of the Il-12 were evident to Ilyushin and the design bureau embarked on a major redesign which resolved many of the problems. A completely new and more efficient wing was produced, engine power was increased and the exhaust system altered to incorporate rear thrust augmentation pipes, a new square tail replaced the triangular fin of the Il-12 and the Il-14 was fitted with improved slotted flaps. The result was an aircraft with improved performance and the ability to carry up to thirty-two passengers – although many aircraft still operated with eighteen or twenty-four seats. The Il-14 entered production in 1953, entering service with the Soviet Air Force in 1954 and with Aeroflot in the following year. The Il-14 was exported to TABSO in Bulgaria, CSA, LOT, Malev, Jugoslovenski Aerotransport, CAAC and to the East German Deutsche Lufthansa. Production of the Il-14 was centred at Plant GAZ-34 in Tashkent and at GAZ-301 at Khodinka in the suburbs of Moscow. The aircraft was also built under licence by Avia at Letnany in Czechoslovakia as the Avia-14 and at the Dresden factory of VEB in East Germany. In the case of Avia, the Il-14 design was substantially improved with the introduction of a pressurised version, the Avia-14 Super, which was exported to several other users. It has been suggested that the Il-14 was also built in China but this is almost certainly incorrect.

During the early 1950s, the Ilyushin Bureau was heavily engaged on development of the Il-28 and Il-54 military bombers but, in 1954 they made a return to transport aircraft with the Il-18 which was required by Aeroflot to serve short haul routes and secondary airfields which were unsuitable for the Tu-104. The Il-18 designation had already been used for a sixty-passenger airliner prototype which was built in 1947 but the designation was revived for the new airliner and it was to become the standard workhorse of the Aeroflot system. The Il-18 first flew in July 1957 and after two years of development it entered service with Aeroflot on the route from Moscow to Alma Ata in April 1959. Approximately 30 are still in service with the domestic Aeroflot system and the new airlines in Russia including Domodedovo Airlines. The Il-18 was widely used by airlines in the Warsaw Pact countries and some remain in operation with Balkan Bulgarian and Romavia. It was a modern pressurised design with a low wing and four turboprop engines which could seat eighty passengers in high density configuration. The Il-18 was also built for the military forces and production included the specialised maritime patrol Il-38 and an electronic surveillance version designated Il-20. By 1969, when the production line was closed, 569 examples of the standard transport Il-18 had been completed at the Khodinka plant.

With the successful introduction of the Il-18, the reputation of Ilyushin was established in the transport aircraft field and all future activities of the Bureau were concentrated in this area. The next major project was to meet the urgent need for a long-range jet airliner capable of operating on long-haul internal routes in the Soviet Union such as Moscow to Vladivostock and Novosibirsk and on Aeroflot's international services. There was an

Ilyushin Il-18, RA-75462

increasing requirement to serve destinations such as Havana, Delhi, Montreal and New York. Accordingly, Ilyushin designed the Il-62 which closely resembled the Vickers VC-10 with a low wing, T-tail and a cluster of four engines in two pairs on the rear fuselage.

The prototype Il-62 made its first flight at the beginning of 1961 and the type entered service after a rather prolonged test period in the spring of 1967. The Il-62 was strictly a commercial design and was not delivered in any numbers to the Soviet military forces but it was sold to foreign users such as Cubana, CSA, CAAC, Egypt Air and LOT. Production was handled by the GAZ-22 factory at Kazan and the last of 281 production Il-62s left the production line in the summer of 1993. With the break-up of Aeroflot in the early 1990s, the existing Il-62 fleet was dispersed among a variety of operators and major current users of the type are Domodedovo Airlines, Orient Avia and Uzbekistan Airways.

One of Ilyushin's most important designs is the Il-76 freighter which made its first flight at Khodinka in March 1971. With the An-12 becoming obsolete there was a requirement for a modern jet cargo aircraft to meet the needs of the Soviet forces and to handle Aeroflot's expanding demand for freight capacity. Ilyushin's design team produced a pressurised aircraft with a high-set wing mounting four podded Soloviev D-30KP turbofans. The high wing was mounted on a substantial raised centre section resulting in an unobstructed internal load compartment which was accessed through clamshell doors below the rear fuselage.

In time-honoured fashion, the Il-76 had a glazed section beneath the nose to house the navigator's station and some military versions also had a tail turret. Many Il-76s have been delivered for military use and have been widely modified. More than forty have been converted by Beriev as the A-50 for the AEW role with a pylon-mounted rear fuselage rotodome and associated radars and sensors. Civilian applications include fire fighting. The Il-76 continues in production at GAZ-84 at Tashkent-Chkalowa and at Khodinka although the rate of production is now reduced. Ilyushin has also built a prototype of the Il-76MF in the hope of regenerating demand and this variant has a stretched fuselage and may be built with CFM-56 turbofans if the necessary interest is forthcoming.

In order to meet the challenge posed by the new western wide-body airliners, the Ilyushin OKB started design work in 1971 on a new large transport aircraft with 350 seats and a range of over 2000 miles. The result was the Il-86 which followed the conventional layout pioneered by the Boeing 707 and '747 with a low wing and four podded turbofans on underwing pylons. As with other wide-bodied airliners, the Il-86 fuselage provided an upper passenger deck and a substantial lower cargo hold. For Aeroflot's domestic passenger routes, Ilyushin used this configuration to provide passenger entrances at lower deck level with storage areas for passengers to carry on their own baggage and internal stairs giving access to the seating section. The Khodinka factory started to build the first examples of the Il-86 in 1979 and production was subsequently transferred to the GAZ-64 factory at Voronezh.

In service, the Il-86 was not wholly satisfactory and was unable to comply with the new international noise standards imposed by FAR Part 36/II. It also suffered from excessive fuel consumption which made the aircraft uneconomic. This led to production being discontinued in 1995 and some of the 102 units built have been re-engined with CFM-56 or Aviadvigatel PS-90A turbofans. As a consequence of the problems with the Il-86, Ilyushin embarked on a major redesign of the aircraft. This resulted in what was virtually a completely new aircraft and included a new supercritical wing with wingtip winglets and redesigned flaps and leading edge slats, elimination of the lower-deck passenger boarding system, fly-by-wire control systems, modified tail and undercarriage and new engines. The new Il-96 was offered in standard (Il-96-300) form or as the stretched Il-96M and started to be delivered from the Voronezh plant in 1992 to fulfil a twenty-aircraft order from Aeroflot Russian International Airlines, for Domodedovo Airlines and for Russian Government use. Around thirteen production examples had been completed by the end of 1997 and future operators include Transaero which has ordered six Il-96Ts.

At the other end of the transport scale is the Il-114 regional turboprop airliner which has had an extended development history and is now completing in-service trials with Uzbekistan Airways. Initiated in 1983, the Il-114 is a sixty-four seat aircraft of very similar appearance to the BAe. ATP (Jetstream 61) and it first flew in 1990 powered by Klimov TV7 engines. Russian type certification was received in April 1997 and it is intended that production will be undertaken by the Tashkent Aircraft Production Association factory in Uzbekistan. Ilyushin has also flown a cargo version of the Il-114 and has plans to build a version powered by Pratt & Whitney PW127 engines for American and European airline customers. However, the future of this project is still very dependent on funds being available from the cash-starved airlines of the CIS. Ilyushin is also working on a new high-wing twin turboprop aircraft, designated Il-112 which is intended as a replacement for the large fleet of LET-410s currently in local service in the CIS but this is expected to be a fairly long-term programme.

Production Details

The system of serial numbers used on Ilyushin aircraft has followed the familiar Soviet method of production batches and individual serials within those batches. Generally, the numbers also include a prefix identifying the aircraft type or, in the case of the Il-86 and Il-96, a four or five digit number which is believed to be the project number. Individual serials for the Il-76 are the apparently randomly-generated four-digit computer numbers which have been adopted for other production types. Details of the different serial number systems are as follows.

Ilyushin Il-62M, RA-86126

Il-76TD, RA-76800

Model	C/n example	Details of Serial numbers
Il-12	93013515	Year built (1 digit, e.g. 9 = 1949); Factory (3 digits, e.g. 301 = Tashkent); Batch number (2 digits, e.g. 35); Individual aircraft (2 digits, e.g. 15).
Il-14	4340507	Year built (1 digit, e.g. 4 = 1954); Factory (2 digits, e.g. 34 = Tashkent); Batch number (2 digits, e.g. 05); Individual aircraft (2 digits, e.g. 07).
Il-14	146000715	Khodinka production. Type (2 digits, i.e. 14); Year built (1 digit, e.g. 6 = 1956); Batch (4 digits, e.g. 0007); Individual aircraft (2 digits, e.g. 15).
Avia 14	42704105	Line number (2 digits, e.g. 42); Year built (1 digit, e.g. 7 = 1957); Batch number (2 digits, e.g. 04); Czech production identifier (1); Individual aircraft (2 digits, e.g. 05).
VEB-14	14803056	Type (2 digits, i.e. 14); Unknown (possibly project number) 8030; Individual aircraft (2 digits, e.g. 56).
Il-18	181002901	Type (2 digits, i.e. 18); Year built (1 digit, e.g. 1 = 1961); Batch (4 digits, e.g. 0029); Individual aircraft (2 digits, e.g. 01).
Il-62	31505	Year Built (1 digit, e.g. 3 = 1973); Batch (2 digits, e.g. 15); Individual aircraft (2 digits, e.g. 05).
Il-76	1003403121	Decade and year built (3 digits, e.g. 100 = 1990); Factory (2 digits, e.g. 34 = Tashkent); Individual aircraft (5 digit computer random number).
Il-86	51483209084	Project number (6 digits, 514832); Year built (2 digits, e.g. 09 = 1989); Individual aircraft (2 digits, e.g. 84).
Il-96	7439201007	Project number (5 digits, 74392); Batch (2 digits, e.g. 01) Individual aircraft (3 digits, e.g. 007).

Model Information

The following details are available on Ilyushin post-war transport aircraft.

Type No.	No. Built	Notes
Il-12	663	Low-wing all-metal unpressurised 21-passenger transport with retractable tricycle u/c, triangular vertical tail and powered by two 1650 h.p. Shvetsov Ash-82FN radial engines. 38,030 lb. TOGW. Prot. FF. 15 Aug. 1945. NATO name 'Coach'.
Il-12B		Il-12 with modified de-icing, dorsal fin fairing etc. Main production variant.
Il-12D		Military tactical transport version with dorsal gun turret, parachute door, hardened interior etc.
Il-12T		Cargo version of Il-12 with port rear double freight doors and strengthened cabin floor.
Il-14	839	Il-12 with new constant-taper wing, enlarged square tail fin, modified engine nacelles with overwing exhaust stacks, improved deicing system and powered by two 1900 h.p. Shvetsov Ash-82T engines. 38,580 lb. TOGW. Prot. FF. 15 Jul. 1950. NATO name 'Crate'.
Il-14D		Military Il-14 with 30 utility seats.
Il-14P		Production commercial Il-14 with 18 seats. Also Il-14P-24, Il-14P-28 and Il-14P-32 with 24, 28 and 32 seats.
Il-14M		Il-14 with 3ft 4in fuselage stretch and extra cabin window each side to give max 36-pax capacity.
Il-14PS		8-seat VIP version of Il-14P with deluxe interior.
Il-14S		VIP version with provision for higher density interior and with improved avionics and pax oxygen.
Il-14T		Military cargo version with port side rear double freight doors and inset parachute door. Other specific military models included Il-14FK for photo mapping, LIK-1 for flight research, Il-14TD for parachute dropping, Il-14TS ambulance aircraft, Il-14RR fishery patrol version.
Il-14G		Civil version of Il-14T without parachute door.
VEB Il-14P	80	Il-14P built in East Germany by DDR. Prot. DDR-AVF, FF. Apl. 1956.

Ilyushin Il-86, RA-86065

Type No.	No. Built	Notes
Avia-14P	203	Il-14P built by Avia in Czechoslovakia.
Avia-14-32A		Avia-14 upgraded to 32-passenger capacity.
Avia-14T		All cargo version of Avia-14 similar to Il-14G.
Avia-14 Super		42-pax pressurised version of Avia-14P fitted with wingtip tanks.
Avia-14 Salon		Avia-14-32A with deluxe VIP interior.
Il-18	1	Low-wing 66-pax pressurised transport with low wing and four 2300 h.p. Shvetsov ASh-73 radial piston engines. Prot. FF. 17 Aug. 1946.
Il-18	569	Pressurised medium-haul 75-pax airliner with low wing, tricycle u/c and powered by four 4000 shp Kuznetsov NK-4 turboprops or 3755 shp Ivchenko AI-20 turboprops. 125,660 lb. TOGW. Prot. CCCP-L5811, FF. 4 Jul. 1957. Sometimes named 'Moskva'. NATO name 'Coot'.
Il-18A		Il-18 with uprated 4000 shp AI-20 engines, 89-pax interior and aerodynamic modifications. 127,870 lb. TOGW.
Il-18B		Il-18A with strengthened structure and 134,900 lb. TOGW giving increased payload.
Il-18D		Il-18B with 4250 shp AI-20M engines, improved avionics and increased fuel capacity. Some aircraft converted for special test work as Il-18LL etc.
Il-18E		High density 120-seat version of Il-18D.
Il-18V		Il-18D with modified three-cabin interior and re-sited cabin entry doors.
Il-20DSR		Military ELINT version of Il-18 with external SLAR antenna.
Il-22		Military flying command post version of Il-18.
Il-38	100	Maritime reconnaissance version of Il-18 without windows, fitted with MAD tail, radome under forward fuselage, lengthened dorsal fin and wing positioned forward on fuselage. NATO name 'May'.

Ilyushin Il-114, RA-91002

Ilyushin Il-96M, RA-96000

Type No.	No. Built	Notes
Il-62	281	Intercontinental pressurised 186-pax jet airliner with low wing set to rear of fuselage, T-tail, tricycle u/c and four 23,150 lb.s.t. Kuznetsov NK-8-4 turbofans in podded pairs on rear fuselage. 347,220 lb. TOGW. Prot. CCCP-06156 FF. 3 Jan. 1961. NATO name 'Classic'.
Il-62M		Il-62 with 198-pax seating, additional fuel tanks in fin, improved nav/comm equipment and 25,350 lb.s.t. Soloviev D-30KU turbofans with thrust reversal. 363,760 lb. TOGW.
Il-62MK		Il-62M with strengthened airframe, remodelled cabin, enlarged u/c and 368,170 lb. TOGW.
Il-76	450	Heavy cargo aircraft with anhedralled high wing, T-tail, ventral loading doors, partly glazed nose with chin radar, four-bogie main u/c and powered by four 26,455 lb.s.t. Aviadvigatel (Soloviev) D-30KP turbofans in pylon-mounted underwing pods. 346,125 lb. TOGW. Prot. CCCP-86712 FF. 25 Mar. 1971. NATO name 'Candid'.
Il-76T		Production civil Il-76 with additional centre-section fuel tank and extra internal cargo handling gantries.
Il-76M		Production military Il-76 with ECM jammer/receivers, tail gun turret and u/c fairing mounted 50 mm guns. 374,785 lb. TOGW.
Il-76TD		Il-76T with Aviadvigatel (Soloviev) D-30KP-1 engines, 418,878 lb. TOGW and increased fuel capacity.
Il-76MD		Il-76M with D-30KP-1 engines.
Il-76MF		Il-76TD with fuselage stretch of 21ft 8in, increased fuel capacity and powered by four 35,300 lb.s.t. Aviadvigatel (Soloviev) PS-90A76 turbofans. 462,970 lb. TOGW.
Il-78		Il-76MD modified as convertible freighter/in-flight refuelling tanker. NATO name 'Midas'.
Il-78M		Il-78 non-convertible dedicated tanker.
Il-86-300	102	Wide-body low-wing airliner with double-deck fuselage incorporating lower deck pax. entry, powered by four 29,320 lb.s.t. Samara NK-86 turbofans (or Aviadvigatel PS-90A or CFM56). Prot. CCCP-86000 FF. 22 Dec. 1976. 'Camber'.

Type No.	No. Built	Notes
Il-96	15	Long-haul wide body airliner based on Il-86 with new wing with wingtip winglets, no lower deck pax access, fuselage shortened by 29ft 3in, redesigned tail unit, FBW controls and powered by four 35,275 lb.s.t. Aviadvigatel PS-90A turbofans. 476,200 lb. TOGW. Prot. CCCP-96000 FF. 28 Sep. 1988.
Il-96M	1	Il-96 with 28ft 2in fuselage stretch giving 386-pax capacity, modified vertical tail and powered by four 38,250 lb.s.t. Pratt & Whitney PW2337 turbofans. Il-96 prot (CCCP-96000) converted and FF. 6 Apl. 1993.
Il-96MK		Proposed Il-96 with NK-93 propfan engines.
Il-96T		Freighter version of Il-96M. Prot. RA-96101.
Il-96-500		Proposed two-deck version of Il-96.
Il-112		Proposed pressurised high-wing 32-pax local service airliner powered by two Klimov TV7-117 turboprops.
Il-114	6	Low-wing pressurised 64-pax regional airliner with retractable tricycle u/c and powered by two 2500 shp Klimov TV7/117-3 turboprops with six-blade propellers. 50,045 lb. TOGW. Prot. CCCP-54000 FF. 29 Mar. 1990.
Il-114PC		Proposed Il-114 powered by two Pratt & Whitney PW127F engines.
Il-114T	1	Il-114 freighter with cabin windows deleted, hardened interior and freight floor and cargo door in port rear fuselage. Prot. RA-91005.

Ilyushin Il-76MF, IS-76900

LET   CZECH REPUBLIC

The present day Let company, based at Kunovice in the Czech Republic has its origins in the pre-war Czechoslovak aviation industry which was composed of six major companies – Aero, Avia, Benes-Mraz, Letov, Praga and Zlinska Letecka. The post-war reorganisation which brought Czechoslovakia into the Soviet sphere gave rise to a reorganisation in 1949, which brought all the country's motor vehicle and aircraft manufacturing under a state holding company known as the Ceskoslovenske Zavody Automobilove a Letecke ('CZAL'). In the early stages, CZAL built a wide variety of gliders and powered light aircraft designed by the original factories but, in 1950, responsibilities were divided through the establishment of three new companies – Moravan, Let (sometimes styled as LET) and Aero. Moravan and Let were, broadly, dedicated to civil aircraft and Aero specialised in military types such as the L-29 Delfin and L-39 Albatross jet trainers.

In 1966, Let embarked on the design of a small feeder airliner to meet the needs of the widely spread communities in the Soviet Union and urgently required as a replacement for the elderly Il-12s then in service. The result was the XL-410 which flew in the spring of 1969. The fifteen-passenger Let-410A Turbolet then entered production at Kunovice with the first examples going to the domestic operator, Slov-Air. Let also started on the first aircraft to meet a huge order for Aeroflot and these started to be delivered in 1972. In the case of early production L-410As the powerplant was the widely used Pratt & Whitney PT6 turboprop but the Czech aero-engine manufacturer, Walter, developed a very similar engine designated M-601 and the L-410M was introduced in 1974 with this engine. The Turbolet became widely used in the Warsaw Pact countries and was also delivered to the air forces of the Soviet Union, Poland, East Germany and Czechoslovakia. A handful were exported elsewhere, notably to Kenya, Equatorial Guinea and Sao Tome.

1979 saw the Turbolet updated as the L-410UVP with a larger fuselage and tail, dihedralled tailplane, longer-span wing and improved systems including an anti-skid braking system, automatic pitch trim and a modified propeller feathering system. It was a highly flexible aircraft which was configured for many roles including all-freight operations, sport parachute dropping, fire control, navaid calibration, mapping and survey and an ambulance variant with room for six stretcher cases and up to six attendants or seated patients. The subsequent Let-410UVP-E was given increased fuel capacity and a nineteen-passenger interior. The Turbolet continued in production well into the 1990s but the economic collapse of the Soviet Union left Let with sizeable stocks of completed aircraft which Aeroflot was unable to pay for and as a consequence production of the Let-410 trickled to a halt with over 1100 aircraft having been produced by the beginning of 1996. Aeroflot's existing fleet has progressively become inactive as spares for the Turbolets have run out. Let is still developing the Let-420 version of the Turbolet and is expecting to gain FAA certification under FAR23/41 during 1998.

COMMERCIAL AIRCRAFT AND AIRLINERS

In 1977, Aeroflot issued a specification for a new local service airliner with greater capacity than the Turbolets which were the backbone of their regional fleet. A twenty-five/thirty-seater was required and this prompted Let to design the L-610. The L-610 was, again, a high-wing aircraft with a retractable undercarriage using fuselage-mounted pods for the main gear and featuring a T-tail. The pressurised cabin is fitted with forty passenger seats in twin rows with a centre aisle but a mixed passenger/cargo version with sixteen seats to the rear is available as is an all-cargo variant. The prototype was flown in December 1988 with Czech-built Motorlet M-602 turboprops but, so far, only the military L-610M has been delivered with these engines and the commercial version, the L-610G, is powered by General Electric CT7-9D engines with five-blade Hamilton Standard propellers. This version is targeted at Western markets and will be fitted with a Rockwell Collins EFIS and avionics suite. At the end of 1997, development of the L-610 was progressing slowly, being limited by the funding problems faced by Let. This may be resolved by the acquisition of Let by the American company, Ayres, which was completed in late 1998.

Production Details

Serial numbers for the Let-410 followed the standard Czech and eastern bloc system which combined details of the year built and the production batch with an individual aircraft serial. The prototype Let XL-410 was c/n 69001 which indicated the year built (1969), the batch (00) and the individual aircraft identity (01). Five prototype aircraft were included in this first batch and production aircraft started in 1971 at c/n 710101 with most production batches containing twenty aircraft and the last L-410M having serial number c/n 781120. With introduction of the L-410UVP, Let started a new series of batches with production aircraft starting at c/n 770101. By 1994, L-410UVP production had reached Batch 27 (922730) although the Kunovice factory completed a number of additional airframes for later completion when orders are received. The L-610 prototypes and pre-production aircraft followed a similar system, starting at c/n 8800001.

Model Information

Details of all models are shown overleaf. Production totals are given for the basic production variant in each case and the total includes the sub-variants.

LET-410UVP, UR-67477

LET L-610G, OK-CZD

Type No.	Name	No. Built	Notes
XL-410		5	High-wing 15-pax. civil or light tactical military transport with retractable tricycle u/c, cruciform tail and powered by two 715 shp Pratt & Whitney PT6A-27 turboprops. 11,245 lb. TOGW. Prot. OK-YKE (c/n 690001) FF. 16 Apl. 1969.
L-410A	Turbolet	30	Initial production L-410 for max 19-pax with PT6A-27 engines, seven (instead of eight) cabin windows each side, port rear pax/cargo door and minor changes. 11,905 lb. TOGW.
L-410AB	Turbolet		L-410A fitted with 4-blade Hartzell propellers.
L-410AF	Turbolet		One L-410A (HA-YFA) with nine cabin windows each side and extended glazed nose for aerial photo-survey work.
L-410AS	Turbolet		L-410A with avionics as required by Aeroflot.
L-410M	Turbolet	115	L-410A with two 550 shp Motorlet M601A turboprops.
L-410FG			Special military version of Czech AF. Also L-410T.
L-410MA	Turbolet		L-410 with two 730 shp M601B engines.
L-410MU	Turbolet		L-410M with avionics and equipment required by Aeroflot.
L-410UVP	Turbolet	950	L-410M with 1ft 7in fuselage stretch, enlarged wing with spoilers, larger vertical tail and dihedralled tailplane, anti-skid braking, prop auto-feather and improved cockpit systems. Prot OK-166 (c/n 770001) FF. 1 Nov. 1977.
L-410UVP-E	Turbolet		L-410UVP with wingtip fuel tanks, four extra seats and repositioned toilet, improved systems, increased flap deflection and 750 shp M.601E engines with five-bladed Avia V.510 propellers. 14,110 lb. TOGW. Sub-variants designated UVP-E1, UVP-E2, UVP-E3, UVP-E4, UVP-E9, UVP-E20 etc. depending on customer.

Type No.	Name	No. Built	Notes
L-410UVP-E20		1	L-410UVP-E with two 778 shp Motorlet M.601F engines, central point refuelling, auto beta-range propeller locks, and Bendix-King avionics. 14,550 lb. TOGW. Prot. OK-150 FF. 15 Nov. 1993. Redesignated L-420.
L-420			Revised designation for L-410VP-E20.
L-430			Proposed L-410UVP-E with PT6A turboprops and increased weights.
L-610		2	High-wing 40-pax pressurised transport with retractable tricycle u/c, T-tail and powered by two 1823 shp Motorlet M602 turboprops. 31,970 lb. TOGW. Prot. OK-130/OK-TZB (c/n 880001) FF. 30 Dec. 1988.
L-610G		3	Commercial version of L-610 with 1750 shp General Electric CT7-9D turboprops.
L-610M		6	Military version of L-610 with M602 engines.

LET L-410AF, HA-YFA

LET-410UVP-E14, 2312, Czech AF

LOCKHEED   UNITED STATES

Lockheed's successful wartime role in aircraft production was a continuation of the work which had gone on during the 1930s in developing the Model 10, the Model 12 and the Model 14 twin-engined transports. The Model 14 became the Model 18 Lodestar and then the Hudson and Ventura patrol bombers. Lockheed also built the Lightning twin-boomed fighter and, as war was reaching its end, the first successful American jet fighter, the P-80 Shooting Star, went into production. Even before the war had started, however, Lockheed had established a strong line of experience in transport aircraft design and manufacture. In 1942, Lockheed had initiated the 204-seat Model 89 Constitution project for the U.S. Navy which was primarily intended to meet a Pan American Airways specification and resulted in two prototypes being flown just after the end of the war. However, it was a requirement from Trans World Airlines which resulted in the company's most successful postwar piston engined transcontinental airliner.

Named the Model 49 Excalibur, the airliner was to be fully pressurised and to this end it had a circular section fuselage with a curving contour to maximise aerodynamic efficiency. The aircraft, which was soon renamed Constellation, had a low wing mounting four Pratt & Whitney Double Wasp radial engines and a three-finned tail unit which would allow the aircraft, which stood high on its tricycle undercarriage, to fit into hangars which had been made for an earlier generation of airliners. An alternative version of the

L.1011-1, VR-HOB

L-049 Constellation, 4X-AKB

Constellation was to be fitted with Wright Double Cyclone engines and, in fact, it was this powerplant which was used on all but the prototype aircraft. As it turned out, the United States was being drawn into the war and the initial batch of Constellations under construction at Lockheed's Burbank plant were rescheduled as C-69 military transports and the prototype which flew in January 1943 wore military camouflage.

By the end of the war, eighteen C-69s had been completed and Lockheed went on to build a further batch, designated L-049, for commercial sale to TWA and to BOAC and other international airlines. The -049 was tailored for the needs of the individual customers and in high density form they could carry up to eighty-one passengers. The definitive civil Constellation was the Model 649 which had more powerful engines and was better equipped to provide the comfort required by civil passengers. In practice, the majority of aircraft ordered as Model 649 were delivered as the longer range Model 749. Eastern Airlines was the first recipient of the Model 649 in March 1947 and deliveries of the 749 followed to Transcontinental and Western, Air France, KLM and Qantas. In total, 145 of the 649/749 series were built by the time the last delivery took place in September 1951. Constellations were employed on transatlantic services by Air France with a technical stop at Gander or Shannon and KLM operated from Amsterdam to New York and on to Curacao via Prestwick and Gander.

Pressure from the airlines and from Lockheed's direct competitor, Douglas, led to further developments of the Constellation being considered. The Model 1049 was a lengthened Model 049/749 and, indeed, the prototype was the original -049 prototype with two new sections totalling 18ft 5in spliced in ahead of and behind the wing. The L.1049 could carry up to ninety-two passengers and in commercial production form was powered by four Wright turbo compound engines. Lockheed was also successful in selling almost 400 Super Constellations to the United States military forces as the C-121 and R7V and as the airborne early warning WV-2 (RC-121D) with its prominent roof and belly mounted radomes. The Super Constellation was sold in several different versions including the L1049D freighter which was fitted with a large upward opening cargo door in the port rear fuselage and the long-range L.1049G which was normally equipped with wingtip fuel tanks. Super Constellations started to be delivered to Eastern Airlines in the spring of 1952 and other early users included TWA, KLM, Air France, Trans Canada, Qantas, Air India and Seaboard and Western who were the main operator of the L.1049D. These variants became the backbone of the North Atlantic routes although technical refuelling stops were still required at Prestwick, Shannon or Gander. 183 examples of the commercial L.1049 series were completed by the time production closed in late-1958. The

L.1049 was followed in 1957 by forty-four examples of the L.1649A Starliner which received a completely new wing with straight taper as compared with the eliptical surfaces of the earlier Constellations. However, by this time turboprop airliners were becoming available and the first Boeing 707 pure-jet airliner was on the brink of delivery to Pan Am. The last Starliner was handed over to Air France in February 1958, bringing to an end the remarkable Constellation line.

With major military programmes in hand, Lockheed did not follow Boeing and Douglas into the heavy jet transport business but they had initiated a new short/medium haul turboprop design intended for domestic route operations by American Airlines and Eastern Airlines. The low-wing L.188 Electra was somewhat larger than the Vickers Viscount, which had captured a substantial order from Capital Airlines, and it had almost twice the range. The Electra was powered by four Allison 501D turboprops which meant that Lockheed could draw on a great deal of test information derived during the development of the military C-130 Hercules.

The first Electra flew from Burbank in December 1957, the type certification being received in August of the following year. The Electra order book filled up rapidly with the Eastern and American orders supplemented by batches of four for Qantas, eight for Pacific Southwest, twelve for KLM and eleven for Braniff. Eastern received the first production Electra out of forty-one on order in October 1958 and despite the arrival of DC-9s in later years the L.188s fulfilled an important role on Eastern's shuttle routes between Boston, New York and Washington. In total, 171 aircraft were built with the last example being delivered to Garuda in January 1961. After service with the main line operators, Electras moved on to smaller carriers such as Aerocondor in Colombia, COPA of Panama, Reeve Aleutian and the Danish operator, Sterling Airways. However, the Electra became most popular as a freighter with users such as Zantop, Overseas National and Universal Airlines and a number were sold to travel clubs such as Ports of Call which were attracted by the strong and capacious aircraft. Lockheed also capitalised on the L.188 airframe by developing the P-3 Orion maritime patrol aircraft which was sold in large numbers to the United States Navy and the air forces of Canada, Norway, Australia and The Netherlands.

With major military work in hand, Lockheed had not followed Boeing, Douglas and Convair in developing a four-jet intercontinental transport and, by pinning their civil aircraft strategy on the turboprop Electra, they lost their place on the commercial ladder. In the early 1960s, they became involved in the bidding process for a new heavy military transport. This was successfully won with their C-141 Starlifter design and, when the U.S. Air Force issued a requirement for an even larger transport under the CX-HLS competition in 1964, Lockheed was able to win again with its C-5A Galaxy. The competition for this requirement was fierce and Lockheed was up against Boeing with the '747 and with Douglas which proposed an aircraft which eventually became the DC-10. Despite the loss of the C-5 competition, Boeing decided to press ahead with the '747 as a commercial programme and this opened up the concept of the civil widebody airliner. Lockheed had completed Electra production and realised that it needed to leapfrog the Boeing 707/DC-8 generation of airliners and produce a widebody aircraft if it was to remain in the civil market. They had attempted to market the C-141 as a civil freighter without success and it was clear that their latest military monster, the C-5A, would not offer a suitable basis for a commercial passenger transport.

By 1966, Lockheed was studying a new 250-passenger aircraft to meet the requirements of trunk carriers such as TWA and American on medium haul sectors such as New York to Atlanta and Chicago to Los Angeles. This was the market being addressed by Douglas with the DC-10 and the first order by American Airlines was awarded to Douglas in competition with Lockheed's proposed L-1011. The L-1011 TriStar was similar to the DC-10 in having two wing pylon-mounted turbofans and a third engine in the tail – although the Lockheed design had the engine buried in the rear fuselage rather than having it mounted on the fin in the manner selected for the DC-10. Unlike the DC-10, the TriStar was designed from the outset to use the Rolls-Royce RB.211 powerplant and this brought major difficulties to Lockheed when Rolls-Royce collapsed in 1971, although the engine manufacturer was reconstituted and went on to develop new variants of the RB.211 and the later Trent 'super turbofan'.

Lockheed obtained TWA as a launch customer with an initial requirement for thirty-three aircraft and eleven options and this was followed by orders from Eastern and from the Air Holdings Group which represented a number of airlines including British Airways, Air Canada and Cathay Pacific which all became major TriStar operators. Following the first flight of the prototype on 16 November 1970 Lockheed pressed ahead with certification which was completed on 14 April 1972. The first version of the TriStar was the medium range L-1011-1, the first of which joined Eastern Airlines in April 1972 but the market was also opening up for an intercontinental aircraft with smaller capacity than the Boeing 747 and this resulted in long-range models from both Lockheed and Douglas. The TriStar 500 featured a shortened fuselage and increased fuel capacity and was placed in service by several major carriers including British Airways, Delta, Pan American and TAP. The TriStar has given good service to its customer airlines but was not as successful in the market as the DC-10 – nor did it benefit from the substantial military orders achieved by the Douglas aircraft. The Palmdale, California line was finally closed in 1983 with delivery of the 250th L-1011 to the Algerian Government.

Lockheeds' longest-running success story has been the C-130 Hercules. Initiated to meet USAF requirements in 1951, the high-wing four turboprop Hercules was first flown in August 1954 and went into production at the Lockheed Georgia Division plant at Marietta, Georgia. The C-130 has gone through many variants and many applications and it flies with nearly every significant air force outside the CIS. While it was primarily a military aircraft, the Hercules also had a clear role as a commercial freighter and Lockheed started to market the L-100 civil version in the mid 1960s. This was, essentially, a C-130E with all military equipment removed and powered by a civil version of the military Allison T56 turboprop. The most popular version was the L-100-30 (382G) which had a stretched fuselage and some aircraft were operated as combined passenger/ freighters with a forward section for thirty-five passengers with a galley and lavatory and a rear cargo section. A version with a ninety-seven-seat high-density pallet-mounted interior and eleven cabin windows each side has also been certificated and this has been operated in Indonesia by Merpati Nusantara. The civil Hercules has been used by a wide variety of companies including Airlift International, Aboitiz Air Transport in the Philippines, Angola Air Charter, Heavylift, Pacific Western and Safair Freighters in South Africa.

Production Details

The serial numbers allocated by Lockheed to their various civil production aircraft are as follows.

Models	Batch
L-049	c/n 1961 to 1980, c/n 2021 to 2088 (inc. one Model 549).
L-649, L-749, L-749A	c/n 2503 to 2590 (excl. 2507 to 11, 2516, 17, 36, 37, 39, 42, 43, 63, 67, 68, 69, 70, 71, 74, 75, 76).
L-749A, C-121A	c/n 2600 to 2677.
L-1049	c/n 4001 to 4024, c/n 4501 to 4565, c/n 4572 to 4687 (excl. 4608, 9, 38), c/n 4801 to 4853.
L-1049 (Military)	c/n 4101 to 4202, c/n 4301 to 4499 (WV-2 & C/RC-121), c/n 5500 to 5522 (WV-2).
L-1649	c/n 1001 to 1045 (excl 1043).
L-188	c/n 1001 to 1149, c/n 2001 to 2022.
L-1011	c/n 1001 to 1250.
L-082 to L-382	c/n 1001 to 1002, c/n 3001 to 3231, c/n 3501 to 5435, c/n 5436 up (C-130J).

L-1649A Starliner, LV-GLI

Model Information

Lockheed designations for the Constellation series consisted of three parts and a typical type number for a Model 749 would be c/n 749-79-31. The first part identified the basic model, the second part (Engine Type Code) identified the engines with which it was fitted and the third part (Configuration Code) showed the interior layout and equipment as specified by the customer. While many of the configuration codes were an accurate guide to the identity of the original customer some of the internal layouts were adopted by several customers. The second and third parts of an individual designation are not used in day-to-day reference. This system was also carried on through the Electra series. For convenience, the following table of the piston-engined Lockheed types includes only the model designations and details of the engine type codes and customer codes are given separately.

Type No.	Name	No. Built	Notes
L.049	Constellation	87	Low-wing pressurised military-spec air transport with streamlined circular-section fuselage, tricycle u/c and triple-fin tail unit. Powered by four 2200 h.p. Wright C18-BA1 (or -BA2 or -BA3) radial piston engines (or Wright 739C18-BA1 or -BA2). 86,250 lb. TOGW. Civil and military sales. Military C-69. Prot. NX25600 (c/n 1961) FF. 9 Jan. 1943.
L.049A	Constellation		L.049 with strengthened u/c and wing centre section. 90,000 lb. TOGW.
L.049B	Constellation		L.049A with further strengthening of structure, modified u/c and 93,000 lb. TOGW.
L.049C	Constellation		L.049B with modified u/c shimmy damper and improved elevator boost control.
L.049D	Constellation		L.049C with strengthened wing, modified nose u/c leg, strengthened forward fuselage and 96,000 lb. TOGW.
L.049E	Constellation		L.049D with strengthened wing centre section and improved main u/c legs. 98,000 lb. TOGW.

Type No.	Name	No. Built	Notes
L.149	Constellation		L.049E retrospectively modified with new Model 749 outer wings incorporating integral long-range tanks and 100,000 lb. TOGW.
L.249	Constellation		Unofficial designation for three El Al long-range Model 049.
L.549	Constellation	1	C-69C 43-pax long range transport for USAF. s/n 42-94561 (c/n 2021).
L.649	Constellation	14	L.049 to commercial specification with strengthened airframe, improved brakes and new u/c, additional fuel tankage and 94,000 lb. TOGW. Many converted to 749A.
L.649A	Constellation	6	L.649 with additional structural strengthening and 98,000 lb. TOGW.
L.749	Constellation	60	Long range L.649 with two additional 565-USG wing tanks and upgraded structure for 102,000 lb. TOGW. Military C-121A/C-121B.
L.749A	Constellation	65	L.749 with strengthened u/c and tyres powered by four 2500 h.p. Wright 749-C18BD-1 engines. Some converted from 749. Military C-121A, VC-121A. U.S. Navy PO-1W radar surveillance version.
L.1049	Super Constellation	89	L.749 with fuselage stretch of 10ft 9in forward and 7ft 8in aft of wing, strengthened structure, improved rudder servo boost system raised cockpit roof. Max 88-pax capacity. Powered by four 2700 h.p. Wright 956-C18CA-1 engines. 120,000 lb. TOGW. Prototype designated 049S NX6700 (c/n 1961S) FF. 13 Oct. 1950. Military C-121G, R7V-1, C-121J.
L.1049A	Super Constellation	167	Military L.1049 for radar picket duty with ventral and dorsal radomes, modified fuselage and strengthened structure and 3250 h.p. Wright 872TC18-DA1 Turbo Compound engines. Designated WV-2, WV-3, RC-121D.

L-188A Electra, XW-PKB (AHS)

Type No.	Name	No. Built	Notes
L.1049B	Super Constellation	55	L.1049A with centre section fuel tanks, cargo doors in front and rear port fuselage, strengthened freight floor, powered by four 3250 h.p. Wright 872-TC18DA-1 Turbo Compounds. 145,000 lb. TOGW. R7V-1 for US Navy and VC-121E for USAF with square cabin windows.
L.1049C	Super Constellation	48	L.1049 max. 82-pax commercial airliner with strengthened wing and fuselage structure, rectangular cabin windows, repositioned passenger doors, new u/c, new fuel management system. powered by four 3250 h.p. Wright 972-TC18DA-1 Turbo Compounds. 133,000 lb. TOGW. Some conversions to L.1049E and L.1049G.
L.1049D	Super Constellation	4	L.1049C commercial cargo variant with cargo doors in front and rear port fuselage, strengthened freight floor and wing structure, improved u/c retraction system and strengthened gear, modified propeller spinners. 135,400 lb. TOGW.
L.1049E	Super Constellation	26	L.1049C with strengthened structure for 150,000 lb. TOGW and minor alterations to engine systems. Some converted to L.1049G.
L.1049F	Super Constellation	33	Military C-121C with 137,000 lb. TOGW, round windows, for USAF. Also VC-121E Presidential transport and JC-121E and EC-121S electronic warfare versions.
L.1049G	Super G Constellation	104	Transatlantic development of L.1049E for max 115-pax. with additional 600-USG wingtip fuel tanks, stronger u/c, wing and tail de-icing, improved soundproofing and 3250 h.p. Wright 972-TC18DA-3 engines.
L.1049H	Super Constellation	53	Convertible pax/cargo version of L.1049G with cargo floor and forward and aft freight doors. 140,000 lb. TOGW.
L.1249A		2	L.1049B converted to Pratt & Whitney T-34-P-6 turboprops as military YC-121F. 150,000 lb. TOGW. 110-pax capacity.
L.1649A	Starliner	44	L.1049G with new longer span wing with straight leading and trailing edges, no tip tanks, lengthened radar nose and powered by four 3400 h.p. Wright 988-TC18EA-2 Turbo Compounds. 99-pax. seating. Prot. N1649 (c/n 1001) FF. 11 Oct. 1956.

The numerical type codes given by Lockheed to the Wright engines used in the Constellation series were as follows: Wright 711C18-BA2 srs (code 46), 739C18-BA1 srs (51), 956C18-CA1 (53), 975C18-CB1 (54), 872TC18-DA1 (55), 972TC18-DA1 (55), 923TC18-DA2 (55), 74C18-BD1 (79), 744C18-BD1 (79), 972TC18-DA3 (82), 988TC18-EA2 (98).

The following table shows Lockheed's configuration codes, as used in the last part of the three-digit designation, and the principal customers. Where several codes are shown for

Lockheed L-100-30 Hercules, 7T-WHA

the same customer, this relates to different seating capacity. In many cases the long-range Constellations had alternative day and night configurations with the night flights carrying fewer passengers in sleeper seats.

Code	Type	Customers	Code	Type	Customers
03	049	TWA	51	749A	TWA
04	049	Pan American	59	049	Capital
10	C-69	USAF	60	649A	Chicago & Southern
12	049	Eastern	63	1049B	Seaboard & Western
19	C-69	USAF	64	1049	TWA
22	649/749	Aerlinte, PanAm, TWA, Air France, KNILM	67	1049	Eastern
			73	749A	Air India
			74	749A	Avianca
25	049	KLM, TWA, Panagra, LAV	80	1049	TWA
26	049	BOAC, Air France, PanAm, KLM, TWA Panair do Brasil	81	1049C	KLM, LAV, TAP, Thai, Varig, Qantas, Iberia, PIA
			83	1049C	Eastern
27	049	American Overseas AL	85	1049D	Seaboard & Western
31	749	Qantas	87	1049C	Air India
32	749A	Aerlinte	90	1049E	KLM
33	749A	Capital, KLM	92	1049E	Avianca
34	749A	LAV	93	1049E	Pasquel
35	749A	Air India	94	1049C	Trans Canada
36	749	USAF	98	1049G	Air France
37	749A	Pan American	99	1049G	Iberia
38	749	USAF	100	1049E	LAV
44	749A	Air India	101	1049G	TWA
45	1049	TWA	102	1049G	Northwest
46	749A	Air France	103	1049C	Pakistan International
50	749A	South African AW	105	1049G	Lufthansa

Code	Type	Customers	Code	Type	Customers
106	1049G	Air India	148	1049H	Flying Tiger, Calif Eastern
107	1049E	KLM			
109	1049G	Trans Canada	151	1049G	KLM
110	1049G	TWA (also model 114)	152	1049H	National
112	1049G	Cubana (also model 115)	153	1049G	Qantas
			156	1049H	Flying Tiger
116	1049D	Seaboard & Western	157	1049H	Pakistan International
118	1049E	Qantas (also model 119)	158	1049G	Varig
			159	1049H	REAL
123	1049G	TAP	160	1049H	TWA
124	1049G	KLM (also model 132), Thai	161	1049G	Trans Canada
			162	1049H	KLM
133	1049H	Qantas	166	1049H	TWA
134	1049G	LAV	167	1049H	Calif. Eastern
140	1049E	Qantas	09	1649A	TWA (also model 20, 22)
142	1049G	Eastern			
143	1049H	US Overseas	11	1949A	Air France
144	1049G	TWA (also model 145, 146)	17	1649A	Lufthansa
147	1049H	Seaboard & Western			

Details of Lockheed's turbine-engined airliners – the Electra and L-1011 TriStar series together with the Hercules, Starlifter and Galaxy freighters are shown in the following table.

Type No.	Name	No. Built	Notes
L-188A	Electra	115	All-metal, pressurised, max. 96-pax. low-wing airliner with tricycle u/c and powered by four 3750 shp Allison 501-D13 turboprops. 113,000 lb. TOGW. Prot. N1881 (c/n 1001) FF. 6 Dec. 1957. Some converted to L-188AF cargo configuration with forward and aft port-side cargo doors and freight floor or L-188PF convertible pax/freighter.
L-188B	Electra		Internal designation for International version of L-188A with modified internal fittings.
L-188C	Electra	55	L-188A with increased fuel capacity and modified nose u/c leg. 116,000 lb. TOGW. Some converted to L-188CF cargo configuration or L-188PF convertible pax/freighter.
L-1011-1	TriStar	163	Wide-body max. 400-pax twin-aisle medium-range airliner with low wing and three 42,000 lb.s.t. Rolls-Royce RB211-22B turbofans mounted in two underslung wing pods and third installation in base of fin. 430,000 lb. TOGW. Prot N1011 (c/n 1001) FF. 16 Nov. 1970.
L-1011-50	TriStar		L-1011-1 converted with strengthened structure to 450,000 lb. TOGW.

Type No.	Name	No. Built	Notes
L-1011-100	TriStar	12	Longer range L-1011-1 with gross weight increased to 466,000 lb. and additional centre section fuel tanks. Some earlier aircraft converted.
L-1011-150	TriStar		L-1011-1 upgraded to 470,000 lb. TOGW.
L-1011-200	TriStar	24	L-1011-100 with 50,000 lb.s.t. RB211-524B4 engines, improved hot and high performance. 474,000 lb. TOGW.
L-1011-250	TriStar		L-1011-1 converted with 50,000 lb.s.t. RB211-524B41 engines, optional extra centre section fuel tanks and 510,000 lb. TOGW.
L-1011-500	TriStar	50	L-1011-200 for 315-pax. capacity with 13ft 6in shorter fuselage and 9ft wingspan increase and modified wing root fairings. 510,000 lb. TOGW. Some converted to freighters with forward port cargo door and cargo floor.
L-082-44	Hercules	2	Military high-wing freighter with fuselage-mounted u/c, ventral tail loading ramp, forward port cargo door and powered by four 3750 shp Allison T56-A-1 turboprops. Prot. YC-130 s/n 53-3396 (c/n 1001) FF. 23 Aug. 1954.
L-182	Hercules C-130A	233	Production C-130A for USAF and other users with increased fuel capacity and 3750 shp Allison T56-A-1A turboprops with 3-blade props. Also C-130D.
L-282	Hercules C-130B	230	C-130A with increased fuel capacity and 4050 shp Allison T56-A-7 turboprops with 4-blade props. Also C-130F.
L-382	Hercules C-130E	491	Long-range C-130B with additional fuel tankage, no forward cargo door, 124,200 lb. TOGW.
L-382	Hercules C-130H	1,129	Developed C-130E with 4508 shp T56-A-15 turboprops and new wing centre section. Also C-130K, C-130T, HC-130N, HC-130P etc.
L-382B	L-100	21	Commercial freighter version of L-382 with military equipment removed. 4050 shp Allison 501-D22 turboprops. 155,000 lb. TOGW. Prot. N1130E (c/n 382-3946) FF. 20 Apl. 1964.
L-382E	L-100-20	27	Commercial L-382B with fuselage stretch of 5ft forward and 3ft 4in aft of wing. Powered by 4508 shp Allison 501-D22A turboprops.
L-382F	L-100-20		L-382B converted to L-100-20 configuration. 4050 shp Allison 501-D22.
L-382G	L-100-30	65	Civil and military L-382F with extra 6ft 8in fuselage stretch. 4508 shp Allison 501-D22A turboprops. 155,000 lb. TOGW. Some converted from 382B and 382E.
L-382U	C-130J-30	12	New generation C-130J Hercules based on C-130H with 15ft fuselage stretch, redesigned EFIS cockpit with HUD, modernised electrical and hydraulic systems, powered by four 4591 shp Allison AE2100D3 turboprops with 6-blade Dowty props. Prot. ZH865 (c/n 5408) FF. 5 Apl. 1996. Civil version to be L-100J.

Type No.	Name	No. Built	Notes
L-300	Starlifter C-141	285	Large high-wing military freighter powered by four Pratt & Whitney TF33-P-7 turbofans. C-141B with 23ft fuselage stretch. No commercial version.
L-500	Galaxy C-5A	135	Very large military freighter with high wing, T-tail and nose and tail loading doors, powered by four 43,000 lb.s.t. General Electric TF39-GE-1C turbofans in underwing pods. Prot. 66-8303 FF. 30 Jun. 1968.

Once again, Lockheed allocated customer numbers to the Electra, although this system was not carried on to the TriStar. A typical Electra designation would be L-188C-08-09 with the second number-group (08) applying to all aircraft and indicating the standard Allison 501 engines and the third number-group (09) indicating the internal fit specified by the customer – in this case, Pacific Southwest. In some cases, the same interior arrangement was specified by more than one customer and the full type number applied to all relevant customers. In practice, the full model number is very rarely quoted for Electras. Details of the customer numbers are:

Code	Customers	Code	Customers
02	Eastern Airlines	14	Northwest
03	Western Airlines	15	National Airlines
06	Qantas, TEAL	16	KLM
08	Braniff Airways	17	Garuda
09	Pacific Southwest	18	Capital
10	American, Ansett, TAA	19	Western Airlines
11	Cathay Pacific		

Lockheed C-5A Galaxy, 60006

McDONNELL DOUGLAS   UNITED STATES

Donald Wills Douglas, with a background as chief engineer in the Glenn Martin Company, formed what was to become the Douglas Aircraft Company in the early 1920s. In 1932 Douglas was contracted to build the prototype Douglas Commercial One – the DC-1 which would form the basis for an aircraft which is arguably the most famous commercial transport of all time. This low-wing all-metal monocoque aircraft was developed into the DC-2 and then the DC-3 which arrived, fortuitously, at the moment when World War Two was on the horizon. The DC-3, produced under many names and designations including Skytrain, Dakota, DST, C-47, C-49, C-53, Li-2 and R4D, became the workhorse of the allied air forces during the war and an aircraft of such strength and flexibility that many of the 13,000 which were built are still flying around the world in 1998. The Russian Li-2 continued to be built until 1950.

Douglas Aircraft also became a major wartime manufacturer through programmes such as the Boston, Havoc and Invader light bombers but it was their expertise in transport design which was to stand them in good stead as the war moved on towards its conclusion. Shortly before the war started, Douglas had designed two aircraft – a twin-engined follow-on design to the DC-3 designated DC-5 which did not result in commercial orders and the much larger DC-4. The DC-4E was a low-wing four-engined transport with twice the capacity of the DC-3, a tricycle undercarriage and a three-fin tail. With forty-two passenger seats it was a large aircraft for the times but its relative sophistication left it without airline orders as the threat of war approached. Nevertheless, the work done on the DC-4E bore fruit through a complete redesign which, somewhat confusingly, carried the type number DC-4.

This aircraft was lighter and less complex but still carried forty passengers in an un-pressurised cabin. It had a single fin and rudder assembly and a higher-aspect ratio wing than the earlier prototype. The onset of war for the United States meant that the DC-4 became the C-54 Skymaster – and the recipient of large orders from the United States Air Force. The first C-54 flew in February, 1942 and production lines were established at Santa Monica, California and at the Douglas plant in Chicago. The new Douglas transport quickly established itself as a valuable long-range carrier at a time when the allied forces sorely needed this capability. Long-range tanks were fitted to give the Skymaster trans-Atlantic and Trans-Pacific performance and when the post-war crisis in Berlin materialised in 1948 the Skymaster provided the capacity and capability required for the Airlift.

Peacetime brought orders for the civil DC-4 from airlines with the first DC-4-1009 being delivered to Western Airlines in January 1946. However, commercial DC-4 production was limited by the early availability of military surplus C-54s and post-war users included

American Airlines, Eastern Airlines, Capital Airlines and Pan American in the United States and overseas carriers such as Air France, Australian National Airlines and Iberia. Many foreign air forces acquired C-54s and a significant number are still serving, principally as cargo aircraft, with civil and military operators. The DC-4 was also built by Canadair with Rolls-Royce Merlin engines as the C-54M (as described in the chapter on Bombardier) and formed the basis of the Carvair freighter conversions. The ATL-98Carvair was engineered by Aviation Traders of Southend, England to meet the need for a replacement for Bristol Freighters on car ferry operations across the English Channel. The extensive modification, carried out on twenty-one DC-4/C-54 airframes involved replacement of the forward fuselage with a bulbous nose including a new flight deck above the fuselage roof line and a hinged nose door through which cars or freight pallets could be loaded with the use of a ground based scissor-lift platform. Carvairs were operated by British Air Ferries and by a variety of other airlines including Aer Lingus, Iberia, Ansett and Hawaii Pacific Air.

The immediate post-war period found Douglas in the midst of multiple programmes of military and civil aircraft production. There were military contracts for the Skyraider, the Skyknight and the heavy military Globemaster I and II transports – and later came development of the Skyray and Skyhawk fighters. On the civil front, Douglas turned its attention to new developments of the DC-4 because it had become clear that the airlines required a pressurised aircraft with better performance and passenger capacity. The DC-6 was a fairly straightforward upgrade of the DC-4 with a fuselage stretch of almost seven feet, more powerful engines, an improved cockpit with more sophisticated radio and navigation equipment and a modernised cabin with square windows. A military version was also produced as the C-118 for the U.S. Air Force and the R6D for the Navy. First deliveries of the DC-6 were made in late 1946 to American Airlines who were anxious to receive the new aircraft in order to compete with TWA who had purchased Lockheed Constellations. United Airlines was another major DC-6 user and other DC-6s went to Panagra, National Airlines and Braniff. A number of subsequent variants of the DC-6 were produced including the highly successful DC-6A freighter which had a further fuselage stretch and increased power and its passenger transport equivalent, the DC-6B. Many DC-6s continued in later life as freighters, some of which were equipped with hinged swing tails, and several were converted as fire bombers for service in the United States and France with large semi-external tanks to contain the retardant mixture.

The final Douglas piston-engined commercial transport was the DC-7 which was a further extrapolation of the DC-6 theme and positioned to compete with Lockheed's Super Constellation and Starliner on long haul transatlantic and American transcontinental routes. A further fuselage stretch was introduced together with Wright Turbo Compound R-3350 engines and DC-7s, DC-7Bs and DC-7Cs with varying range capabilities were

Douglas DC-9-14, N1056T

Douglas C-54D, RP-C325

delivered to many existing DC-6 users. The DC-7C Seven Seas was specifically designed for transatlantic routes with BOAC, Sabena and Pan American and it had the largest fuel capacity and longer wings, a further stretched fuselage and a taller tail unit. The first of these long-range aircraft entered service in late 1956 but within two years the first Boeing 707 jet transports were being delivered and the appeal of piston-engined airliners collapsed. The last DC-7C was completed in November 1958. DC-7s continued in service for some years but their appeal was never as great as that of the 'workhorse' DC-4s and DC-6As and none now remain in commercial operation.

By the start of the 1950s, it was quite clear that future transport aircraft would be turbine powered and the de Havilland Comet and Boeing 367-80 were a sharp reminder to Douglas that they must embark on a jet replacement for the DC-7 or retire from the commercial airliner business. Initial intentions were to produce a turboprop aircraft but this was soon shelved in favour of a pure jet design and studies for the DC-8 were launched in 1952. The Douglas design followed a similar low-wing layout to that of the Boeing 367-80 (Model 707) with four jet engines mounted on underslung wing pylons but it was a somewhat larger aircraft with a wider fuselage capable of accommodating six-abreast seating. Initial customers for the DC-8 came from airlines which had successfully operated the DC-6 and DC-7 including United, National, KLM and JAL. Despite having purchased the first Boeing 707s, Pan Am also placed an order for twenty-five of the long-range DC-8-30.

The first DC-8 was flown from Long Beach, California in May 1958 and the aircraft received its type certificate on 31 August 1959. The first deliveries were made to Pan Am and United in the spring of 1960. Douglas offered the DC-8 in several different versions with varying combinations of engines and fuel capacity. The basic DC-8-10 was a medium range aircraft with JT3C turbojets for domestic operations, the DC-8-21 was fitted with JT4A engines for improved hot and high performance and the DC-8-30 series were longer range versions of the Series 21 with several fuel capacity options for intercontinental routes. Douglas also offered the DC-8-30 series with Rolls-Royce Conway engines as the DC-8-41, -42 and -43.

In 1961, Douglas installed Pratt & Whitney's new JT3D turbofans on the DC-8 to produce a new and more efficient range of aircraft which were, again built in several different range and gross weight options as the DC-8-50 series. A number of existing Series 10 and Series 30 aircraft were upgraded to the same standard. The company also introduced a convertible freight/passenger version, the DC-8-50CF Jet Trader, which was fitted with a strengthened main deck floor and a forward port-side cargo hatch. A few examples of an all-freight equivalent, the -50AF, were completed for United Airlines and these lacked cabin windows or passenger emergency exits.

The DC-8 had, thus far, suffered relatively little change to the airframe but the -60 Series was given a substantial fuselage stretch, in this case a total of thirty-six feet, which allowed high density passenger capacity to be raised from around 190 to 260 seats. It also provided a substantial increase in underfloor third-party freight space. Once more, the -60 series was offered in various forms for medium or long routes and as combi or all-freight variants. The DC-8-60 series became very popular as a load hauler with cargo and package freight air carriers and the majority of the 1998 active fleet of around 250 aircraft are used in this role. A number of Series 60 aircraft have been upgraded to Series 70 with CFM56 turbofans and major users include United Parcel Service with nearly fifty aircraft, Emery Worldwide with over thirty and Airborne Express with a thirty-six-strong fleet.

While the DC-8 was effective in meeting the needs of trunk carriers, the short-haul market was also developing in the early 1960s and Sud Aviation had already put the first Caravelles into service with United Airlines. Douglas initiated its DC-9 project in early 1963 as a ninety-passenger airliner and they followed the rear engined twin layout adopted by the Caravelle and under development for the competing BAC-111. The low-wing DC-9 made its first flight in February 1965 and the accelerated flight development programme resulted in award of the type certificate in the following November and entry into service during the following month by the first Delta Air Lines' aircraft. As with the DC-8, Douglas offered various different powerplant and gross weight options for the basic DC-9 together with convertible MC (Multiple Change) and RC (Rapid Change) models for local service airlines needing to gain the maximum flexibility on mixed routes.

Douglas, which became McDonnell Douglas Corporation (MDC) in April 1967 through merger with McDonnell Aircraft, had become expert in stretching their airframes to upgrade and develop a product line. The DC-9 was designed from the outset to be enlarged and while it started out with a 104-ft long fuselage it eventually ended up as the MD-83 with a 147-ft overall length. It was not long before the basic DC-9-10 series was given a fifteen feet increase in fuselage length to become the -30 Series and then a further six feet extension as the -40 series, which was specifically developed for the requirements of SAS, and a further eight foot stretch to form the -50 series.

With such a choice of passenger capacity and with multiple range and powerplant options the DC-9 found many customers with U.S. regional and trunk carriers such as Delta, American, TWA, Eastern, Continental, North Central, Bonanza and West Coast who all took large fleets. Major foreign customers included KLM, Alitalia, Air Canada, Ansett, Iberia and SAS. Production of the basic DC-9 models (up to the -50 series) continued at Long Beach until the middle of 1982 and McDonnell Douglas also delivered twenty-one examples of the C-9A Nightingale (based on the DC-9-32CF) to the USAF, fifteen of the similar C-9B Skytrain to the United States Navy, two to the Marines and three USAF

Douglas DC-6, OB-R-611

VIP versions of the DC-9-30 designated VC-9C. Several other world air arms have also used the DC-9 including those of Italy, Kuwait and Venezuela.

At this stage, the DC-9 received its ultimate stretch – and a marketing identity change. Renamed the MD-80, the DC-9-80 series was lengthened by fourteen feet three inches and had a wing of greater span and area, a larger vertical fin with a distinctive bulged tip and a new refanned version of the Pratt & Whitney JT8D. The Super 80 as it was sometimes known could accommodate 172 high-density passenger seats. McDonnell Douglas achieved certification on 25 August 1980 for the MD-81 (DC-9-81) which was the first of a line of variants including the MD-82, MD-83, MD-87 and MD-88. The MD-87 featured a shorter fuselage than the other MD-80 models and later aircraft in the production sequence were progressively upgraded with modern EFIS cockpits and other improvements. A co-production agreement was reached with Shanghai Aviation Industrial Corporation for MD-83s to be built in China and twenty-eight examples were completed between 1986 and the completion of the programme in 1992. McDonnell Douglas also experimented with the installation of a pusher propfan PW-Allison 578-X engine on the prototype MD-80 in contemplation of a production twin propfan version of the MD-80 but this was abandoned after extensive testing in 1989. The MD-80 has also been sold to some corporate operators as a business aircraft.

In 1993, the company flew the first MD-90 which offered improved economics to the DC-9 airframe by the use of International Aero Engines V2500 engines with improved emission and noise levels and further advances in the electronic flight instrument system and flight management system. The cabin interior was also redesigned and McDonnell Douglas offered the MD-90-30 with a 155-ft fuselage and 158 passenger seating, the 171-ft MD-90-40 with 180 passenger seating and the short fuselage MD-90-10 with 116 seats. The MD-90 series joined the MD-80 on the Long Beach production line and first deliveries to Japan Air System took place in June, 1995 followed by aircraft for SAS, Delta, Alaska Airlines and AOM. The agreement with China's Shanghai Aviation Industrial Corp. now involves production of 20 MD-90-30T Trunkliners, although none had been completed by mid-1998.

The most recent version of the DC-9 is the MD-95 which is a 100-seat aircraft aimed at airlines with a low density short range requirement and the BMW-Rolls-Royce BR715 turbofan was adopted to power this variant. In mid-1997, while the prototype of the MD-95 was under construction at Long Beach, it was announced that Boeing was to acquire McDonnell Douglas and this took place on 4 August 1997. The takeover put the DC-9 programme into question since the MD-80 and MD-90 were in direct competition with the Boeing 737 series. Eventually, in January 1998 it was decided that the MD-80 variants and the MD-90 would be discontinued after completion of outstanding orders but that the MD-95 would be continued and would be re-titled Boeing 717-200. In this respect it reintroduced the Boeing designation originally allocated to the military Boeing

ATL.98 Carvair, G-APNH

Douglas DC-8-43, N153FA

707. Boeing is also contemplating production of other variants of the '717 including the eighty-seat 717-100 and the 120-seat 717-300 and is expected to find a market among existing DC-9 operators in search of fleet modernisation.

In parallel with the long process of DC-9 development, Douglas also entered the large widebody jet market in 1967. At this time, Boeing was already forging ahead with its Model 747 project and Douglas found that its traditional customers had a need for a large aircraft with less capacity than the '747 but with a similar three-aisle cabin layout. Initial designs were for a 250-passenger aircraft but the design grew to a 340-seater and the Douglas project emerged as a three-engined aircraft with two of the engines mounted on underwing pylons and the third engine mounted on the lower portion of the vertical tail. In general layout the DC-10 was similar to that of the Lockheed 1011 which was also under development and in competition for the orders of leading airline customers. Douglas found a launch customer in American Airlines who awarded orders and options for fifty aircraft and this was followed by a sixty-aircraft order from United. The choice of engines was left to the customer and this provided the option of the Pratt & Whitney JT9D, the General Electric CF6 or the Rolls-Royce RB.211, although most early orders specified the General Electric powerplant.

The prototype DC-10-10 flew in August 1970 and certification was achieved on 29 July 1971. Deliveries to American Airlines took place almost immediately followed by aircraft for United, National, CP Air, Varig and KLM. Laker Airways also used the DC-10-10 for its transatlantic 'Skytrain' services. Over 350 DC-10s were delivered during the next ten years. While the DC-10-10 was primarily intended for American domestic routes the DC-10-30 was soon introduced as an intercontinental version with increased fuel capacity and this version had an enlarged wing and an additional centre fuselage mounted undercarriage unit. Douglas offered convertible versions of both the DC-10-10 and DC-10-30 with a forward port side freight door and also the all-cargo DC-10-30F which went into service with Federal Express in the mid-1980s. In 1981, Douglas handed over the first of a large batch of 60 KC-10A Extender air-refuellers to the USAF. These were externally similar to the standard DC-10-30CF but had a few cabin windows and a ventral tail refuelling boom linked to the bladder fuel tanks which were fitted in the belly cargo area. With a reinforced main deck floor, the KC-10A doubles as a cargo or occasional passenger transport.

The DC-10 achieved reasonable success although it was competing directly with the TriStar for orders until 1983 when the Lockheed production line closed. The DC-10 achieved a reputation for reliability although its image was damaged by the May 1979 crash of an American Airlines aircraft at Chicago caused by the separation of the port wing-mounted engine and an accident to a THY aircraft caused by the in-flight opening of an external baggage door. Production of the DC-10 continued until completion of the

446th example at the end of 1988 by which time the DC-10 fleet had transported over 701 million passengers, had flown over 13.7 million revenue flying hours and had totalled 4.5 million landings.

With DC-10 production tailing off, McDonnell Douglas announced the enlarged and upgraded MD-11 in December 1986. The MD-11 was essentially the same airframe as the DC-10 but with a fuselage stretch of eighteen feet six inches giving a maximum of 405 passenger seats, modified wings with wingtip winglets and a new EFIS equipped two-crew flight deck. The MD-11 was also fitted with improved engines with the customer still having a choice of three manufacturers – Pratt & Whitney, General Electric or Rolls-Royce. Freighter and convertible models were available. The first MD-11 was flown at Long Beach in January 1990 and Delta and Korean Air were the first airlines to take delivery at the end of that year. Other airlines ordering the MD-11 included American Airlines, Thai Airways, Varig, Alitalia, Swissair, Garuda and Japan Air Lines. Federal Express also took delivery of seventeen MD-11F freighters for their package freight operation. By the end of 1997 production of the MD-11 was approaching a total of 170 aircraft and it had been renamed 'Boeing MD-11' but the takeover of McDonnell Douglas by Boeing left the future of the MD-11 open to question, and it was finally confirmed in 1998 that the line will be closed.

Production Details

McDonnell Douglas allocates each aircraft a construction number in an overall Douglas sequence which started with the original pre-war Douglas Cloudster (c/n 100) and has now reached approximately c/n 53500. These numbers cover all the models in production at any time but McDonnell Douglas, in a similar fashion to Boeing, also uses a system of Line Numbers which indicate the sequential position of each aircraft on the production line for that type. The line numbers do not appear on the subsequent official airworthiness paperwork or on the aircraft data plate. There is no relationship between the two numbering systems but line numbers for individual types generally run in the same order as the construction numbers. The line numbers for transport aircraft were first used for the C-54 (DC-4) and were allocated in two different sequences with 'DO' and 'DC' prefixes (e.g. DO.183, DC.288) to indicate production at the main Santa Monica plant and the second line at Chicago. In a number of cases, serial numbers have become unused due to customer order cancellations.

Douglas has allocated fairly large batches of serial numbers to individual types but the serial number sequence covers all models – including military wartime production of A-20s, A-26s and B-17s built for Boeing. Post-war, the batches have included the C-124 and C-133 together with substantial numbers of Boeing B-47 bombers which were produced under sub-contract. The general allocation of postwar serial numbers of Douglas transports is as follows:

MD-83, 9Y-THN

Douglas DC-10-30, SE-DFD

Type	Dates Built	Number Built	First c/n	Last c/n
C-54	1942–1946	1,235	3050	36326
DC-4-1009	1945–1947	79	42904	43157
Canadair C4	1946–1950	71	101	171
DC-6 series and C-118	1946–1958	702	42854	45564
DC-7 series	1953–1958	338	44122	45553
C-74	1946–1948	14	13913	13926
C-124	1950–1955	448	43160	43998
C-133	1957–1961	50	44705	45587
DC-3S	1950–1953	105	43158	43400
DC-8 series	1958–1972	550	45252	46163
DC-9 series and C-9	1965–1982	975	45695	48166
MD-80 series	1979–current	1305	48000	53593
DC-10 series and KC-10A	1970–1988	447	46500	48319
MD-11	1990–current	177	48401	48786

Model Information

Type No.	Name	No. Built	Notes
DC-4E		1	Pre-war large 42-pax airliner with low wing, triple tail and four Pratt & Whitney R-2180-S1A1-G radial engines. Prot. NX18100 (c/n 1601) FF. 7 Jun. 1938.
DC-4	C-54	76	New max 40-pax transport with low wing, single fin tail unit, tricycle u/c and four 1450 h.p. Pratt & Whitney Twin Wasp R-2000-3 radial engines. Prot. s/n 41-20137 (c/n 3050) FF. 14 Feb. 1942. All built as military C-54 with 26-seats and fuselage long range fuel tanks.
DC-4	C-54A	200	C-54 military pax/freighter with rear port cargo door, seating for 50 troops, strengthened floor and R-2000-7 engines. US Navy R5D-1. One converted as VC-54C presidential transport.
DC-4	C-54B	220	C-54A with increased wing fuel and reduced fuselage tankage. US Navy R5D-2 (C-54P).

COMMERCIAL AIRCRAFT AND AIRLINERS

Type No.	Name	No. Built	Notes
DC-4	C-54D Skymaster	380	C-54B with 1350 h.p. R-2000-11 engines. Sub variants inc. SC-54D/HC-54D for search & rescue, EC-54D for airways calibration, VC-54D staff transports. US Navy R5D-3 (C-54Q).
DC-4	C-54E Skymaster	125	C-54D with additional wing tanks in place of fuselage tanks. C-54M as freighter for Berlin Airlift coal transport. MC-54M for casualty evacuation. US Navy R5D-4 and R5D-4R (C-54R).
DC-4	C-54G Skymaster	162	C-54E with R-2000-9 engines. US Navy R5D-5 (C-54S).
DC-4	XC-114	2	C-54E with 6ft 9in fuselage stretch and powered by four 1620 h.p. Allison V-1710-131 piston engines. Prot. s/n 45-874 (c/n 36327). Second aircraft designated YC-116 with modified de-icing.
DC4-1009		79	Post-war unpressurised 44-pax civil airline version of C-54 without cargo door.
DC-4M	North Star		Canadair-built C-54G. *See* Bombardier chapter.
ATL.98	Carvair		21 C-54 airframes converted to pax/cargo layout by Aviation Traders with new bulbous nose section containing nose opening cargo door and overhead cockpit. Powered by four P&W R-2000-7M2 engines. Prot. G-ANYB FF. 21 Jun. 1961.
Li-2		500	Postwar production of Russian-built DC-3 at Komsomolsk, 1946–1950.
DC-3S	Super DC-3	3	Postwar 30-seat production derivative of DC-3 with 3ft 3in forward fuselage stretch, strengthened structure, redesigned outer wings with square tips, new tail with squared off surfaces, fully enclosing wheel wells and doors. Powered by two 1475 h.p. Wright Cyclone R-1820-C9HE or 1450 h.p. Pratt & Whitney R2000-D7 engines. Prot. N30000 (c/n 43158) FF. 23 Jun. 1949. Also 100 military R4D-8 and C-117 converted from existing R4D aircraft.
415A	C-74 Globemaster I	14	Large military 125-troop pax/freighter of conventional low-wing layout with crew cockpit bubble above nose, tricycle u/c and port fuselage forward cargo door. Powered by four 3500 h.p. P&W R-4360-49 engines. 172,000 lb. TOGW Prot. s/n 42-65402 FF. 5 Sep. 1945. Some converted as civil freighters.
1129A	C-124A Globemaster II	205	Development of C-74 with new deeper double-deck fuselage and integral flight deck and double cargo-loading doors under nose. Powered by four 3500 h.p. P&W R-4360-35A engines. 175,000 lb. TOGW. Prot. s/n 42-65406 FF. 27 Nov. 1949. One YC-124B (s/n 51-072) with four P&W YT34-P-1 turboprops.

Type No.	Name	No. Built	Notes
1317	C-124C Globemaster II	243	C-124A with increased fuel tankage, 194,500 lb. TOGW and four 3800 h.p. P&W R-4360-63A engines.
DC-6		174	Civil development of DC-4 with pressurised fuselage incorporating 81in stretch, rectangular cabin windows, stronger u/c and max. 86-pax seating. 97,200 lb. TOGW. Powered by four 2100 h.p. P&W R-2800-CA15 Double Wasp radial engines. Prot. NX90701 (c/n 42854). FF. 29 Jun. 1946. US Navy R6D-1 (C-118B). USAF C-118.
DC-6A		66	All-cargo development of DC-6 with 5ft fuselage stretch, no cabin windows, port side freight doors forward and aft of wing, improved electrical system and cargo floor. Powered by four 2400 h.p. P&W R-2800-CB16 Double Wasp radial engines. Prot. N30006 (c/n 42901) FF. 29 Sep. 1949.
C-118A		167	DC-6A for USAF with 2500 h.p. P&W R-2800-52W Double Wasp radial engines. R6D-1 (C-118B) for US Navy.
DC-6B		289	DC-6A for max 102 passenger transport with cabin windows, no freight doors and standard cabin floor. Many later mod as freighters. Some fitted with swing tail.
DC-6C		6	Convertible pax/freight version of DC-6A with cabin windows. Some retrospectively converted from DC-6A.
DC-7		106	Developed DC-6B with 40in fuselage stretch, strengthened u/c and four 3250 h.p. Wright R-3350-18DA-2 Turbo-Compound radial engines. 122,200 lb. TOGW. Prot. N301AA (c/n 44122) FF. 18 May, 1953.
DC-7B		112	DC-7 with four 3250 h.p. Wright R-3350-18DA-4 Turbo-Compound radial engines in lengthened nacelles containing extra fuel. 126,000 lb. TOGW.

McDonnell Douglas MD-11, HL7375

Type No.	Name	No. Built	Notes
DC-7C	Seven Seas	120	Long-range DC-7B with 42 inch fuselage stretch, 10ft wingspan increase with additional tankage and 143,000 lb. TOGW. Powered by four 3400 h.p. Wright R-3350-18EA-1 engines. Prot. N70C (c/n 44872) FF. 20 Dec. 1955.
C-133	Cargomaster	50	High wing heavy military freighter with main u/c housed in fuselage fairings, ventral rear loading ramp and powered by four 5700 shp Pratt & Whitney T34-P-3 turboprops. Prot. s/n 54-135 FF. 23 Apl. 1956.
DC-8-11		5	Heavy four-jet transport for US domestic operations with low swept wing mounting four 13,000 lb.s.t. Pratt & Whitney JT3C-6 turbojets in underslung pylon-mounted pods and max 176-pax capacity. 265,000 lb. TOGW. Prot. N8008D (c/n) FF. 30 May 1958. Some converted to DC-8-12, DC-8-21 or DC-8-51.
DC-8-12		25	DC-8-11 with wing leading edge slots and extended wingtips and 273,000 lb. TOGW. Some -11 aircraft upgraded as DC-8-11/12. Some -12 aircraft upgraded to DC-8-21 or DC-8-51.
DC-8-21		33	DC-8-12 for hot and high operations with 15,800 lb.s.t. JT4A-3 (or -5, -9, -10, -11, or -12) turbojets and 278,000 lb. TOGW.
DC-8-31		4	Long-range version of DC-8-21 with 34% (5,900 USG) fuel increase and 302,000 lb. TOGW.
DC-8-32		47	DC-8-31 with modified drooped flaps and increase to 310,000 lb. TOGW and higher payload. Some converted to DC-8-53.
DC-8-33		6	DC-8-32 with further increase in TOGW to 318,000 lb. Some -32 aircraft upgraded as model 32/33.

Super DC-3, N99857

Type No.	Name	No. Built	Notes
DC-8-41		4	DC-8-31 with four 17,500 lb.s.t. Rolls-Royce Conway 509 engines. Some upgraded to DC-8-41/43.
DC-8-42		8	DC-8-32 with four 17,500 lb.s.t. Rolls-Royce Conway 509 engines. 312,000 lb. TOGW. Some upgraded to DC-8-42/43.
DC-8-43		20	DC-8-32 with four 17,500 lb.s.t. Rolls-Royce Conway 509 engines. Some upgraded to DC-8F-54.
DC-8-51		29	DC-8-21 with four 17,000 lb.s.t. Pratt & Whitney JT3D-1 (or -3 or -3B) turbofans and 278,000 lb. TOGW. Some converted from DC-8-12.
DC-8-52		21	Long-range version of DC-8-51 with JT3D-1 (or -3 or -3B) turbofans and 302,000 lb. TOGW.
DC-8-53		25	DC-8-52 with 318,000 lb. TOGW and increased useful load.
DC-8F-54		30	Freighter version of DC-8-51 without cabin windows, strengthened cabin floor, forward port side cargo door and 318,000 lb. TOGW.
DC-8-54CF			Convertible pax/freight version of DC-8F-54 with cabin windows. Converted from earlier models.
DC-8-55		6	DC-8-51 passenger transport with JT3D-1, -3 or -3B engines and 328,000 lb. TOGW.
DC-8F-55		26	DC-8F-54 with JT3D-3 or -3B engines and 328,000 lb. TOGW.
DC-8-55CF			Convertible pax/freight version of DC-8F-55 with cabin windows. Some converted from earlier models.
DC-8-61		78	DC-8-55 for short/medium range routes with fuselage stretch of 20ft forward and 16ft 8in aft of wing and max 259-pax capacity. 328,000 lb. TOGW.
DC-8-61F		10	All-freight version of DC-8-61. 331,000 lb. TOGW. Most built as DC-8-61CF convertible pax/cargo version.
DC-8-62		31	Long-range DC-8-61 with fuselage stretch of 3ft 4in forward and 3ft 4in aft of wing JT3D-3B or JT3D-7 engines in modified nacelles, extended wings and increased fuel. 335,000 lb. TOGW. Convertible pax/freight model -62CF.
DC-8-62H		20	DC-8-62 at 350,000 lb. TOGW.
DC-8-62F		8	Freighter version of DC-8-62 at 353,000 lb. TOGW.
DC8-862CF		9	Convertible pax/freight version of DC-8-62F.
DC-8-63		41	DC-8-62 with shorter fuselage of DC-8-61 and 259-pax capacity.
DC-8-63F		7	Freighter version of DC-8-63 at 358,000 lb. TOGW and strengthened u/c.

Type No.	Name	No. Built	Notes
DC-8-63CF		51	Convertible pax/freight version of DC-8-63F.
DC-8-63PF		6	All-passenger version of DC-8-63F without cargo door.
DC-8-71			DC-8-61 re-engined under Cammacorp programme with four 22,000 lb.s.t. CFM56-2-C1 turbofans with modified wing leading edges and engine pylons. 328,000 lb. TOGW.
DC-8-71F			Freight version of DC-8-71. 331,000 lb. TOGW. Also convertible DC-8-71CF.
DC-8-72			DC-8-62 with mods similar to DC-8-71. 353,000 lb. TOGW.
DC-8-72F			DC-8-62F with mods similar to DC-8-71F.
DC-8-73			DC-8-63 with mods similar to DC-8-71. 358,000 lb. TOGW.
DC-8-73F			DC-8-63F with mods similar to DC-8-71F.
DC-9-11		3	Short-range, max. 90-seat twin-engined jet airliner with low wing and T-tail powered by two tail mounted Pratt & Whitney 12,000 lb.s.t. JT8D-5 turbojets. 104ft 5in overall length. 77,700 lb. TOGW. Prot. N9DC (c/n 45695) FF. 25 Feb. 1965. Some converted to other Series 10 models.
DC-9-12			DC-9-11 with 14,000 lb.s.t. JTD-1 (or -7) engines and 85,700 lb. TOGW.
DC-9-14		54	DC-9-11 with 14,000 lb.s.t. JTD-1 (or 12,000 lb -5) engines and 76,300 lb. TOGW.
DC-9-15		56	DC-9-11 with 14,000 lb.s.t. JTD-1 (or -7) engines and 90,700 lb. TOGW.
DC-9-15F		24	All-freight version of DC-9-15 without cabin windows. Also -15MC and -15RC convertible pax/cargo versions. All with forward port cargo door.
DC-9-21		10	DC-9-11 with improved short field performance with 24in wingtip extensions, leading edge slats and 14,500 lb.s.t. JT8D-9 (or 14,000 lb. -11) turbofans.
DC-9-31		239	DC-9-21 with forward fuselage stretch of 15ft. and max. 115-seat capacity. 119ft 5in overall length. 98,000 lb. TOGW. Powered by two 14,000 lb. JT8D-1 (or -7) turbofans.
DC-9-32		341	DC-9-31 with 14,000 lb.s.t. JT8D-7 (or higher thrust -9, -11 or -15) turbofans and 108,000 lb. TOGW. Also VC-9C for USAF.
DC-9-32F		10	Freighter version of DC-9-32 without cabin windows and with forward port cargo door.
DC-9-32CF		39	Convertible pax/cargo DC-9-32 and equivalent USAF.C-9A, C-9B Nightingale.
DC-9-33F		22	DC-9-32F with strengthened u/c and 115,000 lb. TOGW.

Type No.	Name	No. Built	Notes
DC-9-34		7	DC-9-33 with 16,000 lb.s.t. JT8D-17 turbofans and 121,000 lb. TOGW.
DC-9-34F		5	Freighter version of DC-9-34 at 122,000 lb. TOGW.
DC-9-41		70	DC-9-31 with 6ft 2in fuselage stretch and max. 125-pax capacity. 125ft 7in overall length. 115,000 lb. TOGW. Powered by 14,500 lb.s.t. JT8D-9 (or -11 or -15) turbofans.
DC-9-51		95	DC-9-41 with 8ft fuselage stretch and max. 139-pax capacity. 133ft 7in overall length. Powered by 16,000 lb.s.t. JT8D-17 engines. 121,000 lb. TOGW.
DC-9-81	MD-81	168	Developed DC-9-51 with forward and aft fuselage stretch totalling 14ft 3in and max 172-pax capacity. 147ft 10in overall length. Fitted with rear passenger door, enlarged fin with bulged tip, 14ft increase in wingspan, modified flap system and slats, strengthened u/c, increased fuel tankage and modernised cockpit with HUD and autoland. 140,000 lb. TOGW. Powered by two 18,500 lb. JT8D-209 turbofans (or -217, -217A, -217C or -219 at different gross weights) Prot. N980DC (c/n 48000) FF. 18 Oct. 1979.
DC-9-81	MD-80UHB		Prototype MD-80 fitted with PW-Allison 578-X propfan engine in port nacelle. FF. 17 Jun. 1987.
DC-9-82	MD-82	565	DC-9-81 with 20,000 lb.s.t. JT8D-217 (or -217A) turbofans for hot and high operation. 147,000 lb. TOGW.
DC-9-82	MD-82	28	MD-80 built by Shanghai Av. Ind. Corp.
DC-9-83	MD-83	200	Increased range DC-9-81 with additional two belly tanks and 160,000 lb. TOGW.

DC-8-62F, N803MG

Type No.	Name	No. Built	Notes
DC-9-87	MD-87	76	Reduced capacity DC-9-81 with 119ft 1in fuselage (shortened by 28ft 9in) and max. 139-pax seats. Taller fin and no rear passenger door. 150,500 lb. TOGW. Powered by two JT8D-217A turbofans (or -217C or -219 at different gross weights).
MD-88	MD-88	154	MD-82 with improved cockpit with EFIS, FMS etc.
MD-90-30	MD-90	59	MD-88 with 135ft 5in overall length for max. 158-pax, new carbon brakes, improved cabin design and powered by two 25,000 lb.s.t. IAE V2528-D5 turbofans. 156,000 lb. TOGW.
MD-90-30ER	MD-90		MD-90-30 with additional fuel tankage.
MD-90-40	MD-90		MD-90-30 with 152ft 8in overall length for max. 180-pax. 163,500 lb. TOGW. Not built to date.
MD-90-10	MD-90		MD-90-30 for lower density routes with 135ft 5in overall length and 139,000 lb. TOGW. Not built to date.
MD-90-50	MD-90		MD-90-30 extended range variant with additional fuel and 172,500 lb. TOGW. Not built to date.
MD-90-55	MD-90		MD-90-50 for high density charter operations with 187-pax capacity. Not built to date.
MD-95-30	MD-95		MD-90-55 for low density routes with 119ft 3in overall length for max 100-pax capacity. Powered by two BMW-Rolls-Royce BR715 turbofans. Prot. N717XA (c/n 55000) FF. 2 Sep. 1998.
MD-95-20	MD-95		MD-95 with shorter fuselage and 80-pax capacity.
MD-95-50	MD-95		MD-95 with stretched fuselage and 120-pax capacity.
MD-95-20	MD-95		80-seat version of MD95-30. Boeing 717-100.
MD-95-50	MD-95		120-seat version of MD-95. Boeing 717-300.
Bo.717-200			New designation of MD-95-30 following Boeing takeover of McDonnell Douglas in 1997.
Bo.717-100			Boeing designation for proposed MD-95-20.
Bo.717-300			Boeing designation for proposed MD-95-50.
DC-10-10		122	Heavy, wide-bodied, medium range jet passenger transport with low wing mounting two engine pods and conventional tail incorporating third engine pod in lower fin. Max. 380-pax capacity. Powered by three 39,300 lb.s.t. General Electric CF6-6D (or -6D1, -6D1A or -6K) turbofans. Max. 458,000 lb. TOGW. Prot. N10DC (c/n 46500) FF. 29 Aug. 1970.
DC-10-10F		9	DC-10-10 for freight operations with forward port-side cargo door. Also known as DC-10-10CF as convertible pax/freight version.

Type No.	Name	No. Built	Notes
DC-10-15		7	DC-10-10 with 46,500 lb.s.t. CF6-50C2F turbofans.
DC-10-30		164	Long-range DC-10-10 with 48,000 lb.s.t. CF6-50A turbofans (or higher thrust -50C, -50CA, 50C1, 50C2, 50C2B, 50C2-R or 50H) and max 575,000 lb. TOGW. Fitted with additional central undercarriage leg.
DC-10-30ER		3	DC-10-30 with additional rear belly tankage and 54,000 lb.s.t. CF6-50C2B engines. Military tanker for USAF as KC-10A.
DC-10-30F		40	All-freight version of DC-10-30 without cabin windows and with forward port cargo door. Also convertible DC-10-30CF.
DC-10-30F	KC-10A	60	Military tanker KC-10A for USAF. KDC-10 tanker conversions for other customers.
DC-10-40		42	DC-10-30 with three 47,000 lb.s.t. Pratt & Whitney JT9D-20 (or -59A or -59B) turbofans. 575,000 lb. TOGW.
DC-10-40			All-freight version of DC-10-40 without cabin windows and with forward port cargo door.
MD-11		140	Re-engineered DC-10-30 with fuselage extensions of 8ft 4in forward and 10ft 2in aft of wing, wingtip winglets, redesigned tailplane and tail cone, modernised flight deck. Max. 405-pax capacity. 605,000 lb. TOGW. Powered by three 60,000 lb.s.t. Pratt & Whitney PW4460 or 60,690 lb.s.t. General Electric CF6-80C2D1F or Rolls-Royce Trent 650,660 turbofans. Prot. N111MD (c/n 48401) FF. 10 Jan. 1990. MD-11 Combi has rear port cargo door for convertible pax/freight operations.
MD-11F		37	All-freight version of MD-11 without cabin windows and with forward port cargo door. 613,000 lb. TOGW. Also known as MD-11C or -11CF as convertible pax/freight aircraft.
MD-17			Proposed civil version of C-17 military freighter. Not built.

Lisunov Li-2 (DC-3)

PEOPLE'S REPUBLIC OF CHINA

The modern aircraft industry of the People's Republic of China (the PRC) dates from 1951 when a new Plan was created with the assistance of the Soviet Union to build a number of aircraft under licence. Factories were constructed to produce not only finished aircraft but also engines and components and to provide overhaul facilities and the first task was to set up production of the Yak-18 trainer (designated CJ-5) and its M-11 engine by the end of 1955 followed by production of the MiG-15bis by the end of 1957.

China has established two design bureaux (at X'ian and Shanghai) and six manufacturing plants for transport aircraft – at Harbin, Nanchang, Xi'an, and Shaanxi, Shanghai and Shijiazhuang. The first transport aircraft was the venerable Antonov An-2 which started to be produced by the Nanchang factory in 1958 as the Fongshu 2 Harvester. This was later renamed Yunshuji Y-5 and the line was moved to the Shijiazhuang factory in 1970. It is reported that 727 aircraft were built at Nanchang and the Shijiazhuang factory had built 221 by 1986. It is believed that the grand total of Chinese-built Y-5s has now reached around 1150. At around the same time, the Peiping Institute of Aeronautical Engineering designed and built the first indigenous transport aircraft – the Peking-1 which first flew in September 1948. It would seem, however, that this did not progress beyond prototype stage. Another aircraft, probably built only as a prototype, was the Shoudu-1 (Capital-1) which was a high-wing light twin with an upswept twin-fin tail and rear loading doors. This is believed to have been a copy of the Russian An-14 Pchelka.

In 1974, Harbin designed a new small aircraft which was intended to supplement the fleet of Y-5s in the agricultural and general utility role. The high-wing Y-11, which was similar to the Britten-Norman Islander in general layout, was powered by two radial engines and had a fixed tricycle undercarriage braced on fuselage sponsons and a square section fuselage. The first aircraft flew in 1975 and went into production two years later with a total of forty having been built when production ended in the mid-1980s.

The Y-11 gave good service with provincial agricultural collectives but it had a fairly small cabin in relation to fuselage size and Harbin was also anxious to improve its performance. This resulted in the substantially redesigned Y-12 which retained the strut-braced wing and undercarriage sponsons but had a longer and wider fuselage and used a pair of Pratt & Whitney PT6A turboprop engines so as to make the aircraft more attractive to export customers. The Y-12 has been quite successful in gaining overseas orders with examples delivered to Mongolian Airlines, Berjaya Air Charter in Malaysia, Lao Aviation, Nepal Airways and the air forces of Sri Lanka, Eritrea, Peru, Zambia, Tanzania, Mauretania and Iran.

A requirement for an effective fifty-passenger regional transport led the X'ian Aircraft Design Institute to produce a Chinese version of the Antonov An-24 turboprop airliner.

Built by the X'ian factory, the prototype was completed in December 1970 but development was prolonged and the Y-7 did not receive its Chinese type certificate until July 1982. The majority of Y-7s have been delivered to CAAC for services commencing in 1986 and were subsequently passed on to new domestic carriers including Air Great Wall, China Southern, China Northern and Guizhou Airlines most of which have been established during the early 1990s. Over 100 examples of the Y-7 had been completed by mid-1997. Several variations on the An-24 have been introduced including the Y-7H which is the equivalent of the Antonov An-26 cargo aircraft with a ventral rear loading ramp. Considerable assistance has been provided to the X'ian factory by Hong Kong Aircraft Engineering Company (HAECO) who have developed improved cabin interiors and flight deck layouts for several of the transport designs.

The PRC also used an Antonov design when it came to producing a large utility transport for CAAC and the Chinese military forces. The four-turboprop An-12 was adopted by the X'ian factory in 1968 and was given the designation Y-8. The first Y-8 made its maiden flight in the latter part of December 1974 but production was handed over to the Shaanxi factory who flew their own prototype in December 1975 and achieved certification in February 1980. Shaanxi has subsequently developed a number of variants including a maritime reconnaissance version with a forward radome and a fully pressurised version for civil and military users.

The progressive development of Chinese aircraft manufacturing led to the establishment in 1973 of an Aircraft Design Institute associated with the Shanghai state aircraft factory which was tasked with producing a new long-range airliner for use by CAAC. The resultant Y-10 was a 'Chinese copy' of the Boeing 720 and was fitted with four podded JT3D engines as used on the CAAC fleet of Boeing 707-320s. The first airframe was used for exhaustive static tests and the second airframe became the flight test article, making its maiden take-off on 26 September 1980. In a subsequent 167-hour test programme the Y-10 made proving flights to most of the main Chinese cities and even to Lhasa in Tibet but the programme was abandoned in 1985 when it became clear that it would be more efficient to manufacture or buy-in equivalent western airliners. In April 1985 an agreement was signed for production by the Shanghai Aviation Industrial Corporation of an initial twenty-five examples of the McDonnell Douglas MD-82 which would be provided in kit form and would fulfil the need for a domestic trunk route airliner. Twenty-eight examples of the MD-82 were eventually delivered between 1986 and 1992.

Harbin Y-12, T3-ATI

COMMERCIAL AIRCRAFT AND AIRLINERS

Production Details

Generally, Chinese aircraft have adopted a similar pattern of serial numbers to those used in the Soviet bloc. The Y-5 has a separate serial sequence for each factory which has produced it, consisting of the batch number (e.g. 12) the factory number (32 for Nanchang, 164 and 7055 for Shijiazhuang) and a number within the batch. Thus, the twenty-ninth Nanchang-built aircraft in batch 12 would be 1232029. Batch sizes have varied but are frequently up to a maximum of fifty aircraft. Latterly, the factory number has been omitted from the serial system. The Y-8 system consists of the batch number, the number 08 to indicate the type, and the number within the batch. For instance, the 4th aircraft in Batch 7 is c/n 070804 and it appears that batches contain five aircraft. The Y-12 has a much simpler numerical system which runs from c/n 001 to, currently, around c/n 0089.

Model Information

The transport aircraft manufactured by the state factories of the PRC are all prefixed Y- or Yun- (e.g. Y-5 or Yun-5) to denote 'Yunshuji' or 'Transport Aircraft'. Details of known designs are shown in the following table.

Type No.	Name	No. Built	Notes
Peking-1		1	Low-wing 8-pax feeder liner with retractable tricycle u/c and powered by two 260 h.p. Ivchenko AI-14R radial piston engines. FF. 24 Sep. 1958.
Shoudou-1		1	Strut-braced high wing light transport with fixed tricycle u/c, twin fins, boom tail and rear clamshell loading doors, powered by two 160 h.p. M-11FR radial piston engines in helmeted cowlings.
Y-5		1,150	An-2T built in China at Shijiazhuang and Nanchang factories. Production includes Y-5B agricultural model, Y-5C passenger version with deluxe interior and Y-5D high density transport version. Prot. FF. 7 Dec. 1957.
Y-7		20	X'ian built version of 50-pax Antonov An-24 with two Harbin WJ5A-1 turboprop engines. Prot. FF. 25 Dec. 1970.

X'ian Y-7H-500, B-546L

Type No.	Name	No. Built	Notes
Y-7-100		80	Y-7 modified by HAECO with 52-seat cabin, new 3-crew flight deck and wingtip winglets. Prot. B-3499 (c/n 03702).
Y-7-100C1		4	Y-7-100 with five-crew flight deck. Y-7-100C2 and Y-7-100C3 with minor equipment variations.
Y-7-200A		3	Y-7-100 with 1ft 6in forward fuselage stretch, combi 60-pax interior, modified flight deck windows, shorter nose, modified flaps and two 2750 shp Pratt & Whitney PW127 turboprop engines. Prot. FF. 26 Dec. 1993.
Y-7-200B		1	Y-7-100 with 2ft 5in fuselage stretch, no winglets and Dongan WJ5A-IG turboprops.
Y-7E		1	Y-7-100 for hot and high operations with modified APU.
Y-7H		2	Chinese-built version of An-26 military all-cargo aircraft based on Y-7 with ventral rear loading ramp and two 2790 shp Dongan WJ5E turboprops. 48,060 lb. TOGW.
Y-7H-500		1	Civil version of Y-7H with 52,910 lb. TOGW.
Y-8		45	Chinese Antonov An-12 built at X'ian and Shaanxi factories with pointed glazed nose and four 4250 shp Wojiang WJ-6 turboprop engines. Prot. FF. 25 Dec. 1974.
Y-8A			Y-8 with enlarged interior for carrying helicopters.
Y-8B			Civil version of Y-8 without military equipment and improved avionics.
Y-8C			Pressurised version of Y-8 with improved rear loading ramp, longer internal cargo hold and no tail turret. Prot. FF. 17 Dec. 1990.
Y-8D			Export version of Y-8C with western avionics.
Y-8E			Military version of Y-8C for carrying two underwing drones.
Y-8F			Civil freighter with hardened interior for carrying livestock.
Y-8H			Aerial survey version of Y-8C.
Y-8X			Y-8C for military maritime patrol.
Y-10		1	Intercontinental jet 178-passenger transport with low wing, retractable tricycle u/c and powered by four 19,000 lb.s.t. Pratt & Whitney JT3D-7 turbofan engines in underwing pylon-mounted pods. Prot. B-0002 FF. 26 Sep. 1980.
Y-11		40	8-seat light utility and crop spraying aircraft with strut-braced high wing, forward and rear port-side doors, fixed tricycle u/c with sponsons mounting twin-wheel main gear and powered by two 285 h.p. Housai HS6D radial piston engines. Prot. FF. 30 Dec. 1975.
Y-11B			Y-11 re-engined with two 350 h.p. Continental TSIO-550-B turbocharged flat-six piston engines.

Type No.	Name	No. Built	Notes
Y-11T1		3	Y-11 with redesigned, 17-pax stretched fuselage, longer span wings with leading edge slats and extra fuel capacity, simplified wing/undercarriage strut bracing, single-main wheels and two 500 shp Pratt & Whitney PT6A-11 turboprops. First of two flying Prots. FF. 14 Jul. 1982. Redesignated Y-12I.
Y-11T2		3	Y-11T1 without leading edge slats. Redesignated Y-12II.
Y-12-I	Turbo Panda	27	Production Y-12 (former Y-11T1) built at Harbin with larger dorsal fin, deeper cabin windows and 620 shp PT6A-27 engines.
Y-12-II		59	Production version of Y-12-I without leading edge slats (former Y-11T2).
Y-12-IV		2	Y-12 with revised control systems, new braking system, extended wingtips and 19-pax interior. Prot. B-569L FF. 1993.
Y-14-100			Original designation for Y-7H.

X'ian Y-8

SAAB   SWEDEN

In common with many other world manufacturers the Svenska Aeroplan Aktiebolaget A.B. (Saab) entered 1944 with the prospective ending of World War II in sight and questions about its future production plans. While Sweden remained neutral during the conflict, the ever-present danger of annexation of Germany meant that Saab had been kept busy with production of the B.17 and B.18 military aircraft but the expectation of peace made it turn its attention to potential civil projects.

A specification was drawn up for a new short-haul airliner for ABA-Swedish Airlines to replace DC-3s which were then in operation. The company's proposed design, the Saab 90 Scandia, was a modern low-wing all-metal design with a maximum of thirty-two passenger seats. It was unpressurised but plans were also made to produce a pressurised version at a later stage. Saab decided on a pair of the reliable Pratt & Whitney R-2000 piston engines to power the Scandia and the prototype was flown in November 1946. It became clear that the Scandia was underpowered and the production version was fitted with larger R-2180 engines but, apart from modification to the nose gear and a redesign of the engine cowlings the production Scandia was very similar to the prototype.

Saab delivered the first of ten Scandias ordered by Scandinavian Airlines System (into which ABA had been absorbed) on 3 October 1950. The extended production delay

Saab 2000, HB-IZK

combined with rationalisation of the SAS fleet structure resulted in SAS only taking delivery of six aircraft but Saab had gained a six-aircraft order for the Scandia from the Brazilian airline, VASP. This batch, which included the Scandia prototype, was delivered between March 1950 and July 1951. Saab then received further orders for another six Scandias but the increasing pressure of work on the J.29 jet fighter resulted in a sub-contract being let to Fokker and this final Scandia batch was built at the Aviolanda factory at Papverweg in the Netherlands. SAS continued to use the Scandia until 1957 at which time the whole fleet was sold to VASP. Scandias were eventually withdrawn from VASP service during the late 1960s.

Saab did not return to commercial aircraft manufacture until 1979 when they entered into a partnership with the American manufacturer, Fairchild Industries to design a new pressurised local service airliner which would offer greater capacity than the Bandeirante, Twin Otter and Swearingen Metro which were in widespread use with the commuter carriers. The low-wing SF.340 was designed to seat thirty-five passengers in 2-1 seating and Saab-Fairchild selected a pair of General Electric CT7 turboprop to power the aircraft. The prototype flew in January 1983 and it offered operators a clearly 'bigger aircraft' than the light turboprops which had gone before. Flight testing of the three development aircraft proceeded rapidly with JAR and FAA certification being awarded on 29 June 1984. Production of the SF.340 was shared between Saab and Fairchild with wings, engine nacelles and tail units coming from Fairchild and the fuselage, undercarriage and final assembly handled by Saab at Linkoping.

The European launch customer was the Swiss operator, Crossair who had ordered ten aircraft and eventually received twenty-four, and the first American operator was Comair with a fifteen-aircraft order. These started to be delivered from the middle of 1984 and other airlines receiving early deliveries included Wichita-based Air Midwest, Birmingham Executive Airways in the United Kingdom, Swedair and the Australian operator, Kendell Airline who eventually built up a fleet of sixteen Saabs to complement their Fairchild Metros.

Not long after commencement of production, Saab and Fairchild announced that the whole programme was being handed over to Saab and by late 1987 manufacture of wings and tail units had been passed over to the Swedish factory. Over 100 had been delivered by the beginning of 1988, the majority going to the United States but with deliveries to many European countries and to further flung areas such as Argentina, China, Japan and Taiwan, Saab also sold a number of 340As to business companies such as Mellon Bank and Philip Morris as corporate shuttle or executive aircraft. One '340A was sold to the Swedish Air Force for VIP transportation and Saab has offered a special military surveil-

Saab 340, G-GNTE (AHS)

Scandia, PP-SQZ

lance version (340AEW&C) with a roof-mounted SLAR antenna. Two Saab 340s were also sold to the Japanese Maritime Safety Agency as search and rescue aircraft with a belly-mounted search radar and a rear fuselage mounted FLIR. The '340B was introduced from the 160th aircraft and this featured more powerful engines with larger propellers to give better climb and cruise speeds and a higher gross weight. The first '340B was delivered to Crossair in September 1989 and the 300th Model 340 left the factory in May 1992 and the 400th in August 1996.

In 1988, Saab carried out new market studies to define the next generation of the '340. Earlier reviews had suggested that the aircraft should be enlarged with forty-four seats and discussions took place with customers on this Saab SF.440. However, they settled for a stretched version with up to fifty-eight seats and with higher cruise performance, improved soundproofing and longer range than the basic aircraft. Crossair immediately committed itself to purchasing twenty-five of the new Saab 2000 and the development programme culminated in the first flight in March 1992. Three aircraft were used for the test programme and the Saab 2000 was certificated by the JAA on 31 March 1994. With production at Linkoping at full capacity, Saab (now reorganised as Saab Aircraft AB within the Saab-Scania Group) subcontracted manufacture of wings to CASA in Spain. The first customer delivery was made to Crossair in 1993 with other aircraft going to Deutsche BA and to SAS Commuter. As with the '340, the Saab 2000 was attractive to business users and three were sold to General Motors for inter-factory transport.

By the end of 1997 with forty-four examples of the Saab 2000 delivered, the market for the two Saab aircraft was starting to dry up with potential customers opting for the Canadair and Embraer regional jets rather than turboprops. With a backlog of around twenty aircraft, Saab followed Fokker and British Aerospace by announcing that it was closing its marketing operation and would cease production by the middle of 1999 due to growing losses in the commuter aircraft division.

Production details

The prototype Saab Scandia was allocated serial number c/n 90.001 and Saab-built production aircraft ran from c/n 90.101 to 90.111. Production in Holland by Aviolanda/de Scheldt ran from c/n 90.112 to 90.117. Saab 340s commenced with the prototype at c/n 001 and have continued to approximately c/n 435 at the end of 1997 with production expected to continue to approximately c/n 442 by the time the line is closed. The Saab 2000 has its own serial sequence commencing with the prototype, c/n 001 and reaching c/n 053 by the end of 1997.

Model List

Type No.	Name	No. Built	Notes
Saab 90A-1	Scandia	1	Low-wing all-metal unpressurised 32-pax short haul airliner with retractable tricycle u/c and powered by two 1450 h.p. Pratt & Whitney R-2000 piston engines and 3-blade props. Prot. SE-BCA (c/n 90.001) FF. 16 Nov. 1946.
Saab 90A-2	Scandia	17	Production Scandia with modified u/c and 1825 h.p. R-2180-E1 engines in repositioned and reshaped cowlings and four-blade props.
Saab SF.340A		159	Low-wing pressurised 35-pax regional airliner with retractable tricycle u/c and powered by two 1630 shp General Electric CT7-5A2 turboprops with 4-blade props. 26,000 lb. TOGW. Prot. SE-ISF (c/n 001) FF. 25 Jan. 1983.
Saab 340B		276	Saab SF.340 with 1735 shp CT7-5A2 engines and larger propellers. 27,275 lb. TOGW. Available with cargo door as combi version.
Saab 2000		53	SF.340 with fuselage stretch of 23ft 11in and max 58-pax. seating, enlarged wing, improved cabin sound suppression, improved cockpit and two 4125 shp Allison AE2100A turboprops. 48,500 lb. TOGW. Prot. SE-001/SE-LSI (c/n 001) FF. 26 Mar. 1992.

Saab 340, N72LP

TUPOLEV   SOVIET UNION

Andrei N. Tupolev was probably the most prolific of all Russian aircraft designers. Throughout the 1920s and 1930s he conceived a large range of transport and bomber aircraft and his Tu-2 light bomber made a major contribution to the Russian effort in the Second World War. One of the responsibilities of the Tupolev OKB was to produce a copy of the Boeing B-29 heavy bomber and around 900 of these were built as the Tu-4 to become principal equipment of the Soviet Air Force as the Cold War developed. The Tu-4 formed the basis for a long-range pressurised airliner, the Tu-12, which was built in 1946 and a cargo derivative designated Tu-75 but these designs did not advance beyond prototype stage and Tupolev moved forward to concentrate on a range of combat designs of which the Tu-16 twin-jet bomber and Tu-95 four-turboprop bomber and patrol aircraft became the most significant.

The Tu-16 was a mid-wing aircraft with a pair of turbojets positioned in the wing roots. This basic design was used by Tupolev to produce the Tu-104 which used the Tu-16 wing and engine installation married to a new pressurised fuselage. The Tu-104 made a dramatic debut in March 1956 when it brought General Serov on an official visit to London. It was the world's first medium-capacity twin jet airliner and, while it had poor operating economics compared with the contemporary Sud Caravelle, the Tu-104 brought fast efficient service to Aeroflot, the Soviet forces and to the Czech airline, CSA.

Tupolev Tu-114A, CCCP-L5611 (AHS)

Tupolev Tu-124, OK-TEA

However, a reminder of its military background was provided by the navigator's station in a glazed 'bomb-aimer's' nose which remained a feature of several later Tupolev airliner designs.

Five prototypes were built at the Moscow-Bykovo factory (GAZ-400) using existing Tu-16 components. These were followed by a pre-production batch of Tu-104Gs, variously reported as ten or fifteen aircraft, built with Tu-16 wings before two full production lines were opened in 1956 at Kharkov (GAZ-135) and Omsk (GAZ-166). Production was subsequently moved, in 1958 to Kharkov. The Tu-104 was put into revenue service by Aeroflot between Moscow and Irkutsk in September 1956 and remained in operation until the late 1970s. Tupolev also developed a four-engined version of the Tu-104B, designated Tu-110 and flew two prototypes but this did not reach production.

The four-turboprop Tu-95 (Nato name 'Bear') bomber was soon given the same treatment as the Tu-16. With the wings, engines, undercarriage and tail joined to a 220-seat fuselage the resultant Tu-114 provided Aeroflot with long-range capacity for routes from Moscow to the eastern cities of the Soviet Union and was also able to fly to New York or, with a refuelling stop at Shannon, on the route to Cuba. The Tu-114 was designed with a main passenger deck and a lower section which combined luggage and freight compartments with an in-flight galley to provide passenger meals. Tupolev also designed a long-distance VIP version, the Tu-116, which retained the original narrow Tu-95 bomber fuselage with an appropriately modified interior to carry up to thirty passengers. A total of thirty-six Tu-114s were completed and they operated with Aeroflot for just over ten years until they were replaced in service by the Il-62.

The Tu-104 design provided the Tupolev OKB with the basis for a range of airliners which have become the standard short/medium range equipment for Warsaw Pact airlines. The first variation was the Tu-124 which was a scaled-down forty-four-seat Tu-104 to replace the worn out Aeroflot fleet of Il-12s and Il-14s. Its performance and operating economics were superior to those of the Tu-104 and first deliveries were made in 1962. In addition to Aeroflot, the Tu-124 was used by Interflug in East Germany, CSA and Iraqi Airways. Three were delivered to the Indian Air Force and the Chinese Air Force also received a small number. In due course, however, it was plain that the Tu-124 was noisy, overweight and had a very high fuel consumption. This led to a further major redesign which resulted in a much more efficient aircraft which resolved most of the problems experienced by Aeroflot with its predecessors. The Tu-134 was instantly identifiable by its T-tail and by the twin Soloviev D-30 turbofans which were relocated from the wing roots to pods on the rear fuselage. It first flew in 1963 and was eventually put into production at the GAZ-135 plant at Kharkov, entering service in September 1967. A number were still in service in the mid-1990s with Russian airlines such as Volga Airlines, Tyumen Airlines, Kaliningrad Avia and Bashkirian Airlines together with foreign examples with Estonian Air, Air Moldova and CSA.

Growth in internal travel in the Soviet Union inevitably led to a requirement for more capacity and, in October 1968, the three-engined Tu-154 made its first flight. Developed from the Tu-134 with an enlarged fuselage, this aircraft was targeted at the same 130/160 passenger market for which Boeing had built the '727 but it had more powerful engines than the '727 and was designed to operate from the poor surfaces of the shorter and more remote Russian airfields. The GAZ-18 plant at Kyubishev (Samara) was designated to build the Tu-154 which was to become the most widely used of all Tupolev's transport aircraft and remains in service with most of the new airlines of the former Soviet Union and with other operators as varied as Air Great Wall in China, Cubana, Kish Air, Belavia and Tarom. Two examples were taken over by the German Luftwaffe after the collapse of East Germany. The Tu-154-100 was still in production by the Aviacor factory at Samara in 1996 to meet new orders and more than 920 have been built to date.

The most spectacular achievement of the Tupolev Bureau has, undoubtedly, been the conception of the Tu-144 supersonic airliner. As with the BAC-Sud Concorde, this was targeted at a cruise speed of Mach 2.4 and it emerged as a very similar slender delta design with its four engines clustered in a belly mounting. As with the Concorde, the problem of poor visibility in the landing configuration was resolved by fitting a drooping nose. Testing of the prototype revealed numerous problems and the second aircraft had a completely redesigned wing, longer fuselage and retractable foreplanes set into the forward fuselage to give improved low-speed handling.

Eventually, the Tu-144 went into service with Aeroflot on cargo flights between Moscow and Almaty in late 1975 followed by passenger services at the end of 1977. However, these services were halted in the spring of the following year, due to a combination of the high operating cost, insufficient range and as a result of an accident to another Tu-144 (CCCP-77111), and the type was abandoned. A total of sixteen Tu-144s are known to have flown from the production plant at Voronezh, recording a total of some 4,110 hours and many were consigned to storage at the Russian Test Centre at Zhukovskiy although two aircraft were used for a while for ozone research. One of the lower time aircraft, CCCP-77114 was revived and re-engined to be used in the NASA High Speed Civil Transport programme, making its first flight for this purpose in November 1996.

In 1983, Tupolev started design work on a new medium-haul airliner which would replace the highly successful Tu-154. With increasingly powerful engines becoming available, this 200-seat aircraft was able to use just two Soloviev PS-90A turbofans and externally it closely resembled the Boeing 757. Development was protracted with the prototype flying in January 1989 and Russian type certification being achieved six years later. The financial crisis resulting from the break-up of the Soviet Union meant that the anticipated customer orders for the Tu-204, which totalled over sixty aircraft at the time of certifi-cation, were heavily scaled back and production of the Tu-204 at the Aviastar factory in

Tupolev Tu-134A, ES-AAK

Ulyanovsk moved at a sluggish pace with completed aircraft remaining undelivered for protracted periods.

The main operator to date has been Vnukovo Airlines which received three and others have been ordered by Rossiya ARIA, Kazakhstan Airlines and Oriol-Avia. Problems have arisen with the Aviadvigatel-Perm PS-90A engines and the Tu-204 has been offered also with Rolls-Royce RB211-535E4 engines. Aviastar has established a leasing company, Sirocco Aerospace International, in conjunction with the Egyptian group, Kato Aromatic, and this organisation is marketing the Rolls-Royce powered Tu-204-120 and claimed twenty-one firm orders at the end of 1997 with KrasAir as the lead customer. They are also marketing the Tu-214 combi version of the aircraft (also known as Tu-204-200C) and the Tu-224/234 which has a shortened fuselage and 166 seats.

In addition to the Tu-204, the Tupolev bureau has also produced the Tu-334 which is a short-haul aircraft intended as a replacement for the large fleet of Tu-134s which remain in service. The Tu-334 prototype was rolled out in 1995 but, again, was a victim of the severe lack of funds which has affected the whole aviation industry. The prototype had still not flown by the end of 1997 and its future remains uncertain.

Production Details

As with other aircraft built in the various State factories, construction numbers were normally allocated to Tupolev aircraft according to a standard formula. This system (referred to in the table as the Standard system) is to have a four-part serial consisting of the Year Built (one digit indicating the last number of the year), Factory Number (two digits, e.g. 35 for factory GAZ-135 at Kharkov), Batch Number (two digits) and the Individual Aircraft in the batch (two digits). A typical example would be a Tu-104 manufactured in 1958 at Kharkov with the construction number 8 35 07 04. Many variations exist, however, with parts of the serial structure frequently being omitted. The most recent system involves long numbers without any obvious pattern which appear to be computer-generated and do not clearly indicate the individual number of the aircraft concerned. The systems used for each of the Tupolev types are as follows.

Model	C/n example	Serial – Part 1	Serial – Part 2	Notes
Tu-104	9350805	Standard system	Standard system	Built at GAZ-22 Kazan, GAZ-135 Kharkov and GAZ-166 Omsk.
Tu-114	Unknown	Unknown	Unknown	Built at GAZ-31 Samara.

Tupolev Tu-104B, CCCP-42444

Tupolev Tu-144, CCCP-77110

Model	C/n example	Serial – Part 1	Serial – Part 2	Notes
Tu-124	3341003	Standard system	Standard system	Built at GAZ-135 Kharkov.
Tu-134	8350403	Standard system	Standard system	Built at GAZ-135 Kharkov.
Tu-134	17112	Random computer number		Built at GAZ-135 Kharkov.
Tu-144	04-2	Batch number (from 01 to 09)	Individual number	Built at Voronezh. System shown is Line Number. c/n system unknown.
Tu-154	7-05	Prefix 7	Individual number	9 prototypes c/n 7-01 to 7-09.
Tu-154	72A-029	Year Prefix and A	Individual number	c/n 71A-010 to 96A-1016.
Tu-204	1450741364011	145074, Year and quarter (2 digits)	Individual number (5 digits)	Built at Ulyanovsk

Model Information

Details of all Tupolev civil transport models is as follows:

Type No.	No. Built	Notes
Tu-70	1	72-pax low-wing pressurised airliner based on Boeing B-29/Tu-4 wings and tail with new fuselage. Powered by four Wright R-3350-57 Double Cyclone radial engines. Prot. FF. 27 Nov. 1946. NATO name 'Cart'.
Tu-75	1	Unpressurised cargo version of Tu-70. Prot FF. Jul. 1960.
Tu-104	5	Pressurised all-metal low wing 50-pax airliner with anhedralled wings from Tu-16 bomber incorporating twin jet engines set into wing roots, retractable tricycle u/c with main units in wing fairings. Glazed nose with chin radar. Powered by two 14,880 lb.s.t. Mikulin RD-3 turbojets. Prot CCCP-L5400 FF. 17 Jun. 1955. NATO name 'Camel'.

Type No.	No. Built	Notes
Tu-104G	15	Pre-production Tu-104 with various changes including under-floor cargo holds.
Tu-104A	103	Tu-104 with 70-pax capacity and powered by two 19,180 lb.s.t. Mikulin AM-3M turbojets.
Tu-104B	104	Tu-104A with 3ft 11in forward fuselage stretch, altered cabin window layout, larger flaps, repositioned baggage doors and 21,385 lb.s.t. RD-3M-500 engines.
Tu-104D		Tu-104B modified for 85-pax interior.
Tu-104V		High-density Tu-104A with 100-pax seating and restricted toilets etc.
Tu-107	1	Tu-104B for military use with cargo door and tail gun turret.
Tu-110	2	Tu-104B in four-engine configuration with extra AL-7 engine in each wing root and modified centre section. Prot. CCCP-L5600. FF. 11 Mar. 1957.
Tu-114	1	Transport development of Tu-95 'Bear' with 170-pax fuselage married to low wing and engine installation from Tu-95, retractable tricycle u/c with main units in wing pods, glazed nose and chin radar. Powered by four 12,000 shp Kuznetsov NK-12M turboprops each with two 4-blade counter-rotating props. Prot CCCP-L5611. FF. 15 Nov. 1957. NATO name 'Cleat'. Also named 'Rossiya'.
Tu-114A	2	Tu-114 with modified interior layout.
Tu-114B	32	Tu-114 with modified interior layout.
Tu-114D	1	Tu-114 with slim fuselage based on Tu-95 with no lower cargo area and with 120-pax seating for high speed long distance VIP transport. Prot. CCCP-7480.
Tu-116	2	Precursor of Tu-114 based on Tu-95 with rear pressurised cabin for 30-pax. Prot. 7801 FF. 1958.
Tu-124	112	Scaled-down short haul version of Tu-104 with 44-pax seating and powered by two 11,900 lb.s.t. Soloviev D-20P turbofans. Prot CCCP-L45000 FF. 24 Mar. 1960. NATO name 'Cookpot'.

Tupolev Tu-154B-2, RA-85498

Tupolev Tu-334, RA-94001

Type No.	No. Built	Notes
Tu-124K		Convertible pax/cargo version of Tu-124.
Tu-124V		Tu-124 with revised three-cabin interior for 56-pax seating.
Tu-134	853	Low-wing short-haul airliner based on Tu-124 with enlarged wing centre section, 5ft 3in fuselage stretch for 72-pax capacity, T-tail and engines moved to rear fuselage pods. Powered by two 14,990 lb.s.t. Soloviev D-30 turbofans. Prot. CCCP-45075 FF. 29 Jul. 1963. NATO name 'Crusty'.
Tu-134A		Tu-134 with 6ft 11in fuselage stretch, 84-pax capacity, tailplane/fin bullet deleted, strengthened u/c, solid radar nose and APU.
Tu-134B		Tu-134A with revised interior for 90-pax, new spoilers, modernised cockpit. Tu-134B3 has higher density seating and upgraded engines.
Tu-134UBL		Military Tu-134 with long radar nose for training Tu-16 bomber crews.
Tu-144	1	Supersonic long-range 140-seat passenger airliner with slim delta wing, droop nose and four reheated 38,580 lb.s.t. Kuznetsov NK-144 turbofans in parallel box installation below centre section. Prot. CCCP-68001 FF. 31 Dec. 1968. NATO name 'Charger'.
Tu-144	10	Production standard Tu-144 with redesigned wing, 20ft 8in fuselage stretch, forward retractable canard, modified u/c with 8-wheel main bogies and 44,090 lb.s.t. NK-144A engines in two paired nacelles. First aircraft CCCP-77101 FF. 1 Jul. 1971.
Tu-144D	6	Tu-144 with uprated 48,500 lb.s.t. RD-36-51A engines. Prot. FF. Nov. 1974.
Tu-144LL		Tu-144D fitted with Kuznetsov NK-321 engines, strengthened wing, modified fuel and control systems for joint supersonic research project with NASA. One aircraft RA-77114 FF as -144LL on 29 Nov. 1996.

Type No.	No. Built	Notes
Tu-154	923	Medium-haul airliner with airframe similar to scaled-up Tu-134, 167-pax capacity and powered by three Kuznetsov NK-8-2 turbofans in tail cluster. Prot. CCCP-85000 FF. 3 Oct. 1968. NATO name 'Careless'.
Tu-154A		Tu-154 with additional centre-section fuel tanks, 23,150 lb.s.t. Kuznetsov NK-8-2U engines, upgraded avionics and additional emergency exit doors.
Tu-154B		Tu-154A with 180-pax capacity, modernised flight control system, new spoilers and two extra entry doors.
Tu-154B-2		Tu-154B with crosswind landing system, modified fuel system and new radar.
Tu-154S		Tu-154B for freight operations with strengthened rollamat floor, forward port-side cargo door and hardened interior.
Tu-154M		Tu-154B with three 23,150 lb.s.t. Aviadvigatel D30KU-154 turbofans with thrust reversers, larger spoilers, new inertial nav. system, redesigned cabin interior.
Tu-154M2		Tu-154M with 35,275 lb.s.t. Aviadvigatel PS-90A turbofans.
Tu-154-100		Tu-154M with modernised cockpit and redesigned cabin interior.
Tu-156M2		Tu-154M for cargo operations with LNG-fuelled NK-89 engines.
Tu-204	28	Medium haul 212-pax airliner of conventional design with low wing mounting two underslung 35,580 lb.s.t. Aviadvigatel-Perm PS-90A turbofans. Prot. CCCP-64001 FF. 2 Jan. 1989.
Tu-204C		Cargo version of Tu-204 with forward port-side freight door, no cabin windows, reinforced rollamat floor etc.
Tu-204-100		Long-range version of Tu-204 with additional tanks.
Tu-204-100C		Tu-204-100 combi with increased payload and restricted range.
Tu-204-120		Tu-204-100 with 43,100 lb.s.t. Rolls-Royce RB211-535E4 turbofans.

Tupolev Tu-204, CCCP-64006

Type No.	No. Built	Notes
Tu-204-122		Tu-204-120 with avionics package by Rockwell-Collins.
Tu-204-200		Tu-204-100 with additional centre-section fuel tank and increased gross weight. Redesignated Tu-214.
Tu-204-200C		Tu-204-200 combi with increased payload and restricted range.
Tu-204-220		Tu-204-200 with 43,100 lb.s.t. Rolls-Royce RB211-535E4 turbofans.
Tu-204-300		Initial designation for Tu-234.
Tu-214		New designation for Tu-204-200.
Tu-224		New designation for Tu-204-220.
Tu-234	1	Tu-204 with 19ft shorter fuselage and 166-pax capacity powered by PS-90A engines. Prot. RA-64001.
Tu-334-100		Short-haul airliner with low wing, wide-body fuselage, T-tail and two Ivchenko-Progress D-436T-1 turbofans in rear fuselage pods. FF. 8Feb. 1999.
Tu-334-120	1	Tu-334 powered by two BMW-Rolls-Royce BR70-48 turbofans. Prot. RA94001.

Tupolev Tu-234, RA-64001

YAKOVLEV SOVIET UNION

The majority of post-war Yakovlev design activities have centred on military combat aircraft such as the Yak-25 and Yak-28 and the basic trainers based on the Yak-18 low-wing light aircraft. However, in 1964, the bureau was tasked with producing a new small airliner to serve short-haul routes with a thirty-two-passenger maximum seating capacity. The small Yak-40 was in many ways the precursor of the regional jets which became fashionable twenty years later. It had a straight unswept low wing set well to the rear of the fuselage and was designed to meet the Aeroflot requirement for operation from remote unpaved airfields.

To facilitate this, the Yak-40 was powered by three small rear-mounted Ivchenko AI-25 turbofans which gave it an excellent power-to-weight ratio and a high degree of safety margin but resulted in relatively high operating costs. The first Yak-40 was flown in October 1966 and first deliveries took place in 1968. Over 1000 were built for Soviet users and for military and airline operators in the Warsaw Pact countries with production taking place at GAZ-292 at Saratov and ceasing in 1980. Some effort was made to export the Yak-40 in the west with a reported total of 123 being delivered to seventeen countries and a project was launched in the United States to sell a version of the Yak-40 fitted with Garrett TFE731 turbofans but this was not finalised. Sales were made in Western Europe to the German airline, General Air who acquired five and to Aertirrena in Italy who received three but their fuel consumption was high and both airlines ceased operating

Yak-42, RA-42411

Yak-40, HA-YLR

them after a short time. Nevertheless, the Yak-40 remains in widespread operation with CIS airlines and as a business and charter aircraft.

In the early 1970s, Yakovlev took on the assignment of designing a regional jet airliner to replace the large fleet of Il-18s and Tu-134s which were in service. The Yakovlev Bureau followed a similar design layout to that of the Yak-40 with three tail-mounted turbofans but, in this case they used a mildly swept wing to improve long-range cruise performance. The Yak-42 had a wide body fuselage arranged with 120 seats in six-abreast single-aisle configuration and the four-wheel main undercarriage bogies were, again, designed to facilitate operation from secondary airports. Following the prototype first flight in the spring of 1975, the Yak-42 was found to need modifications to improve low speed handling and further such changes were made to production aircraft with the wing area being increased following operational experience by Aeroflot and as a result of an accident which saw the type being temporarily grounded in 1982. The first Yak-42s were delivered from the Smolensk factory in 1980 and it is believed that around 190 had been completed by the end of 1997. These are used by the former Aeroflot domestic network and by various operators including Macedonian Airlines, Lithuanian Airlines, Cubana, Air Ukraine, and China General Airlines. A number of derivatives of the Yak-42 have been proposed including the Yak-46 with Progress D-27 propfan engines and the Yak-242 which is extensively redesigned and has twin underwing-mounted engines – but none of these have yet reached prototype stage.

Production Details

Yakovlev aircraft built at the Saratov and Smolensk factories received serial numbers in line with the general Soviet modular system. For the Yak-40, this system consists of a four-part serial containing the Factory Number (9 for GAZ-292 at Saratov), Year Built (one digit indicating the last number of the year and commencing at 8, indicating 1968), Quarter of that Year (i.e. 1 to 4), Individual aircraft serial number (two digits between 01 and 20) and the Batch Number (two digits). A typical example would be a Yak-40 with the serial c/n 9030713 built in the third quarter of 1970 in batch 13 with the individual number 7. The Yak-42 was not so clearly defined and several systems have been used. Generally, these contain the Factory Code, the year of manufacture, the individual aircraft number and the batch number but there are several anomalies and some of the Yak-42 serial numbers contain a random computer-generated number. Early Yak-42 serials run from c/n 11820201 to approximately 11140305. Later aircraft have a prefix number '452042' and serials which run from c/n 2202030 to 4404018. Thus, a typical serial number would be 4520423304016.

Model Information

Type No.	No. Built	Notes
Yak-40	1,136	Low-wing pressurised 32-pax local service airliner with T-tail, retractable tricycle u/c, ventral rear airstair entry door and powered by three 3300 lb.s.t. Ivchenko AI-25 turbofans. 35,275 lb. TOGW. Prot. CCCP-1966 FF. 21 Oct. 1966. NATO name 'Codling'.
Yak-40K		Yak-40 with port-side forward cargo door.
Yak-40TL		Proposed conversion of Yak-40 to use two Lycoming LF507-1H turbofans.
Yak-42	190	Medium haul pressurised 120-pax regional airliner with T-tail, retractable tricycle u/c, swept wing and powered by three 14,325 lb.s.t. Ivchenko D-36/1 turbofans in rear fuselage cluster. Prot. CCCP-1974 FF. 7 Mar. 1975. NATO name 'Clobber'.
Yak-42B		Yak-42 with Allied Signal EFIS cockpit etc.
Yak-42D		Yak-42 with additional fuel tankage.
Yak-42F		Environmental survey version of Yak-42 with underwing sensor pods etc.
Yak-42T		Cargo version of Yak-42 with forward port cargo door.
Yak-142		Improved Yak-42D with new spoiler system and modified flaps, redesigned cabin, Allied Signal 5-screen EFIS flight deck.

Yakovlev Yak-42, RA-42424

OTHER MANUFACTURERS

AEROSPACE TECHNOLOGIES
OF AUSTRALIA

AUSTRALIA

On 1 July 1987, Aerospace Technologies of Australia ('ASTA') was established following the public flotation of the Government Aircraft Factory ('GAF'). GAF was originally formed on 1 July 1939 and its early post-war activity involved military production of Avro Lincolns, Canberras, Jindivik targets and Mirage III fighters. In 1967, GAF designed a twin turboprop utility aircraft aimed at the needs of the Australian Army and commercial operators. The N2 Nomad was a strut-braced high-wing monoplane with twin 400 shp Allison 250-B17 turboprops, a square-section twelve-passenger fuselage with an upswept rear section and a cruciform tail. It had a retractable tricycle undercarriage, the main units of which were housed in external sponsons attached to the lower fuselage.

The Nomad prototype was flown in July 1971. The initial production models which were handed over in 1975 were the Australian Army N.22 and the N.22B which was for civil customers and export military users including the Philippines Air Force, Indonesian Navy and the Thai Navy and Air Force. Civil customers for the N.22B included Douglas

GAF Nomad N.24A, N244E

229

Airways in New Guinea, Forrestair and the Royal Flying Doctor Service and Northern Territories Medical Service. GAF further developed the Nomad into the stretched N.24A which could accommodate up to seventeen passengers and several of these reached the United States to serve with Century Airlines, Princeton Airways and the optimistically titled ASAP Airlines. The United States Customs Service also acquired a fleet of Nomads for anti-drug operations. The Nomad was used for a while in Europe by Rotterdam Airlines on services between Rotterdam and short haul destinations such as Southend.

The Nomad suffered from various problems including a number of premature prop reduction gearbox failures and sales of the aircraft were slow with the result that GAF closed the Nomad line in 1984. The Nomad prototypes were c/n N2-01 and N2-02 and production aircraft were given serial numbers from c/n 1 to 170 in an integrated series covering all models. These serials were prefixed by the identity of the model concerned (e.g. N22SB-103; N24A-44). Details of the Nomad models are as follows.

Model	Number Built	Notes
N.22	14	Basic short fuselage aircraft with strut-braced high wing, retractable tricycle u/c with main units housed in external sponsons. Max seating for 2 crew and 13 passengers. Powered by two 400 shp Allison 250-B17B turboprops. Largely Australian Army deliveries. Prot. VH-SUP (c/n N2-01) FF. 23 Jul. 1971.
N.22B	96	N.22 configured for civil use with increased TOGW. All-cargo version, N.22C.
N.22SB	6	Coastal patrol 'Search Master B' model with nose radome containing Bendix RDR1400 search radar. Also N.22SL with external radome beneath nose and Litton APS.504 radar.
N.24	44	N.22 with fuselage plugs ahead of and behind wings totalling 5ft 9in., two extra windows each side, four extra seats, 8500lb TOGW. Prot. VH-DHF (c/n 10) FF. 17 Dec. 1975. N24A with 9400 lb. TOGW. N.24SB modified to Searchmaster B standard and N.24BF floatplane version.

AIRSPEED   UNITED KINGDOM

Airspeed Ltd, a small company formed in 1931 to build light aircraft, gained prominence during World War II as a manufacturer of the Oxford twin-engined trainer and the Horsa troop-carrying glider. At the end of the war, Airspeed found a short-term market for the AS.65 Consul 5-passenger feeder liner. 161 Consuls were converted from Oxfords which

Airspeed Ambassador, G-ALZZ

were bought as surplus from the RAF and the changes involved little more than a re-positioning of the tailplane, modified baggage carrying nose and a change to the internal cabin furnishings.

The major post-war preoccupation of the company was the AS.57 Ambassador which was yet another response to Brabazon Committee specifications for new airliners. The Ambassador was an extremely elegant pressurised all-metal aircraft with a high wing, retractable tricycle undercarriage and a triple-finned tail unit. During its design development, the AS.57 grew from being a twenty-five-seater to being capable of carrying up to fifty-five passengers. It was powered by two, 2700 h.p. Bristol Centaurus 661 piston engines but numerous tests were done with the second prototype Ambassador with Bristol Proteus and then Rolls-Royce Tyne turboprops, and had suitable support been forthcoming the Ambassador could have beaten the Fokker Friendship in the race for the fifty-seat turboprop market.

Airspeed flew the prototype Ambassador, G-AGUA (c/n 61) on 10 July 1947 from their Christchurch base followed by the second prototype (G-AKRD c/n 62) in August of the following year. The first order was for twenty aircraft for British European Airways and the first contracted delivery was made in 1952. The AS.57 (named 'Elizabethan' class by BEA) was a success in service but became overtaken by the turboprop Viscounts which were also being delivered to BEA. It also suffered from the bad publicity of the March 1952 crash of G-ALZU at Munich which killed the Manchester United football team. Only twenty production aircraft and a production prototype were built (c/n 5210 to 5230) and when the fleet was withdrawn from service by BEA in 1958 the nineteen surviving aircraft went to various operators including BKS, Globe Air, Autair, Butler Air Transport, Dan-Air and the Royal Jordanian Air Force. The last Ambassadors were finally withdrawn from use in mid-1971.

AVIATION TRADERS   UNITED KINGDOM

In 1955, Aviation Traders (Engineering) Ltd. of Southend designed the ATL.90 Accountant short-range airliner. The ATL.90 was a modern pressurised aircraft with a low wing and two 1740 shp Rolls-Royce Dart 514 turboprops mounted well above the wing to give suitable propeller clearance. The Accountant 1 was configured for twenty-eight passengers and the proposed Accountant 2 was to have had a stretched fuselage to give forty-two-seat capacity. Aviation Traders flew the prototype (G-41-1/G-ATEL c/n ATL.90) on 9 July 1957 and it was demonstrated at the Farnborough Show later that year. Despite its promise, Aviation Traders were unable to face the high development costs which would be required to achieve certification and the Accountant which was aimed at

Aviation Traders ATL.90 Accountant G-41-1

the market requirement later met by the Avro 748, was scrapped in 1960. Aviation Traders subsequently carried out the engineering design and conversion of twenty-one DC-4s as the Carvair freighter. This is further described under the Douglas chapter.

AVRO CANADA   CANADA

The British company, A.V. Roe & Co. formed Avro Canada Ltd in 1945 and successfully completed nearly 800 examples of the CF-100 Canuck all-weather fighter. In 1946, Avro Canada started work on a four-engined jet airliner which owed much to the design of the Avro Tudor transport. The C-102 Jetliner was a low-wing pressurised aircraft with a cruciform tail, a tricycle undercarriage and accommodation for fifty passengers. The four 3600 lb.s.t. Rolls-Royce Derwent 5 turbojets were mounted in pairs fitted closely under the inboard wing sections. The prototype, CF-EJD-X, was flown at Malton on 10 August 1949 and was extensively tested during the following year. Despite some promising proving flights, the Jetliner failed to attract any airline orders and the certification effort was abandoned.

Avro Canada Jetliner, CF-EJD-X

BERIEV   RUSSIA

The Russian design bureau named after Georgy Beriev is best known for its series of flying-boats. However, in 1966 construction commenced on the prototype of a new sixteen-passenger local service airliner, the Be-30. The Be-30 was a high-wing turboprop twin with a retractable undercarriage and the first of eight examples flew on 3 March 1967. In the event, the market for which the Be-30 was intended was taken up by the Let-410 Turbolet which had slightly larger capacity and was acquired in large numbers by Aeroflot for its local service network. In 1993, the Be-30 project was reopened and the aircraft redesigned as the Be-32K with two 1100 shp Pratt & Whitney PT6A-65B turboprops which were to be manufactured by Klimov under licence. The first Be-32K, RA-67205 was tested extensively and an order for fifty examples for Moscow Airways was announced but the programme appears to have been shelved due to lack of further development finance.

Beriev Be-32K, RA-67205

BREGUET   FRANCE

The Breguet Provence was one of the most impressive of the post-war piston-engined airliners. With its double-deck fuselage (resulting in the more commonly used name 'Deux Ponts') the low-wing Br.763 served with Air France on its domestic routes between Paris and the Côte d'Azur and to London and other European capitals with efficiency and distinction during the 1950s. Avions Louis Breguet had a well established history of building large aircraft and the Br.763 owed much to the Br.730 Sirius and Br.731 flying-boats built in the mid-1930s.

The concept of the Provence was as a freight and passenger transport with the upper deck dedicated to fifty-nine seats and the lower deck being used for cargo, including small vehicles, loaded through clamshell doors in the underside of the rear fuselage. Alternatively, the lower deck could be fitted with a further eighty seats and Air France used the aircraft in this configuration on its shuttle flights from Paris to Nice. The proto-type Br.761 (F-WFAM c/n 01) flew for the first time on 15 February 1949 powered by four Gnôme Rhône radial engines and this was followed by three Br.761S development aircraft which had a higher (99,200 lb.) gross weight and used 2100 h.p. Pratt & Whitney R-2800-B-31 engines in place of the French powerplants.

The Air France version, the Br.763 had a further increase in weight to 113,770 lb. and the more commonly available R-2800-CA-18 engines. Air France took delivery of the first Provence (F-BASN, c/n 1) on 9 August 1955 and this was followed by eleven further examples (c/n 2 to 12). Breguet also built four examples of the military Br.765 Sahara for the Armée de l'Air (c/n 501 to 504). The Air France fleet of Br.763s was finally replaced

Breguet Br.763, F-BASV

by Caravelles in 1964 and six aircraft were converted to become 'Universel' dedicated freighters. Several of the surviving Br.763s were subsequently transferred to the Armée de l'Air and flew until the late 1960s. Although certain Provences were painted in other airline colours (Air Algerie and Silver City), Breguet never managed to make any further sales of the type. Breguet did subsequently develop the Breguet 941 STOL transport which was tested by Eastern Airlines in the United States and was seen as a possible commercial commuter airliner but, in the event, only four production aircraft were built for the French Air Force.

BUDD   UNITED STATES

The quest for a post-war replacement for worn out ex-military C-47s and DC-3s was addressed by many aircraft manufacturers. The Philadelphia-based E.G. Budd Company came up with a solution which not only surpassed the freight carrying ability of the venerable Dakota but also found a solution for the perceived scarcity of aluminium for aircraft construction. Budd, which was skilled in manufacture of railroad cars and had built the Pioneer flying-boat, proposed a military cargo transport built of welded stainless steel. The Budd RB-1 Conestoga foreshadowed the Fairchild C-123 and Lockheed C-130 in having a high wing and upswept rear fuselage with a ventral hydraulically-operated cargo loading ramp.

Powered by two Pratt & Whitney Twin Wasp S1C3G piston engines it was awarded an order from the United States military forces for 1000 aircraft, the first of which would be delivered to the U.S. Navy as the RB-1 and later examples were to go to the U.S. Air Force as the C-93. Budd's prototype, NC41810 (c/n 001) was first flown on 31 October 1943 but by the time acceptance testing took place the war was reaching its close and further development was cancelled with seventeen aircraft completed (c/n 001 to 017) and a further nine in final assembly. The completed aircraft were mainly sold to the newly formed Flying Tiger Line commercial freight company and four Conestogas were delivered to Shell Aircraft in Ecuador where they took over from a group of Ford Trimotors the arduous supply operations to remote oil sites. The Conestogas were underpowered and in some respects had poor handling characteristics. They were soon replaced by DC-4s in Flying Tiger service and while they soldiered on for a while in Ecuador they were all scrapped in 1947 due to spar fatigue and shortage of spare parts.

CESSNA   UNITED STATES

In common with the other major light aircraft manufacturers, Cessna has been a major supplier of small twin-engined aircraft for the commuter market. In 1962, Cessna flew the first of its medium cabin twins, the Model 411 which was aimed, primarily, at the corporate market. This had a comfortable interior for four to six passengers, an airstair entry door and sufficient power, range and avionics to meet the stringent operating demands of company users. The Model 411 gave the design base for numerous variants including the Model 402 and stretched 404 for third level airline operation. The Model 404 formed the starting point for the F.406 Caravan II with Pratt & Whitney PT6A turboprop engines. This was jointly developed by Cessna and its French affiliate, Reims Aviation and when Cessna eventually discontinued production of the 400-series aircraft in Wichita the F.406 continued in production at Reims and is still built for the third level and utility markets.

Together with the Citations, the other current production model from Wichita is the high wing Model 208 Caravan I. This is the largest single-engined Cessna to have been built and is sold in standard or stretched versions powered by a single Pratt & Whitney PT6A turboprop. The majority of the early production Caravan Is were sold to Federal Express who use the type extensively on mini-hub freight operations but the Model 208 has been sold in executive configuration, on amphibious floats and in Grand Caravan passenger layout. It is widely used by commuter operators as varied as Brasil Central, Japan

Regional Airlines, Aerolineas Paraguayas, SANSA in Costa Rica and the Caribbean airline, Air St. Martin. Details of the main Cessna models used by commuter airlines are as follows.

Type No	No. Built	Notes
208 Caravan I	270	Large all-metal high-wing utility aircraft with fixed tricycle u/c and 14 seat/cargo interior with 4 doors including port side double cargo door. Powered by one 600 shp Pratt & Whitney PT6A-114 turboprop. 8000 lb. TOGW. Prot. N208LP (c/n 699) FF. 9 Dec. 1982. Military U-27A. Special Missions model has large roller-blind door. Later fitted with 675 shp PT6A-114A engine (introduced as standard, 1998).
208A Cargomaster		Model 208 for all-freight operation with hardened interior, no cabin windows or starboard rear door, taller vertical tail and belly pannier.
208B Super Cargomaster	600	208A with 4ft fuselage stretch aft of the wing, no windows and larger belly pannier. 675 shp PT6A-114A engine. 8750 lb. TOGW. Prot. N9767F FF. 3 Mar. 1986.
208B Grand Caravan		208B with windows and passenger seating for passenger/cargo operations.
208B Pathfinder	1	Soloy-remanufactured '208B with 6ft aft fuselage stretch, under-fuselage cargo section and Soloy Dual-pac PT6A turboprop. Prot. N5010Y (c/n 208B-0304).
401	545	Model 411 with broader vertical tail, lower (6300 lb.) TOGW, six-seat executive interior and two 300 h.p. Cont. TSIO-520-E engines set further out on wings. (Note: Production total includes Model 402, *q.v.*).
402		401 with utility interior for freight or nine-seat commuter use.
402A	129	402 with 26 cu.ft. baggage compartment in lengthened nose, optional crew entry door and other minor changes.

Cessna F.406, G-DFLT

Type No	No. Built	Notes
402B Utililiner	835	402A with minor changes. 1973 model has larger cabin and five square cabin windows each side instead of four portholes. Businessliner has deluxe cabin trim.
402C	681	402B with 6850 lb. TOGW, longer span bonded wet wing without tip tanks, new trailing link u/c without wheel well doors and 325 h.p. TSIO-520-VB engines.
404 Titan	396	Stretched '402C with enlarged vertical tail, dihedralled tailplane, trailing link u/c legs, 8400 lb. TOGW and two 375 h.p. Cont. GTSIO-520-M engines. Titan Courier has cargo interior; Titan Ambassador is 10-seater. Prot. N5404J (c/n 627). FF. 26 Feb. 1975.
F406 Caravan II	80	14-seat development of '404 Titan with two P&W PT6A-112 turboprops. Built by Reims Aviation. Prot. F-WZLT. FF 22 Sep. 1983.

DASSAULT   FRANCE

The noted designer, Marcel Bloch had been responsible for a number of pre-war transport and military aircraft designs and after the war he personally changed his name to Marcel Dassault (because of the German origins of Bloch) and renamed his company accordingly. Avions Marcel Dassault designed a two-engined low-wing light transport, the MD.303, which was developed into the definitive MD.315 and MD.312 Flamant military communications and trainer aircraft. The Flamant had a circular section, unpressurised fuselage, a tricycle undercarriage and distinctive large twin fins. The prototype MD.315 flew on 6 June 1947 and a total of 318 production aircraft were built between 1949 and 1953. Although several Flamants were transferred to various foreign governments, none was used by commercial operators.

While primarily a military aircraft producer, Dassault achieved success with its Falcon business jets. In 1967 this opened up the opportunity for the company to consider filling an existing market niche building a short-haul passenger airliner with 150-seat capacity. The low-wing Dassault Mercure (no numerical designation was allocated) was externally similar to the Boeing 737 with two 15,500 s.h.p. Pratt & Whitney JT8D-15 turbofans positioned on small pylons under the wings. The Mercure had a wide cabin capable of allowing six-abreast seating with a central aisle and had a full-length underfloor baggage and cargo hold. The prototype Mercure (F-WTCC c/n 01) made its maiden flight at Bordeaux on 28 May 1971 and was supported in the flight test programme by a second

Dassault MD.312 Flamant

Dassault Mercure, F-BTTD

prototype (F-WTMD, c/n 02). The French Type Certificate was awarded on 12 February 1974 by which time only one airline order had been placed – for ten aircraft for Air Inter. The first delivery was made on 16 May 1974 and by December 1975 Dassault had handed over the last of the batch (with serial numbers c/n 1 to 10) and had attracted no further airline customers. Eventually, despite plans to produce a larger and longer range Mercure 200, the line was dismantled although the Air Inter fleet continued to give good service on French domestic routes until they started to be retired in 1990.

DE HAVILLAND AUSTRALIA   AUSTRALIA

Formed in March, 1927 as a subsidiary of the British de Havilland Aircraft Company Ltd, de Havilland Aircraft Pty. Ltd. ('DHA') brought its wartime production of the Mosquito FB.40 to a close and looked for new production programmes to fill its Bankstown factory. A requirement was published for a small feeder airliner type of aircraft for operation by the Royal Flying Doctor Service to replace Rapides on remote ambulance services.

DHA came up with the DHA-3 Drover 1 which was a six/eight seat low-wing aircraft with a fixed tailwheel undercarriage and three 145 h.p. Gipsy Major 10/2 piston engines with variable pitch metal propellers. The alternative Drover 1F had fixed pitch propellers. In general appearance it followed the lines of the new DH.114 Heron and DH.104 Dove which were under development by the parent company in Britain and the prototype (VH-DHA c/n 5001) was first flown on 23 January 1948. A total of twenty Drovers was

DHA-3 Drover, VH-ADN

237

built (c/n 5001 to 5020) between 1950 and September 1953 and five of these were Drover 2s with double-slotted flaps. In eight-passenger configuration the Drover also operated scheduled routes with Trans Australian Airlines on its services in Queensland and in Fiji with Fiji Airways. At least one Drover was used in Australia for aerial seeding of pastures in Queensland. In May 1960 the first Drover Mk. 3 flew at Bankstown, re-engined with 180 h.p. Lycoming O-360-A1A flat-four piston engines. A number of aircraft, notably the six used by the R.F.D.S., were modified to this specification.

FIAT   ITALY

Originally formed as Aeronautica Ansaldo, Fiat became a part of the well-known engineering company and motor vehicle manufacturer in 1926. During the war it built a range of fighters and bombers for the Italian Air Force. Prior to commencement of World War II, Fiat had designed a sixteen-passenger three-engined airliner for use by *Avia Linee Italiane* on European medium-haul routes. The G.12 became an important general military transport and was built in substantial numbers. In the post-war period of reconstruction of the Italian airline industry, a combined fleet of seven G.12s was used by Avia Linee Italiani and Airone on their domestic services.

During the mid-war years Fiat looked at an enlarged version of the G.12 designated G.212. Construction of a prototype was delayed until the end of the war came and this aircraft (MM61634 c/n 1) was first flown on 20 January 1947. The G.212 was an all-metal aircraft with a low wing, retractable tailwheel undercarriage and three 860 h.p. Alfa Romeo 12B-RC18 (later changed to 1215 h.p. Pratt & Whitney R-1830-S1C3-G) radial engines. In standard airline passenger layout it could accommodate twenty-six first-class or thirty-four to thirty-eight high density seats and was built as the G.212CP Monterosa passenger aircraft, the G.212AV military crew trainer and the G.212TP Monviso freighter. A total of nineteen were built (c/n 1 to 19) of which eleven (with porthole windows) went for military use and the other eight (with rectangular cabin windows) were delivered to *Avia Linee Italiane* and to the Egyptian airline, Services Aérien Internationaux d'Egypte (SAIDE) which used them for services to Libya, the Lebanon and Italy. The Fiat G.212s were retired in the mid-1950s.

Fiat G-212, I-ESTE (MJH)

GRUMMAN   UNITED STATES

After the war, Grumman Aircraft Engineering Corporation was able to develop new business in its core activity of military production but it also carved a market niche for

Grumman G-159C Gulfstream, C-GPTN

itself in the design and sale of amphibious aircraft such as the G.73 Mallard. The company's experience with the S2F Tracker and TF-1 Trader naval patrol aircraft provided the opportunity for the company to produce a civil executive transport. In fact, after much design deliberation the G-159 Gulfstream owed little to the Grumman Tracker. It was much larger, with accommodation for twenty-one passengers, had a low wing and was powered by two Rolls-Royce Dart turboprops. N701G, the prototype, first flew on 14 August 1958, followed quickly by two further prototypes, and the type certificate (1A17) was awarded on 21 May 1959.

Production of the Gulfstream started in 1959 and Grumman eventually finished building the Gulfstream in early 1959 having completed 200 examples including five TC-4Cs for the U.S. Navy. While most aircraft were ordered by corporate customers as executive aircraft, a substantial secondary market developed for the aircraft with commuter airlines with some sixty-seven aircraft being transferred to public transport service. Royale Airlines was the largest user and other Gulfstreams were acquired by Chaparral Airlines, Air Provence, Air Inuit and Birmingham Executive Airways. A number went into service with package freight carriers such as Purolator Courier. In 1979, the company announced a new version of the G-159 aimed specifically at the commuter airline market. The GAC-159-C (later known as the G-159C) featured a fuselage stretch of 9ft. 6in. to allow a maximum payload of thirty-eight passengers. The prototype (N5400C c/n 116) was converted from a standard Gulfstream and first flew in this form on 25 October 1979. Grumman converted a further five existing G-159s (c/n 27, 83, 88 and 123) but did not put the G-159C into full production. Gulfstream 1s were allocated serial numbers from c/n 1 to c/n 200 together with c/n 322 and 323 (but excluding c/n 13 and 113).

IPTN   INDONESIA

In 1974, the Indonesian state oil company, Pertamina and its transport subsidiary, Pelita Air Service, represented by Dr B.J. Habibie, entered discussions with CASA for licence production of the C.212 in Indonesia. This led, in August 1976 to the establishment of IPTN (Industri Pesawat Terbang Nusantara) – otherwise known as Nurtanio which commenced production of the C.212 at the former Lipnur factory at Bandung and has also built the MBB Bo-105, Aérospatiale Super Puma and Bell 412 helicopters. IPTN subsequently also formed Airtech as a joint development company with CASA to develop the CN235 forty-four-passenger transport and utility aircraft and both the C212 and CN235 are described in more detail in the chapter on CASA.

In 1989, IPTN (now named Nusantara Aircraft Industries Ltd) announced a new project for a fifty-seat local service airliner which they would develop independently from their existing partnership with CASA. The N.250 bore a close relationship to the CN.235 but

IPTN N-250, PK-XNG

was a rather larger aircraft without the sharply upswept rear fuselage of the CASA designs. It had a high wing mounting two 3271 shp Allison AE2100C turboprops driving six-blade Dowty propellers, a fly-by-wire control system, fuselage mounted main under-carriage units retracting into external fairings and a high T-tail. The prototype CN.250 (PK-XNG, c/n PA1) was first flown on 10 August 1995 and at this time a decision was made to increase the capacity of the production N.25-100 to sixty-eight seats and the first aircraft to this standard flew in December 1996. Further versions including the seventy-seat N.270 are planned. IPTN also has plans for the N2130 regional jet but the financial pressures of IPTN during 1997 and 1998 have thrown doubt on the future of these programmes.

MARTIN   UNITED STATES

The Glenn L. Martin Company was a major producer of military aircraft during the Second World War and built a wide range of types including the B-26 Marauder, the Mars and Mariner flying boats and, in the 1950s, the B-57 jet bomber based on the English Electric Canberra. Martin's sole venture into airliner manufacture came immediately after the war with the design of the Martin 2-0-2. This unpressurised low-wing twin-engined aircraft was a contemporary of the rather more successful Convair 240 and addressed the

Martin 404, N40448 (AHS)

same need for a DC-3 replacement. The 2-0-2 was a modern all-metal monocoque design with a retractable tricycle undercarriage and it featured a retractable passenger entry stair under the rear fuselage. Power was provided by two 2400 h.p. Pratt & Whitney R-2800-CA18 Double Wasp engines mounted conventionally on the inboard wing sections. Martin's 40-passenger design, referred to as the 'Martin-Liner' became the first post-war twin-engined commercial transport to receive CAA certification. The prototype, NX93001 (c/n 9122) was first flown on 21 November 1946 and type approval was granted on 13 August 1947. The first delivery was to Northwest Airlines who needed forty examples and other substantial orders included fifty for Eastern Airlines and thirty-five for Penn Central. TWA, Delta and Braniff also placed orders for the aircraft.

With the 2-0-2 in production, Martin set about enhancing the design. A powerplant change to the R-2800-CB16 and increased fuel capacity resulted in the 2-0-2A and thirteen of the total of forty-six production 2-0-2s were this version. The 2-0-2 started to gain a poor safety record with no fewer than five Northwest aircraft being written off in crashes between August 1948 and January 1951. Martin also realised that without pressurisation the aircraft was unappealing to the major airlines and they carried out a major redesign fitting the 2-0-2 prototype with a pressurised cabin in which form it became the Martin 3-0-3 (with the new c/n 9222). The aircraft was further changed with a 3ft 3in fuselage stretch and R-2800-34 engines to become the Model 4-0-4.

The second prototype 2-0-2 (NX93002 c/n 9123A) became the 4-0-4 prototype and certification was gained on 5 October 1951. Despite its questionable reputation TWA and Eastern ordered the 4-0-4 or converted earlier orders to the new model. TWA received the first of forty-one aircraft in February 1952 and Eastern received sixty. The only other customer for the 4-0-4 was the United States Coast Guard who took the last two production aircraft designated RM-1Z (VC-3A) in the third quarter of 1952. With major military orders in hand, Martin closed the production line and never returned to civil aircraft programmes. Serial numbers of the thirty-four Martin 2-0-2s (including prototypes) were c/n 9122 to 9136, c/n 9142 to 9150 and c/n 9158 to 9167. The thirteen Martin 2-0-2As were c/n 14071 to 14083. The 103 production Martin 404s were c/n 14101 to 14176, c/n 14223 to 14247 and the Coast Guard's RM-1Zs were c/n 14290 and 14291.

NAMC   JAPAN

The Nihon Aircraft Manufacturing Co. Ltd (NAMC) was formed in May 1957 as a joint venture company between the major Japanese aircraft manufacturers, Fuji, Kawasaki, Mitsubishi, Japan Aircraft Manufacturing, Showa and Shin Meiwa. Its purpose was to design and build a short haul airliner to meet the needs of the Japanese domestic carriers. The NAMC solution was a fairly conventional low-wing twin turboprop aircraft of

NAMC YS-11, N912AX

rugged construction and capable of carrying sixty passengers in pressurised single class accommodation. NAMC selected the well proven Rolls-Royce Dart as the powerplant for the YS-11 and flew the first of two flying prototypes (JA8611, c/n 1001) on 30 August 1962.

Almost exactly two years later Japanese type certification was granted and production examples of the YS-11 started to emerge with the first passenger service being operated by Toa Airways, who acquired four aircraft, in April 1965. Other early deliveries were made to All Nippon (seven aircraft) and Japan Domestic Airlines (eleven aircraft) together with four of a military variant to the JASDF and two to the JCAB. In due course, NAMC developed further variants of the YS-11 and was able to penetrate the American market with a sale to Piedmont Airlines. Several other United States operators used the YS-11 including Reeve Aleutian, Mid Pacific Airlines and Airborne Express which flew the YS-11 on small package services. Elsewhere, the YS-11 flew with Olympic Airways in Greece, Cruzeiro do Sul and VASP in Brazil and Philippine Airlines. Serial numbers of the 180 production YS-11s ran from c/n 2003 to 2182, the flying prototypes were c/n 1001 and 1003 (later changed to c/n 2001 and 2002) and static test airframes, c/n 1002 and 1004. YS-11 variants were as shown in the following table. Each purchaser had a specific designation relating to the selected interior fit (e.g. YS-11-101 for Toa Airlines, YS-11-211 for VASP, YS-11-306 for Transair Canada).

Type No.	No. Built	Notes
YS-11-100	50	Low-wing pressurised max. 64-seat local service airliner with retractable tricycle u/c and powered by two 3060 shp Rolls-Royce Dart Mk.542-10K turboprops. 50,265 lb. TOGW.
YS-11A-200	94	YS-11 with 54,010 lb. TOGW and higher useful load.
YS-11A-300	16	Convertible pax/freight version of YS-11A with port side forward cargo door and 46-pax seating in mixed configuration.
YS-11A-400	8	All-freight military version of YS-11A without cabin windows for JASDF.
YS-11A-500	5	YS-11A-200 with 55,115 lb. TOGW and increased useful load.
YS-11A-600	9	YS-11A-300 with 55,115 lb. TOGW and increased useful load.

PILATUS – BRITTEN NORMAN

UNITED KINGDOM/SWITZERLAND

Established in the Isle of Wight in 1953, Britten Norman built up a reputation for good engineering, mainly with products for the aerial agriculture industry, during the following decade. In June 1965 they flew the prototype BN-2 Islander. This nine/ten-seat all-metal twin-engined utility aircraft had a minimum of refinement and was fitted with a fixed undercarriage and simple systems. It was certificated on 18 August 1967 and went into production at Bembridge, Isle of Wight, shortly afterwards. Islanders were sold worldwide to air taxi and commuter operators as varied as the Scottish operator, Loganair, Air Tahiti, Vieques Air Link in Puerto Rico, Munz Northern in Alaska, Botswana Airways and Aerial Tours of Port Moresby in Papua-New Guinea. Such was the success of the Islander that basic production of the aircraft was subcontracted to IRMA in Romania. Initially, kits of parts were sent from Britain for local assembly (starting with aircraft c/n 85 – later c/n R.601) but IRMA soon reached the stage of full production of the aircraft.

In 1968, Britten Norman saw the opportunity for a stretched version of the BN-2. The company rebuilt the second BN-2 (G-ATWU) as the prototype BN-2A Mk.III Trislander with an enlarged strengthened vertical tail and a third Lycoming engine

BN-2 Islander, J6-SLV

mounted on the fin. In this form, the Trislander could carry seventeen passengers and it found favour with operators such as Aurigny Air Services in the Channel Islands, Air Seychelles and Aero Cozumel in Mexico. The Islander was also developed for military purposes as the Defender with underwing armament points and other equipment to fit the aircraft for light troop transport and ground support roles. However, this success brought with it severe financial pressures and, in August, 1971 a receiver was appointed. Britten Norman then passed through the ownership of the Fairey Group and, when that company faced its own business crisis, Britten Norman was sold to Pilatus in January 1979. By this time the company had launched the Turbo Islander project which involved re-engining of the basic aircraft with a pair of Lycoming LTP-101 turboprops. This engine proved to be too powerful and the final design which emerged was the BN2T Turbine Islander which used a pair of Allison 250 turboprops. The BN-2B-20 is the major production model in 1998 with the Turbine Islander and BN-2B-26 being produced in smaller numbers. The company is also building the larger BN2T-4S Defender 4000 for military customers. Several other variants have been built, including the CASTOR Turbine Islander with a nose-mounted Ferranti surveillance radar and the AEW Defender with a bulbous nose radome housing a Thorn-EMI Searchwater radar. The Trislander is no longer manufactured although some uncompleted airframes may emerge in due course as flyable aircraft.

Production of Islanders had totalled 1188 examples by mid-1992 and seventy-two Trislanders have been built. Islander serial numbers started with c/n 1 (the prototype) and ran to c/n 599 and followed by Romanian built aircraft c/n 601 to 919 (excluding c/n 917). A new Islander series started in 1977, running from c/n 2001 to 2043 and then from c/n 2101 to current production aircraft at around c/n 2301. Production by Philippine Aerospace Development Corporation started at c/n 3001 and finished at c/n 3015. The newly-announced Defender 4000 (BN-2T-4S) military variant has serial numbers commencing at 4001 and production had reached c/n 4014 by late 1996. Trislanders were given serials c/n 1001 to 1072. The various models of the Islander are as follows:

Type No	Notes
BN-2	High wing all metal 10-seat cabin monoplane with fixed tricycle u/c and two 260 h.p. Lyc. O-540-E4B5 piston engines. 5700 lb. TOGW. Prot. G-ATCT (c/n 1). FF 13 June 1965. Designated BN-2A with minor modifications and TOGW increased to 6300 lb.
BN-2A-2	BN-2A with modified flaps, wing leading edges and 300 h.p. Lyc. IO-540-K1B5 engines. BN-2A-3 has increased wingspan and extra wingtip fuel tanks. These variants at 6600 lb. TOGW are designated BN-2A-20 and -21. BN-2A-21 with lengthened nose is BN-2A-23.

BN-2A-III Trislander, G-BEPH

Type No	Notes
BN-2A-6	BN-2A with wing leading edge modifications and 260 h.p. O-540-E4C5 engines. BN-2A-7 has increased wingspan and extra wingtip fuel tanks. BN-2A-8 and -9 are these variants with droop flaps and, at 6600 lb. TOGW are designated BN2A-26 and -27. With lengthened nose they are BN-2A-24 and -25.
BN-2A-10	BN-2A-8 with 5070 lb. TOGW and 270 h.p. turbocharged Lyc. TIO-540-H1A engines.
BN-2A-41	Turbo Islander with lengthened nose, droop flaps and two Lyc. LTP-101 turboprops. Prot. G-BDPR (c/n 504) FF. 6 Apl. 1977.
BN-2B	New variant based on Defender with 300 h.p. IO-540-K1B5 engines, four underwing hardpoints, optional nose radar and military hardened interior. BN-2A-21, -26 and -27 can be converted with these mods as BN-2B-21, -26 and -27.
BN-2B-20	BN-2A-20 with improved soundproofing, increased landing weight and other detailed improvements.
BN-2S	Islander Super. BN-2A with 33in fuselage stretch.
BN-2T	Turbine Islander. BN-2A-26 with two 320 shp Allison 250-B17C turboprops and 7000 lb. TOGW.
BN-2T-4S	Defender 4000 16-seat military variant with 2ft 6in fuselage stretch, larger strengthened wing, larger vertical tail, deeper windshield, 8500 lb. TOGW, 40% increase in fuel capacity and Allison 250-B17F turboprops. Prot. G-SURV (c/n 4005) FF. 17 Aug. 1994.
BN-2T-4R	Turbine Islander with Westinghouse radar in bulbous nose radome and other multi-sensor equipment for military surveillance duties. Named 'MSSA'.
BN-2A-III-1	18-seat stretched BN2A with three 260 h.p. Lyc. O-540-E4C5 piston engines, extended wing and 9350 lb. TOGW. Prot. G-ATWU (c/n 2) FF. as Trislander, 11 Sep. 1970. BN-2A-III-2 is Trislander with lengthened nose and 10,000 lb. TOGW and BN-2A-III-3 is certificated for US operation.

The parent company of Britten Norman, Pilatus, had a background in military contracts and manufacture of the Porter utility aircraft. In 1989, it launched the PC-XII which has started to penetrate the third level commuter airline market. The PC-XII is a single-engined multi-purpose utility aircraft with a low wing, retractable tricycle undercarriage and a T-tail. It is powered by a 1200 shp Pratt & Whitney PT6A-67B turboprop. The nine-

Pilatus PC-XII, HB-FOE

passenger pressurised fuselage has an internal capacity of 330 cubic feet and is fitted with a large cargo hatch behind the wing. Available configurations include a mixed four passenger and cargo ('PC-12 Combi') model, a six passenger 'PC-12 Executive' layout or an All-Cargo version. Two prototypes of the PC-12 (HB-FOA and 'FOB, c/n P-01, P-02) were built, the first of which first flew on 31 May 1991. Pilatus delivered the first production aircraft from Stans in October 1994 and has now built more than 100 examples (c/n 101 to 200). One of the first users is Kellner Airways in Canada.

PIPER UNITED STATES

Piper Aircraft is well known for its range of low-wing single-engined light aircraft and for the high-wing private and club machines originating in the Piper Cub of the 1930s. These are documented in the companion volume, *Airlife's General Aviation*. At the heavier end of the product line, in the early 1960s Piper built the prototype of an eight-seat low-wing cabin-class twin which was received its type certificate on 24 February 1966. It went into production the following year as the PA-31 Navajo and was the design basis for all Piper's subsequent large twins. This basic airframe was sold in stretched form (as the PA-31-350

PA-31-350 Navajo Chieftain, VH-KGN

Navajo Chieftain) and with a pressurised cabin as the PA-31P Pressurised Navajo. The PA-31P, fitted with PT6A turboprops became the Cheyenne.

For the most part the PA-31 series were sold for executive use but a considerable number were used for low-density operation by small commuter carriers and by the small package freight and night mail companies. In general, these were the stretched Chieftain version but Piper did sell a small number of dedicated commuter models of the PA-31 as the T-1020 and T-1040. Details of the principal Navajo models are as follows.

Type No.	Name	No. Built	Notes
PA-31	Navajo	1785	6–8 seat all-metal low wing cabin class twin. Prot. N3100E (c/n 31-1) named 'Inca' FF. 30 Sep. 1964. 6200 lb. TOGW. Powered by two 300 h.p. Lyc. IO-470-M engines or optional turbocharged 310 h.p. TIO-540-A engines.
PA-31	Navajo B		PA-31 with turbocharged TIO-540-E engines, optional pilot entry door, engine nacelle baggage lockers, better air conditioning etc. 6500 lb. TOGW.
PA-31	Navajo C		Navajo B with TIO-540-A2C engines and minor changes.
PA-31-325	Navajo C/R		Navajo B with counter rotating 325 h.p. TIO-540-F2BD engines and extended nacelles.
PA-31-350	Chieftain	1825	PA-31 with 2ft. fuselage stretch, one extra window each side, cargo door, 10-seat interior and 7000 lb. TOGW. Powered by two counter-rotating Lyc. TIO-540-J2BD engines. Originally named Navajo Chieftain. Prot. N7700L (c/n 31-5001).
PA-31-350	T-1020	21	Chieftain for commuter use with hard interior, improved u/c, new fuel system, crew entry door.
PA-31-353	Chieftain II	2	PA-31-350 with 4ft longer span wings, modified tailplane, 350 h.p. TIO-540-X48 counter rotating engines. Prot. N353PA (c/n 31-8458001).
PA-31T3	T-1040	24	Chieftain with pressurised fuselage, wings, tail and nose of PA-31T1 Cheyenne business aircraft and two 500 shp PT6A-11 engines, 9050 lb. TOGW. Prot. N2389Y (c/n 31T-8275001). FF 17 Jul. 1981.

RAYTHEON   UNITED STATES

Much of early post-war commercial aviation in the United States was founded on war surplus Douglas DC-3s and the popular and economical Beech 18 light transport. The Beech 18 continued in production until 1969 and from it grew a large range of Beech twins, many of which went into service with local service 'commuter' airlines. Beech Aircraft Corporation, based in Wichita, Kansas has gained an important reputation for producing strong and reliable aircraft for General Aviation users and, since 8 February 1981 it has been a subsidiary of the Raytheon Company.

In 1958 it developed the ten-seat Model 65 Queen Air, derived from the Model 50 Twin Bonanza/Seminole and initially intended to meet a military requirement. This aircraft was sold successfully to executive users and also as the Queen Airliner to carriers as diverse as Masling Airlines in Australia, Lap-Air in Sweden, Trans-Cal Airlines and Air Texas in the United States and the French operator, Transazur.

The next growth development for the Queen Air was the addition of turboprops and pressurisation which resulted in the incredibly successful King Air which has dominated the turboprop sector of the corporate executive market for three decades. As a part of this King Air design effort, Beech also produced a light airliner which combined a stretched version of the Queen Air 80 fuselage with the turboprop engine installation of the King Air 90. The Beech LR-1 (Model PD.208) first flew in 1966 and, with suitable modification, was awarded a type certificate on 2 May 1968. The first delivery took place in 1968 to Commuter Airlines and the last of 239 examples went to Rio Airways in 1987. The Beech 99 competed with the Twin Otter and the Bandeirante in the fifteen to twenty-seat commuter category. Major users of the Beech 99 included Henson Airlines, Mid-State Commuter, Cal-State Airlines, SMB Stagelines, Hub Airlines, Royale and Air Midwest. France was a major destination for the Model 99 with some twenty-three seeing service there with various airlines including Air Alpes, many Beech 99s ended up in Canada and the Chilean Air Force acquired a fleet of eight.

Beech progressively developed the King Air line with the stretched King Air 100, followed by the T-tail Model 200 Super King Air and its derivatives. The local service airlines were now demanding pressurised aircraft in place of the unpressurised early turboprops and Beech came up with an extensive redesign of the King Air 200 to compete with the Embraer Brasilia and the Jetstream 41. The Beech 1900 was a nineteen-seat aircraft, powered by a pair of Pratt & Whitney PT6A-65B turboprops and featuring a large rear cargo door to allow dual use of the aircraft.

Loyal users of the Beech 99 including Business Express and Bar Harbor Airlines became customers for the Beech 1900C and the first aircraft were handed over to Bar Harbor and Cascade Airways in the spring of 1984. The Beech 1900C continues in production but Beech introduced the Model 1900D in 1989 and this featured a much deeper stand-up cabin and higher powered engines to provide better hot and high performance. The majority of deliveries are now the 1900D version and customers have included the United Express system and niche operators such as Mesa Airlines. The Beech line of larger cabin twin aircraft, many of which have been used by the commuter airline industry, is as follows.

Type No	Name	No. Built	Notes
65	Queen Air	445	7/9 seat low-wing all-metal cabin monoplane for corporate, military or commuter use developed from Model 50 with new fuselage and tail, 7700 lb. TOGW and two 340 h.p. Lyc. IGSO-480-A1A6 engines. Prot. N821B (c/n L-1) FF. 28 Aug. 1958. U.S. Army L-23F Seminole (later U-8F/U-8G). Model A65 with swept vertical tail, fourth stbd cabin window and optional certification at 8200 lb. TOGW as Model 79 Queen Airliner. Model 70 based on A65 with longer B80 wings and up to 11 seats.
65-80	Queen Air	511	Model A65 with swept tail, 8000 lb. TOGW and two 380 h.p. IGSO-540-A1A engines. Prot. N841Q (c/n LD-1). FF. 22 Jun. 1961. 65-A80 has longer span wing, 11 seats and 8500 lb. TOGW. B80 is A80 with extra starboard cabin window, 380 h.p. IGSO-540-A1D engines, 8800 lb. TOGW and max 13 seats. Also Model 89 Queen Airliner for commuter airlines at 8800 lb. TOGW. Later designated Model 65-A80-8800.

Beech 1900C, N13OUE

Type No	Name	No. Built	Notes
65-88	Queen Air	47	A80 with 10-seat pressurised cabin, round porthole windows and modified cockpit glazing, 8800 lb. TOGW. Powered by two 380 h.p. IGSO-540-A1D engines. Prot. N8808B (c/n LP-1). FF. 2 Jul. 1965. Some conversions to Model 65-90 (King Air).
99		101	17-seat low-wing unpressurised all-metal third level airliner based on Model 65–80 with lengthened fuselage, baggage-carrying nose, twin wheel main u/c, 10,400 lb. TOGW and two 550 shp P&W PT6A-20 turboprops. Prot. (Model PD.208) N599AT (c/n LR-1) FF. 25 Oct. 1966.
99A		43	99 with 680 shp P&W PT6A-28 engines.
A99			99 with 10,650 lb. TOGW and reduced fuel capacity due to elimination of nacelle tanks.
A99A	Airliner	1	A99 with 10,900 lb. TOGW and 680 shp PT6A-27 turboprops.
B99	Airliner	18	A99A with additional 115 U.S. gal. fuel capacity in nacelle tanks.

Beech 99, VH-OXB

Type No	Name	No. Built	Notes
C99	Airliner	77	B99 with 11,300 lb. TOGW and two 715 shp P&W PT6A-36 engines, improved u/c etc.
200	Super King Air		Stretched Beech 100 King Air with T-tail, increased wing span, extra fuel, improved pressurisation system, two 850 shp P&W PT6A-41 turboprops. 12,500 lb. TOGW and detailed systems and trim changes. Prot. N38B (c/n BB-1). FF. 27 Oct. 1972.
1300		14	13-seat commuter version of Model 200 with belly cargo pod and ventral fins.
1900		3	21-seat third-level airliner or business aircraft based on Model 200 with fuselage stretch, dual airstair doors, two 850 shp PT6A-65B turboprops, extra horizontal tail surfaces on lower rear fuselage, tailplane finlets. Prot. N1900A (c/n UA-1). FF 3 Sep. 1982. Military C-12J.
1900C		74	1900 with starboard rear cargo door in place of airstair.
1900C-1		174	1900C with 'wet' wings increased fuel and redesigned fuel system.
1900D		99	1900 with 14-inch deeper fuselage, new pressurisation, larger entry door, larger windows, wingtip winglets and two PT6A-67 turboprops. Prot. N5584B (c/n UE-1) FF. 1 Mar. 1990. Replaced 1900C, Oct. 1991.

SAUNDERS–ROE   UNITED KINGDOM

Among the many major transport projects of the immediate post-war era, the development of the Saunders Roe Princess must stand out as an act of faith which deserved a better ending. With so much water available for landing it seemed natural that large transport flying-boats would have a unique advantage and, indeed, some success has been achieved by the Shorts and Boeing flying-boats in the pre-war years. The SR.45 Princess

Saro Princess, G-ALUN

was intended to carry 140 passengers on its double decks over a range of 5720 miles and was powered by ten 2500 shp Bristol Proteus turboprop engines with four inboard coupled pairs driving counter-rotating propellers and two single outboard engines. The major engineering effort of constructing the three development airframes started in 1948 and the prototype Princess, G-ALUN (c/n SR901) eventually flew at Cowes on 22 August 1952. The intention was that the Princess should operate transatlantic services for BOAC – but, as with many other centrally controlled projects, the theories of the Ministry of Supply and the operational plans of BOAC were at variance and in the end it was clear that nobody wanted to operate the stately Princess even though its performance was promising. In 1953, the Princess project was terminated and the second and third aircraft remained uncompleted and unflown. Eventually, in 1967, the three airframes were scrapped.

SIAI–MARCHETTI ITALY

The long-established Italian company, Savoia-Marchetti is well known for its series of wartime heavy combat aircraft including the three-engined SM.79 Sparviero bomber. The basic design of the SM.79 was developed into the S.73 and the later commercial S.83 ten-passenger transport during the immediate pre-war period and most of the 23 which were completed were impressed into military service with the Regia Aeronautica. Savoia Marchetti (later restyled SIAI-Marchetti) also built the larger S.75 and S.76 transports which were larger trimotors to a similar formula. A few of these remained in military service after the war.

Experience with the Sparviero-based transports led the company to design a much larger troop carrier – the S.82 Canguro. This low-wing aircraft, which could carry forty troops, had a retractable tailwheel undercarriage and was powered by three 950 h.p. Alfa Romeo 128-RC21 radial engines. The prototype flew in 1939 and a number served with the Luftwaffe during the war. It is believed that around 700 were completed and production continued after the war with a number of S.82s wearing airline colour schemes (which were frequently fictitious in order to avoid post-war military restrictions).

The first truly post-war transport built by SIAI-Marchetti was the S.95 which was a smaller, long-range version of the S.82, again with a tailwheel undercarriage and with four 860 h.p. Alfa Romeo 128-RC18 engines and a passenger capacity of eighteen. The first two S.95s were completed in 1943 and, while primarily a transport aircraft were seriously considered for conversion for possible bombing raids on New York. With the end of the war, the company pressed forward with production of a further eighteen of the type and delivered five to Alitalia, four to the Egyptian airline, S.A.I.D.E. and a batch to the Italian Air Force. The total batch of twenty are believed to have carried serial numbers c/n 41001 to 41020. The other transport built by SIAI Marchetti after the war was the SM.102 – a

SIAI S.95, I-DALL (APN)

small eight-seat aircraft built of tube, fabric and plywood which first flew in 1949. It was powered, initially, by two 500 h.p. Ranger SVG-770 in-line engines, but these were replaced by 450 h.p. Pratt & Whitney Wasp Junior radials. A total of twenty-one were completed (c/n 1 to 21) and operated as military communications aircraft. At least five were sold as surplus to commercial operators when the type was retired from military service in 1960.

In more recent times, SIAI-Marchetti has been engaged in production of the S.205 and S.208 four-seat light aircraft and the SF.260 civil and military trainer. They have also been concerned in the development of the SF.600TP Canguro light utility aircraft. This is more fully described in the companion volume *Airlife's General Aviation*.

TRANSALL   INTERNATIONAL

The Arbeitgemeinschaft Transall was formed in 1959 to develop and build a new medium transport for use by European air forces. The companies involved were Nord Aviation in France, Messerschmitt-Bölkow-Blohm in Germany and the bi-national VFW–Fokker who shared production of the aircraft at their factories at Bourges, Finkenwerder and Lemwerder respectively. The Transall C-160 was a high-wing twin turboprop aircraft with an upswept rear fuselage and inbuilt loading ramp. Powered by two 6100 shp Rolls-Royce Tyne R.Ty.20 Mk.22 engines, the prototype (D-9507, c/n V-1) made its first flight at the French air base at Melun Villaroche on 25 February 1963 and was followed by a further two flying prototypes and two test airframes (c/n V-2 to V-5). A further series of six pre-production aircraft were built (c/n A-01 to A-06) followed and then series production of the C-160D (for the German Air Force) and C-160F (for the French Air Force) followed. These production aircraft had a fuselage which was one foot eight inches shorter than the pre-series Transalls.

The serial numbers of Transalls ran from 1 to 160 and were prefixed F (for the French Air Force), D (for the German Air Force) and Z (for foreign deliveries). Parallel production lines were operated with Nord completing fifty-six aircraft, Messerschmitt-Bölkow-Blohm completing fifty-six aircraft and VFW completing fifty-seven between 1967 and 1973. While the Transall was primarily a military transport factory deliveries of nine were made to the South African Air Force and civil examples released from military service have served with Pelita Air Service in Indonesia and with Air France.

Transall C-160, PK-PTQ

VEB   EAST GERMANY

During the 1950s, the factory of VEB (the Vereinegung Volkseigener Betriebe) Flugzeugbau at Dresden built a series of Ilyushin Il-14 piston-engined airliners for use by the national airline, Interflug and for export to other eastern bloc airlines. At about the same time, the company embarked on design of a four-jet transport aircraft, designated VEB-152. Conceived by Prof. Baade, the VEB-152 had a swept high wing with pronounced anhedral on which were mounted two pairs of 7275 lb.s.t. Type 014-A1 turbojets on underwing pylons. The aircraft had retractable nose and main undercarriage units in the belly of the fuselage and outrigger supporting wheels. The prototype (DM-ZYA, c/n 1) was first flown on 4 December 1958 but was written off during testing in the following March. Two static test airframes (c/n 2 and 4) and five further airframes were abandoned when the programme was wound up in March 1961.

VFW   GERMANY

The Vereinigte Flugtechnische Werke (VFW) was formed in 1963 through a merger of Weser Flugzeugbau GmbH and Focke-Wulf GmbH together with Ernst Heinkel Flugzeugbau added in 1964. VFW was a major partner in several transport programmes such as the Transall C-160 and, in 1969 joined with Fokker to form the holding company, Zentralgesellschaft VFW-Fokker. At this time, VFW was in the course of development of a new short-haul airliner, the VFW.614 which, with forty-four-passenger maximum capacity, was intended to be complementary to the Fokker F.28.

The VFW.614 was a low-wing aircraft with a circular section fuselage and conventional tail. Its unusual feature was the mounting of its two 7480 shp Rolls-Royce SNECMA M45-501 turbofan engines on pylons above the rear wing centre section. The intention was that this arrangement would simplify the design of the wing control surfaces and provide jet flow over the tail. The prototype VFW.614 (D-BABA c/n MG.01) was first flown from Bremen on 14 July 1971 but was lost during flight testing in February of the following year. Nevertheless, the other two prototypes (c/n MG.02 and MG.03) completed the test programme and the German type certificate was issued on 23 August 1974. Orders were slow but sales were placed by Cimber Air for five aircraft, the first of which was delivered on 28 August 1975 and by Air Alsace and Touraine Air Transport. The VFW. 614 was not economic in airline service and VFW ceased production with the twentieth production airframe (c/n MG.23), the last four of which were scrapped. Three of the final production units were sold to the German Government for use by the Luftwaffe as VIP transports and one went to the DFVLR for test purposes. By the end of 1981, the remaining airline examples had been withdrawn and scrapped or consigned to museums, and the Luftwaffe aircraft were finally withdrawn at the end of 1998.

VFW.614, F-GATG

INDEX

COMMERCIAL AIRCRAFT AND AIRLINERS